Master Conflict Therapy

Illustrated with case studies, this book teaches couples and sex therapists the comprehensive, integrative treatment approach of master conflict therapy (MCT), which combines psychoanalytic conflict theory and Bowen Theory with the basic principles and practices of sex therapy. MCT suggests that each partner has an internal conflict born out of their experiences from their respective families of origin. Partners then choose one another based on these conflicts, and it is only when they are out of balance that the couple experiences symptoms. The authors help clinicians treat couples by providing them with a solid theoretical foundation, a practical assessment procedure, and highly effective treatment techniques to re-balance a couple and, in turn, alleviate their sexual symptoms.

Stephen J. Betchen, DSW, is a licensed marriage and family therapist, an AAMFT-approved supervisor, and an AASECT diplomate and certified supervisor. He serves as a senior supervisor in the post-graduate Sex Therapy Program at the Council for Relationships and as an adjunct clinical professor in the Department of Couple and Family Therapy at Thomas Jefferson University. He is the author of numerous professional publications on relationships, including the critically acclaimed book, *Intrusive Partners-Elusive Mates*. Dr. Betchen is an official blogger for PsychologyToday.com and currently maintains a full-time private practice in Cherry Hill, New Jersey specializing in couples/sex therapy.

Heather L. Davidson, EdM, MA, is a licensed professional counselor, an EMDR-certified therapist, and an AASECT-certified sex therapist. Ms. Davidson maintains a full-time private practice in Narberth, Pennsylvania, specializing in couples/sex therapy and trauma-related disorders.

Master Conflict Therapy

A New Model for Practicing Couples and Sex Therapy

Stephen J. Betchen and
Heather L. Davidson

NEW YORK AND LONDON

First published 2018
by Routledge
711 Third Avenue, New York, NY 10017

and by Routledge
2 Park Square, Milton Park, Abingdon, Oxon, OX14 4RN

Routledge is an imprint of the Taylor & Francis Group, an informa business

© 2018 Stephen J. Betchen and Heather L. Davidson

The right of Stephen J. Betchen and Heather L. Davidson to be identified as authors of this work has been asserted by them in accordance with sections 77 and 78 of the Copyright, Designs and Patents Act 1988.

All rights reserved. No part of this book may be reprinted or reproduced or utilized in any form or by any electronic, mechanical, or other means, now known or hereafter invented, including photocopying and recording, or in any information storage or retrieval system, without permission in writing from the publishers.

Trademark notice: Product or corporate names may be trademarks or registered trademarks, and are used only for identification and explanation without intent to infringe.

Library of Congress Cataloging-in-Publication Data
Names: Betchen, Stephen J., 1954- author. | Davidson, Heather L., author.
Title: Master conflict therapy: a new model for practicing couples and sex therapy / Stephen J. Betchen and Heather L. Davidson.
Description: Routledge: New York, 2018. | Includes bibliographical references and index.
Identifiers: LCCN 2017055570 | ISBN 9781138726956 (hbk : alk. paper) | ISBN 9781138726963 (pbk: alk. paper) | ISBN 9781315191102 (ebk)
Subjects: LCSH: Couples therapy. | Marital psychotherapy.
Classification: LCC RC488.5 .B492 2018 | DDC 616.89/1562–dc23
LC record available at https://lccn.loc.gov/2017055570

ISBN: 978-1-138-72695-6 (hbk)
ISBN: 978-1-138-72696-3 (pbk)
ISBN: 978-1-315-19110-2 (ebk)

Typeset in Sabon
by Deanta Global Publishing Services, Chennai, India

To Bonnie, Jennifer, and Melanie with abiding love
— SJB

To Antonio, with love always
— HLD

"No body, but he who has felt it, can conceive what a plaguing thing it is to have a man's mind torn asunder by two projects of equal strength, both obstinately pulling in a contrary direction at the same time."
— Laurence Sterne, *The Life and Opinions of Tristram Shandy, Gentleman*

Contents

Preface   x
Acknowledgments   xiii

SECTION I
Understanding Master Conflict Therapy (MCT)   1

1   Introduction: Definitions, History, and Influences   3

The Call for Integration 3
The Freudian Influence 4
The Problem with Choice 6
Choosing a Life Partner 7
The Greeks, Freud, and Conflict 8
Nietzsche, Freud, and Conflict 13
MCT: A Personal Journey 14
Summary 16
References 17

2   Key Features of a Master Conflict   21

Fifteen Fast Facts 22
The Power of a Master Conflict 25
The Development of Relationship Symptoms 27
Summary 29
References 30

3   Master Conflicts   31

Acceptance vs. Rejection 31
Adequacy vs. Inadequacy 32
Closeness vs. Distance 33

Commitment vs. Freedom 34
Conformity vs. Rebellion 35
Control vs. Chaos (Out-of-Control) 35
Getting Your Needs Met vs. Caretaking 36
Giving vs. Withholding 37
Justice vs. Injustice 38
Legitimacy vs. Illegitimacy 38
Person vs. Object 39
Power vs. Passivity 40
Resolution vs. Misery 41
Satisfaction vs. Disappointment 41
Security vs. Risk 42
Self vs. Loyalty (Others) 43
Specialness vs. Ordinariness (Less than Ordinary) 43
Success vs. Sabotage (Big vs. Small) 44
Trust vs. Distrust 45
Others (Conflict Adjustment) 46
Summary 46
Reference 47

SECTION II
Assessment and Treatment 49

4 Assessment 51

Structuring the Therapy 51
Using the Genogram as an Assessment Tool 53
Questions for the Genogram 57
Content and Process 74
Identifying Incongruent Feelings and Behaviors 76
Assessing Sociocultural Factors 85
Summary 99
References 100

5 Treatment 107

The 5-Stage Treatment Process 107
Exercises 112
Neutrality, Balance, and Boundaries 117
Broadening the Process 124
Treatment: Success and Failure 126
Termination and Relapse 128

Summary 130
References 131

SECTION III
Case Studies   **133**

6   Female Sexual Disorders   135

    Female Orgasmic Disorder 135
    Rodrigo and Angela: Closeness vs. Distance 136
    Genito-Pelvic Pain/Penetration Disorder 140
    Frank and Merjan: Giving vs. Withholding 141
    Female Sexual Interest/Arousal Disorder 145
    Adam and Rebecca: Self vs. Loyalty (Others) 146
    Summary 150
    References 151

7   Male Sexual Disorders   154

    Premature (Early) Ejaculation 154
    Jack and Carolyn: Success vs. Sabotage (Big vs. Small) 155
    Erectile Disorder 158
    Gopal and Bernadette: Adequacy vs. Inadequacy 159
    Delayed Ejaculation 162
    Joseph and Kerry: Conformity vs. Rebellion 163
    Summary 168
    References 168

8   Selected Sexual Issues   172

    Open Marriage (Swingers) 172
    Madison and Carl: Conformity vs. Rebellion 173
    Online Infidelity 178
    Jared and Samantha: Security vs. Risk 179
    Sexual Abuse 183
    Tom and Zoey: Specialness vs. Ordinariness 184
    Summary 188
    References 188

    Epilogue   191
    References 194

    Index   197

Preface

Not all therapists who practice couples therapy are comfortable discussing sexual issues with their clients; and there are a fair share of clients who are quite happy about this. Nevertheless, therapists who fail to inquire about a couple's sex life, even if they are not presented with a sexual disorder, may be ignoring information that could lead to a deeper understanding of the couple—a miscue that may rob the couple of a healthier level of functioning. We have witnessed time and again that a couple's sexual dynamics can tell the therapist a great deal about their non-sexual dynamics and *vice versa*. For example, a man who reports with delayed ejaculation—a form of control or the inability to let go—may also withhold affection and positive reinforcement from his mate; he may even be financially stingy. Perhaps this individual was raised in a family of origin that exerted control over his life and his withholding is an effort to maintain a sense of self; it might also be a form of retaliation. All this to say that a couples therapist without sex therapy training is partially trained, and a sex therapist with little to no training in systems is at a similar disadvantage. This is the primary reason we went back for more training in sex therapy.

The call for more training is not without its challengers. Graduate and postgraduate students as well as some colleagues have begged the question: Why do we need to endure extra training and expense if we can refer when a sexual problem is evident? We find this perspective plausible. It was not long ago that couples therapy training was offered exclusively as a postgraduate experience. For most, sex therapy was an additional training, but by this time many therapists were emotionally and financially exhausted. Our response has always been in favor of "one-stop shopping." Couples can "fall through the cracks" when two therapists are working separately on these two issues, especially if the therapists fail to communicate regularly—an all-too-common practice. And what if the therapists follow incompatible treatment models, or possess vastly different skill sets? One of the major challenges of the couples and sex therapist is to discern which symptom—sexual or nonsexual—serves as the trigger point for the relational difficulty. It is usually easier to accomplish this with one therapist on the job.

We are offering a unique, integrative model specifically designed to treat a diverse group of couples who present with a wide variety of relational and sexual problems. The model, master conflict therapy (MCT), has been referred to by those who have studied it as a "counterintuitive" approach that offers therapists a unique way to understand their clients. Some have found it particularly useful in its ability to explain how and why couples get stuck, and how to free them from their destructive dynamics. It was also called a "seamless" approach to treating couples with sexual problems—perhaps the highest compliment that could be paid to the architects of an integrative model. It has without a doubt instilled a confidence in us as we continue to negotiate a demanding specialization. By presenting MCT, we hope to help our readers achieve the same.

The book consists of three major sections and several associated chapters. While time and space have limited us from covering every sexual disorder that an unbalanced conflict can generate in a couple, we have done our best to be as comprehensive as possible. Our main objective is to encourage the reader to think "conflict" when analyzing couples and their symptoms. This, in and of itself, would be quite an accomplishment.

- Section I: Understanding Master Conflicts – In *Chapter 1 Introduction: Definitions, History, and Influences*, a case is made for integrating couples and sex therapy, and the MCT model is offered as a viable approach. An historical analysis of the master conflict is presented beginning with the pre-Socratics and their influence on Freudian psychoanalysis and MCT. How specific symptoms develop and how people choose their life partners are prominent issues. *Chapter 2 Key Features of a Master Conflict* presents several prominent characteristics of the concept. It also addresses both the evolution and strength of the master conflict from both an internal (emotional) and external (environmental) perspective. *Chapter 3 Master Conflicts* lists 19 master conflicts and provides several case examples for each.
- Section II: Assessment and Treatment – *Chapter 4 Assessment* details the evaluation process. The genogram is utilized to determine the origin of the master conflict and its associated symptoms. When and how to ask "focus questions," which will help couples to link non-sexual and sexual problems, is illustrated. This chapter will also address the concept of diversity and how it is incorporated in the MCT model. The objective of this chapter is to demonstrate a relatively quick and accurate way to diagnose a wide variety of couples who suffer from sexual problems. In *Chapter 5 Treatment*, the 5-stage MCT treatment process is examined with the aid of case examples. How to balance a couple, set effective

boundaries and maintain neutrality, evaluate the treatment progress, and negotiate termination are detailed.
- Section III: Case Studies – Chapters 6–8 present detailed case examples of couples suffering from any one of the 19 master conflicts and associated sexual symptoms. *Chapter 6 Female Sexual Disorders* includes: Female Orgasmic Disorder, Genito-Pelvic Pain/Penetration Disorder (GPPPD), and Female Sexual Interest/Arousal Disorder (SAID). *Chapter 7 Male Sexual Disorders* includes: Premature (Early) Ejaculation (PE), Erectile Disorder (ED), and Delayed Ejaculation. *Chapter 8 Selected Sexual Issues* includes: Open Marriage (Swingers), Online Infidelity, and Sexual Abuse. Genograms for each case are provided and used for gathering data, analyzing relational patterns and conflicts, and to aid in the treatment process.

Acknowledgments

We would like to sincerely thank the many couples who have shared their lives with us over the years. Facing one's flaws and attempting to correct them requires a great deal of courage, perseverance, and tenacity. Sadly, for some the price is too steep to pay.

Our gratitude also goes to George Zimmar, Nina Guttapalle, and all others affiliated with Taylor & Francis that have made the publication of this book possible, and to Rachel Cook of Deanta Global Publishing for her expert copyediting. Also deserving of thanks are the administration, staff, and students of the Council for Relationships (formerly the Marriage Council of Philadelphia), where we both trained, but not in the same decade. We also thank those in the Department of Couple and Family Therapy, Jefferson College of Health Professions, Thomas Jefferson University.

Last, we pay homage to our mentors and supervisors who have prepared us to take on a therapeutic model of such scope. We are blessed to have been afforded such diverse guidance and training throughout the course of our careers.

– SJB
– HLD

Section I

Understanding Master Conflict Therapy (MCT)

Chapter 1

Introduction
Definitions, History, and Influences

The Call for Integration

Many couples who present for treatment—even if they initially report with a nonsexual problem such as "poor communication"—also tend to experience some form of sexual dysfunction. The latest research indicates that approximately 40% to 50% of women suffer from a sexual disorder (McCabe et al., 2016), compared to 31% of men (Cleveland Clinic, 2016). Given the obvious connection between couples and sexual issues, it is somewhat bewildering that couples therapy has been more closely linked to family therapy than to sex therapy.

In contrast, some scholars believe that sex therapy has become too associated with the medical establishment (Tiefer, 2004, 1996). It is certainly hard to turn on your television set without being confronted with a commercial advertisement for the medical treatment of Erectile Disorder (ED). And the pressure to develop a drug for Female Sexual Interest/Arousal Disorder, such as flibanserin (Addyi), was quite intense—almost rushed. Vernon (2010) claimed that pharmaceutical companies around the world were obsessed with finding a treatment ever since Pfizer gained FDA approval for sildenafil citrate (Viagra), a billion-dollar-generating drug effective for treating ED.

Advocates for the integration of couples and sex therapy have long called for therapeutic models that join the two specialties (Betchen, 2015, 2010, 2006, 2005, 2001a, 2001b; Hertlein, Weeks, & Gambescia, 2015; Leif, 1977; McCarthy, 2015; McCarthy & McCarthy, 2003; Sager, 1976; Scharff & Scharff, 1991; Schnarch, 1991; Weeks & Hof, 1987). Weeks, Gambescia, and Hertlein (2016) wrote "it is absolutely essential [that] the fields of couple and sex therapy be fully integrated theoretically and pragmatically" (p. 1). Nevertheless, the response has been limited. The major purpose of this book is to teach therapists who practice, or wish to practice couples and sex therapy, the MCT approach (Davidson & Betchen, 2017). MCT contends that in most cases, the sexual symptoms that couples present in treatment are intricately linked to their relationship dynamics and *vice versa*. The therapist must therefore possess sufficient knowledge and skill in both areas, and in many cases, deem them equally important to provide a balanced and effective treatment. MCT is unique in part because it borrows from certain aspects of what is often referred to as psychoanalytic conflict theory (Freud, 1910/1957), the psychodynamic systems approach of Bowen Theory (Bowen, 1978), and basic principles and practice of sex therapy (Kaplan, 1983, 1974).

The Freudian Influence

Couples therapy is perhaps the hardest psychotherapy (Doherty, 2002), and studies have long reported poor results (Christensen, Atkins, & Baucom, 2010; Gottman, 1999; Snyder, Wills, & Grady-Fletcher, 1991). Frustrated with the limitations of our family-of-origin treatment with couples, we looked to add Freudian conflict theory to delve deeper into the psyche of each partner of a couple. The objective was to determine how their internalized conflicts impacted their relational interactions and led to a wide variety of symptoms, especially those of a sexual nature.

Freud (1923/1961) believed that neurosis was the result of an inner conflict between an instinctual sexual drive or impulse—the demands of the libido—and opposing forces in the form of the ego. He wrote:

> By thus getting hold of the libido from the object-cathexes, setting itself up as sole love-object, and desexualizing or sublimating the libido of the id, the ego is working in opposition to the purposes of Eros and placing itself at the service of the opposing instinctual impulses.
>
> (p. 46)

Freud (1933/1964) found that the ego, besieged by this impulse, could only control it—as best as possible—by way of repression. Symptoms developed in disguised form because the repression rendered the conflict unconscious but failed to eliminate it. Waelder (1960) described the pattern: "inner conflict—unsuccessful repression—return of the repressed" (p. 37).

When most couples therapists hear the word conflict, they conjure a disagreement "between" two partners. This is referred to as an external conflict. In tune with Freud, a conflict herein is defined as two conflicting opposites or opposing forces "within" the individual—an internal duality or conflict. One side needs something that the other side opposes. In a previous work (Betchen, 2010), it was likened to having two politicians sitting on opposite sides of a seesaw, each trying to convince you to see their point of view. The arguments are so convincing that the process can paralyze one's ability to choose one side of the conflict over the other, or to negotiate a compromise between the two. For example, a female client said that she was finally in position to achieve her dream of pursuing a law degree from an Ivy League university. She wavered, however, because she found it to be too expensive and time-consuming. "They'll work me to death, and cut into my free time to travel," she said. As an alternative, she considered attending a cheaper, less prestigious law school, but once again she wavered because she considered it an inferior degree. "It will be more manageable, but my dream is to get an Ivy League degree." For several months, the young woman could not decide which degree to pursue. She continued to suffer in the hope that by some miracle a perfect solution to her dilemma would appear. You could see the agony and frustration on her face as the politicians inside of her played point/counterpoint. How specific symptoms emanate from conflicts, sexual and otherwise, will be discussed in the following chapter.

MCT is not psychoanalysis, nor does it pretend to be. It is not specifically concerned with sexual impulses, nor is the origin of the struggle believed to emanate from poorly negotiated conflicts in an individual's psychosexual stages. But it does reflect the dilemma Freud (1923/1961) presented in his use of the Oedipus Complex. Freud coined the term from the Sophocles play, *Oedipus Rex*, to determine the seat of neurosis: A child wants the opposite-sex parent but fears retribution—a conflict, to be sure. MCT borrows the concept of "internalized conflict" and applies it to couples work by viewing it as a struggle between what individuals want or desire and what they can allow themselves to have. This is the dilemma presented by the woman who wanted an Ivy League degree but feared the consequences.

MCT contends that master conflicts largely begin in the family of origin as a child is besieged with contradictory messages that are eventually internalized. These messages can be presented verbally, behaviorally, or both. For example, a man with what we refer to as a *power vs. passivity* master conflict may want power and control in his relationship but simultaneously be averse to responsibility. Perhaps in his youth he experienced his successful father working himself to death; or he may have repeatedly heard his mother complain that his father, albeit successful, was never home. Notice the double messages about taking control in these examples.

If a woman has a *trust vs. distrust* master conflict, a part of her wants to trust her partner, but the other part is very wary. She may have been told repeatedly by her mother that she shouldn't trust anyone—that they will always let her down; or the parent she was closest to or idolized might have disappointed her by having an extramarital affair. The double message here is that the people you trusted were either distrusting or distrustful.

As will be discussed in the following chapter, the extent to which the individual was enlisted in parental conflicts as a child will, in part, determine the intensity or power of their internalized master conflict. Eldest and only children are commonly triangulated into their parents' dynamics and therefore seem to possess their fair share of entrenched conflicts (Toman, 1976); these individuals are referred to as "players." Middle siblings, especially those from large families, are better able to escape direct triangulation or hide from the family dynamics, but this does not exempt them from impact. We refer to these individuals as "witnesses." Given the genesis of the conflict, the process of negotiating with it is a difficult one. Seemingly unrelated symptoms derive from the difficulty people have in making a choice or negotiating a compromise between the two sides.

While some people are aware of one side of their conflict, the other side is usually beyond their grasp. This is often evident when a couple first present for treatment. Contradictions or irrational comments and behaviors can lead the therapist to the specific conflict. For example, if a woman complains that her husband does not speak to her but stops him the minute he tries, the woman might be demonstrating a conflict about what she truly wants from him. But if you tell her that only part of her wants him to engage, she'll vehemently disagree. If the husband complains about her dominance but fails to intervene, he might be in conflict about giving his power away. But if you suggest that he is in conflict about holding onto his power, he may consider you crazy.

The Problem with Choice

Freud (1910/1957) believed the solution of a conflict between instinctual drives and opposing forces can be in favor of negotiating a compromise between the two, or via sublimation of the drive. The solution requires the frustration of one of these forces at the expense of the other, and in our experience clients do not readily appreciate this sacrifice. Growing means change, and deep change can be painful. Confronted with choice, most individuals must give up something or suffer a loss; but they usually gain something in return. What seems to stop people from choosing is the potential loss that change may bring. This loss may result in deep sadness, a temporary state of depression, or significant anxiety. Waelder (1960) likens it to "all weaning processes and to the process of mourning" (p. 226).

To rebalance a master conflict, each partner may also have to challenge the anchored dynamics of their respective families of origin, which gives their conflicts meaning. For example, in a *success vs. sabotage (big vs. small)* master conflict, being "bigger" or eclipsing the success of a parent might be perceived as risking the wrath of that parent. People therefore "want it all," and they may spend years in treatment trying to find a way to accomplish this. Most people prefer to "stay the same without the pain," even at the expense of maintaining their symptoms. Philosopher Sir Isiah Berlin (1958) described this dilemma as "the necessity and agony of choice" (p. 54).

Master conflicts exist even in the healthiest of couples. Some people can better tolerate the anxiety and depression that often comes with change. Problematic relationships can be salvageable, however, if each partner can agree which side of the conflict to choose, or to "integrate" the two comfortably—which most tend to attempt. Their internalized conflicts will then be under control, and symptoms may dissipate. On the other hand, if a conflict is unbalanced for too long, symptoms often ensue and thrive.

Choosing a Life Partner

An important tenet of MCT is that individuals seek out a mate with the same master conflict: their "twin-in-conflict." Albeit unconscious, this choice helps to avert change and the sacrifice it often entails. For example, if an ambitious woman is in conflict about achieving financial success (e.g., one side of her wants to reach her economic goals; the other side feels a need to sabotage them), she would likely feed her conflict by choosing a partner who can serve both sides of her conflict. This individual would need to possess the ability to vacillate between achieving and failing. Typical of a conflict, as the woman neared her goals, she, her partner, or both, would balance their shared conflict by sabotaging the success. The partner would fail as well. In contrast, if either partner was skewed too far toward failure, both would mobilize to avert a disaster. If this woman was not in conflict about achieving success, she would then partner up with someone who couldn't or wouldn't sabotage her. She would not need someone like her to balance her conflict.

As a fail-safe against change, couples may unconsciously put their conflicts on "pause" or temporarily appear to have them under control. While this may prove positive in certain situations, such as avoiding a fight at a social event, they may inadvertently convince themselves that they are no longer in need of treatment. A couple with a *giving vs. withholding* conflict may be intimate on vacation—taking turns meeting one another's needs. But because their conflict remains in their unconscious, a fight might break out on the plane ride home or as soon as they return to familiar surroundings. One couple were so convinced that more vacations were the answer to their relational woes that they prematurely terminated treatment and proceeded to travel the world. The couple did indeed travel, but they apparently fought all throughout Europe. Once they made travel the "constant" in their lives, the conflict flared up again. Master conflicts travel; they go wherever we go. People who think a solution lies in the external world are only trying to solve an internal problem with an external solution—and it usually does not work. No vacation, new car, or cross-country move will escape a master conflict; it has both a visa and a passport (Betchen, 2010).

There is no cure for a master conflict; only management and control via an appropriate balance of conflicting sides. In most cases, this alleviates the symptoms presented in treatment. As mentioned, to "maintain" a balanced-shared conflict and a symptom-free relationship, each partner of a couple must give up something to get something. In those couples with an unbalanced *power vs. passivity* conflict, for example, one partner may have to balance his or her own conflict by giving up a little power or taking less responsibility. This will allow the corresponding mate to take more power, provided he or she is willing to give up the benefits of assuming less responsibility.

The MCT practitioner does not make any decisions for the couple or allow personal values to influence either partner's choice. The therapist can, however, help the couple to explore the potential consequences of their decision. Freud (1917/1963) wrote:

> I can assure you that you are misinformed if you suppose that advice and guidance in the affairs of life play an integral part in analytic influence. On the contrary, so far as possible we avoid the role of a mentor such as this, and there is nothing we would rather bring about than that the patient should make his decisions for himself.
>
> (p. 433)

Waelder (1960) aptly pointed out that it is the job of the therapist "to open the area of conflict widely and clearly, with a view to discovering possible unconscious elements, ultimately to help the patient to 'make peace with himself'" (p. 220). MCT is based on the concept that two opposing forces are necessary to make a whole person, and yet powerful enough to cause the individual pain. It is the aim of MCT to help each partner of a couple to make peace with themselves and one another.

The Greeks, Freud, and Conflict

The concepts of "opposites" and "opposition" (conflict) precede Freud and are well-grounded in Western philosophy. There is little doubt that Freud was influenced by the Greeks. In the article, *Freud and the Greeks: A Study of the Influence of Classical Greek Mythology and Philosophy Upon the Development of Freudian Thought*, Tourney (1965) contended that Freud utilized Greek concepts, analogies, and metaphors to increase the understanding of his psychoanalytic concepts and treatment of neurosis.

Thompson (2000) wrote: "Freud's grasp of and appreciation for Greek philosophy probably exceeded that of many philosophers; his imaginative incorporation of ideas from Socrates, Plato, Aristotle, and Empedocles into his clinical theories and technique demonstrates a gift for practical application that would rival the most gifted artist" (p. 463). Freud made use of the Oedipus Complex as mentioned, as well as narcissism, and his final instinct theory consisting of Eros, or the life or sex instinct, and Thanatos, or the destructiveness or death instinct. In *Group Psychology and the Analysis of the Ego*, he wrote: "In its origin, function, and relation to sexual love, the 'Eros' of the philosopher Plato coincides exactly with the love-force, the libido of psychoanalysis" (Freud, 1921/1955, p. 91).

Perhaps most germane to MCT is the resemblance of Freud's theories as they relate to the Greek "problem of opposites in conflict" (Tourney, 1965,

p. 67). Plato (429–347 BCE) and Aristotle (384–322 BCE) recognized the precedent set by many pre-Socratic thinkers—those who have lived before or during the life of Socrates (469–399 BCE)—to incorporate the concept of opposites in philosophical thought as it related to physical, physiological, or psychological phenomena (Cranney, 2005; Lloyd, 1995). Aristotle claimed that "*all* his predecessors adopted opposites as principles" (Lloyd, 1995, p. 15). The great philosopher was referring to pre-Socratics such as Anaximander, who studied physical change in the world such as the transitionary process from bright to dark, warm to cool, and moist to dry (Wheelwright, 1997). Parmenides also analyzed changes in the physical world "partly in terms of opposites" (Lloyd, 1995, p. 19). He contrasted fire and light, for example, which he saw as equal but opposite.

Pythagoras was a philosopher and mathematician whose many followers were often referred to as Pythagoreans. The Pythagoreans' Table of Opposites has been used by great thinkers including Plato and Aristotle to try and understand some of the most profound questions in philosophy. The table included such opposites as one and many, right and left, light and darkness, and good and evil, to name a few. The pair of "one and many" raises the Platonic question: If the universe is one, then what is its underlying, unifying aspect? This is commonly referred to as the problem of "the one over many" (Aristotle, trans. McKeon, 2001; Matthews & Cohen, 1968, p. 630).

The famed Sophist, Protagoras, was the first to claim that there were two opposing sides to every question. He built his arguments on this premise and was said to be the first "to teach tricks of argument to pleaders on both sides of a question" (Wheelwright, 1997, p. 245). Considered a humanist, Protagoras wrote, "Man is the measure of all things: of things that are, that they are; of things that are not, that they are not" (p. 239).

Some followers of the pre-Socratic Hippocrates, considered the father of medicine, ultimately attributed many diseases to one of a pair of opposites, such as hot and cold and wet and dry. It was believed that the body contained black and yellow bile, blood, and phlegm; substances which increased and decreased depending on the seasons of the year. Those diseases that are predominant in one season won't be in another, and each disease is most prominent during the season that is in keeping with its nature. Black bile and blood were considered strongest in the summer and autumn because these are generally warm, dry seasons; yellow bile and phlegm are at their weakest levels. In winter, yellow bile and phlegm increase; black bile and blood decrease. Disease strikes when the substances become too hot or too cold, or too wet or too dry—when an imbalance occurs. The cure was not to completely rid the body of one or more of these elements, because it was believed that they could not exist without the other; they are interdependent, and life would cease if any were absent. Rather, the treatment process called for a counterbalance of the opposites. For example, if a patient was too cold or wet, as is more likely in the winter, hot and dry food would be considered a remedy (Hippocrates, trans. Chadwick & Mann, 1983; Lloyd, 1995).

Heraclitus, as noted in *The Fragments of the Work of Heraclitus of Ephesus on Nature and Heracliti Ephesii Reliquiae* (Heraclitus of Ephesus, trans. Patrick & Bywater, 2006), proposed the "unity of opposites." The pre-Socratics believed that all things are one, in that each opposite is inseparable from its other; and despite the tension, they depend on one another for their identity. There is unity in their duality: day and night; alive and dead; asleep and awake. Light is different from dark, but both are needed to exist. Up is different from down, but one cannot go up if they weren't already down, and *vice versa*. Heraclitus claimed, "it is harmony by tension" (p. 62). He also saw nonphysical opposites as being the same. For example, good and evil were perceived as two sides of the same coin. He wrote: "The same thing may be good or evil according to the side from which you look at it" (p. 64). Famous for his theory of "flux," Heraclitus believed that all things remained in motion; that nothing stays fixed: "You cannot step twice into the same river, for other waters and yet others go ever flowing on" (Wheelwright, 1997, p. 71). This is in tune with his unity of opposites in that he saw opposites as "continually and reciprocally passing into one another" or "reciprocal transmutations of each other" (Heraclitus of Ephesus, trans. Patrick & Bywater, 2006, p. 63).

In *The Fragments of Empedocles* (Empedocles, trans. Leonard, 2015), the philosopher proposed the theory of four elements: earth, air, fire, and water. When these elements come together, they create love and life; when they separate, they result in strife and death. Empedocles believed that these "conflicting" principles were dynamic, or always in flux. In his famous poem, *On Nature*, Empedocles wrote: "Whiles into One do all unite; Whiles too the same are rent through hate of Strife" (p. 22). The philosopher was referring to the mutual attraction of "like" or Love (φιλία) and the repulsion of the "unlike" as Hate or Strife (νεῖς).

Freud (1937/1964) referred to Empedocles as: "one of the grandest and most remarkable figures in the history of Greek Civilization," whose "mind seems to have united the sharpest contracts" (p. 245). His interpretation of the philosopher's concept was "that two principles governed events in the life of the universe and in the life of the mind, and that these principles were everlastingly at war with each other" (p. 246). Freud admitted that his instinct theory consisting of Eros and Thanatos reflected Empedocles's principles of Love and Strife. Freud wrote:

> The two fundamental principles of Empedocles—φιλία and νεῖς—are, both in name and function, the same as our two primal instincts, *Eros* and *Destructiveness*, the first of which endeavors to combine what exists into even greater unities, while the second endeavors to dissolve those combinations and to destroy the structures to which they have given rise.
> (p. 246)

Influenced by the pre-Socratics, Plato made use of opposites and opposition in his dialogues, often using Socrates as his protagonist. For example, the setting for *Phaedo* takes place in a prison in the village of Philius, some distance from Athens. There, Socrates is imprisoned for corrupting the youth of Athens and rejecting the religious mainstream (Plato, trans. Jowett, 2005). Surrounded by some of his most loyal followers, notably Simmias, Cebes, Crito, and Phaedo—whom Plato employs as the narrator of this work—they engage in a discussion only hours before Socrates is to take the poison that would result in his death. Followers of the great philosopher are understandably distraught with their mentor's plight and beg him to save himself or to allow for an escape. But fearless Socrates refuses, and employs the concept of opposites to show them that there is nothing to worry about because the soul is immortal, and it will not "admit death" (p. 363); that because all things opposite are generated by opposites, he will live on in perhaps an even better place. Consider the following exchange between Socrates and Cebes (Plato, trans. Jowett, 2005, p. 363):

Socrates: And is there any opposite to life?
Cebes: There is ...
Socrates: And what is that?
Cebes: Death.
Socrates: Then the soul, as has been acknowledged, will never receive the opposite of what she brings.
Cebes: Impossible ...
Socrates: And now ... what did we just call that principle which repels the even?
Cebes: The odd.
Socrates: And that principle which repels the musical or the just?
Cebes: The unmusical ... and the unjust.
Socrates: And what do we call the principle which does not admit of death?
Cebes: The immortal ...
Socrates: And does the soul admit of death?
Cebes: No.
Socrates: Then the soul is immortal?
Cebes: Yes ...

Cranney (2005) contended that Plato's biggest contribution to the concept of opposites "was elucidating when it is possible to predicate a pair of opposites of the same subject at the same time" (p. 1). The following exchange between Simmias and Socrates supports this notion (Plato, trans. Jowett, 2005, p. 359):

Socrates: This is your way of speaking; and yet when you say that Simmias is larger than Socrates and shorter than Phaedo, do you not predicate of Simmias both largeness and smallness?

Simmias: Yes, I do.
Socrates: But still you allow that Simmias does not really surpass Socrates, as the words may seem to imply, because he is Simmias, but by reason of the size which he has; just as Simmias does not surpass Socrates because he is Simmias, any more than because Socrates is Socrates, but because he has smallness when compared with the largeness of Simmias?
Simmias: True.
Socrates: And if Phaedo surpasses him in size, this is not because Phaedo is Phaedo, but because Phaedo has largeness relatively to Simmias, who is comparatively smaller?
Simmias: That is true.

In the *Republic* (Plato, trans. Scharffenberger, 2005), Plato offered his Tripartite Theory in which he breaks the soul down into three parts: reason—responsible for thought and understanding; spirit—desires that covet victory; and appetite—where basic cravings come from. As illustrated in the dialogue, *Phaedrus* (Plato, trans. Jowett, 2005), the philosopher presented the metaphor of a chariot with two horses: the charioteer represents the rational; the spirit is represented by the "good horse" that follows directives; and the appetite represents the "bad horse" that refuses direction and prefers to follow unruly passions. Copleston (1993) believed Plato was conveying that "there are frequently rival springs of action within man" and "the ethical interest of insisting on the right of the rational element to rule, to act as charioteer" (p. 210). Freud's Structural Theory bears some resemblance to Plato's concept. Freud (1923/1961) wrote of the conflict between the rational ego and the pleasure-seeking id:

> The functional importance of the ego is manifested in the fact that normally control over the approaches to motility devolves upon it. Thus in its relation to the id it is like a man on horseback, who has to hold in check the superior strength of the horse; with this difference, that the rider tries to do so with his own strength while the ego uses borrowed forces. The analogy may be carried a little further. Often a rider, if he is not to be parted from his horse, is obliged to guide it where it wants to go; so in the same way the ego is in the habit of transforming the id's will into action as if it were its own.
>
> (p. 25)

Aristotle was considered the first to develop a system to analyze opposites (Lloyd, 1995). In *Categories*, the philosopher presented four classes of opposites: correlatives, contraries, privatives and positives, and affirmation and negation (Aristotle, trans. McKeon, 2001). Correlatives are opposites that exist in relation to one another; they are said to be interdependent. As an example, the philosopher offered the terms "knowledge" and "known." Contraries are more straightforward than correlatives; they are distinct and not interdependent. For example: "The good is not spoken of as the good *of the bad*, but as *the contrary of the bad*, nor is white spoken of as the white *of the black*, but as *the contrary of the black*" (p. 29).

Privatives and positive opposites are not interdependent but must be of the same subject. Aristotle used "sight" as an example of a positive and "blindness" as a privative; both are related to the eyes. He wrote: "It is a universal rule that each of a pair of opposites of this type has reference to that to which the particular 'positive' is natural" (Aristotle, trans. McKeon, 2001, p. 30). By this he means that because it is natural to have sight, sight then is a positive; blind must therefore be the opposite of sight. Cranney (2005) uses the example: "If Socrates is blind, and Phaedo can see, then 'blind' and 'seeing' are not, in this instance, true opposites. Socrates is either blind or not—this is a statement that shows how privatives and positives are true opposites" (p. 5).

The fourth and final class of opposites are affirmatives and negatives. These concepts are made up of individual statements and therefore are not interdependent. For example, "good" and "evil" are not considered opposites in this case because they are not statements: "Plato is good" is a statement that is either true or false; Plato is either good or he is not (Cranney, 2005).

Plato saw reality on two levels: the visible world of sights and sounds, and the intelligible world of forms that apparently gives the visible world its being. For example, we can say that something we see is beautiful because we have a concept of what the form of beauty is. (Kleinman, 2013). To Plato, the most real things were eternal forms, which had their opposites (Lloyd, 1995). Aristotle, on the other hand, found Plato's theory of forms too abstract. He contended that the visible world was not illusionary, but very real; too real to base its understanding on metaphysical assumptions (Cranney, 2005). As an example of his interest in real things, Aristotle referred to an artisan making a bronze sphere. While bronze was the matter, sphericity was the real form which was imposed by the maker. Aristotle also postulated that coins or statues could be made of bronze, but that bronze remained the foundational "substance" or "substratum" (Herman, 2013, p. 48), thus making it easier for opposites to be derived at (Cranney, 2005).

Nietzsche, Freud, and Conflict

Freud was said to admire the German philosopher Friedrich Nietzsche (Lehrer, 1995). This is not surprising given that Nietzsche, too, was influenced by Greek philosophy and its contradictions. Nietzsche's belief in conflict, which is "identical" to Freud's primary and secondary function process (Lehrer, 1995, p. 1), is perhaps best illustrated by his use of the legend of Apollo and Dionysus in his book *The Birth of Tragedy* (Nietzsche, 1872/2000). In Greek mythology, Zeus had two sons: Apollo, the God of reason and the rational; and Dionysus, the God of chaos, who appealed to emotion and instinct. The Greeks saw the value in each, and the value of two opposing sides pushing against one another. The tension that conflict produced was perceived to be at the center of great art, music, and literature. Several scholars (Armstrong, 2015; Lehrer, 1995) have claimed that Nietzsche strongly believed in the existence and value of conflict. In tune with Heraclitus, his principles "were not inert, or stable," and he considered "strife" and the courage to face it an essential part of living (Kaufman, 1974, p. 241). He argued "that there is a basic conflict at the root of life" (Armstrong, 2015, p. 37) that should be embraced.

Nietzsche reasoned that "we want order, calm, reason and dignity" and yet there is a need "for wild joy and uninhibited desire" (Armstrong, 2015, p. 37). But he also believed that there is dignity in accepting both sides of a conflict. While both Nietzsche and Heraclitus agreed that both sides of a conflict are necessary, they also believed in "some affirmation of value" (Wheelwright, 1997, p. 66). Nietzsche favored the Apollonian over the Dionysian (Kaufman, 1974); Heraclitus preferred "the superiority of the upward way" (Wheelwright, 1997, p. 68). In this sense, clarity, control, and the rational were preferable.

MCT: A Personal Journey

It was in training analysis that I (Betchen) began to consider the Oedipus complex in trying to formulate a treatment model for couples with sexual problems—my specialty. During an analytic session, I mentioned to my analyst that I wanted to write a book. He paused, and then grunted something inexplicable. Several months later I brought the subject up again only to receive a barely audible, "hmmm." A year passed before I brought the idea up a third time, but I was finally rewarded for my persistence. My analyst's response was: "You could have written it by now." This intervention compelled me to try and understand why I was having difficulty achieving something I claimed to have wanted. Was I in conflict? From this point, we explored the reasons for delaying my dream, which in turn led to guilt over surpassing my father's seventh grade education and being favored by my mother, who saw him as a failure. It seemed as plausible as any other explanation for my contradictory behavior. But I wasn't a true believer until my experience at a gym, which I would come to never forget.

I was in the changing room speaking with an 80-year-old man with little formal education. I had long admired this gentleman for his tenacity and financial achievements, given his limitations. The man was standing to my left. At some point during our conversation, a friend with very impressive academic credentials joined us to my right and began to talk about a rather highbrow subject that my friend to the left knew little about. My first reaction was one of panic. Will my friend to the left feel excluded, insulted, or humiliated by the turn of the conversation? Will he be angry with me for allowing this shift to occur? On the other hand, I was very interested in what my erudite friend had to say. I was in conflict. My initial reaction was to dissociate, or go into what felt like a trance. I took this avenue rather than make a choice between what felt like two fathers struggling for control of my destiny. Luckily, at the precise point that I re-engaged, the elderly man politely excused himself. In discussing this experience in analysis, I came to realize that the man to my left resembled my poor father—the man I admired on some level but didn't necessarily want to model. Although I saw the man to my right as an admirable candidate, I was too anxious and guilty to fully commit to that direction.

With this experience, I soon embraced Freud's Oedipus Complex and conflict theory in general. I began to "think conflict," as my training analyst would put it. This led me to the analytic writings of others: Brenner's (1982) *The Mind in Conflict*; Waelder's (1976) *Psychoanalysis: Observation, Theory, Application*; and Paris's (2000) *The Unknown Karen Horney: Essays on Gender, Culture, and Psychoanalysis*, in which the prominent female psychoanalyst pointedly wrote about her own conflict regarding personal and professional success.

I also began to pay attention to internal conflict or "man vs. self" in the arts, especially in literature. As depicted in *The Picture of Dorian Gray*, author Oscar Wilde uses a man's portrait to illustrate an internal struggle between the man and his darker, hedonistic side. He did so to convey the external conflict between the current aestheticism at the time and a deeper, more authentic beauty. In *Arrowsmith*, Sinclair Lewis describes the ongoing, often painful and exasperating struggle of protagonist Martin Arrowsmith. A physician, Arrowsmith has great difficulty choosing between the financially secure, affluent life of a dedicated private practitioner and that of an idealistic medical researcher.

Somerset Maugham's protagonist, Charles Strickland, in *The Moon and Sixpence*, gives up everything and moves to Paris to become a painter. Using Strickland as a vehicle, Maugham suggests that no matter how single-mindedly one pursues his art, no matter how much is sacrificed in this process he must ultimately be to his nature. Holden Caulfield in J.D. Salinger's *The Catcher in the Rye* is conflicted about the death of his younger brother. He considers his brother better than he is and grows to be an angry young man, intolerant of others and society. Caulfield's internalized conflict regarding his survival causes him to provoke many external conflicts in his world.

In Christopher Marlowe's *Doctor Faustus*, the protagonist makes a deal with the devil for power and pleasure, but eventually struggles with his decision. He follows the advice of "the bad angel," keeps his deal intact, and loses his soul to the devil. And in Shakespeare's *Hamlet* (Brooke &

Crawford, 1993), the protagonist wants to kill his father's murderer but is concerned about taking up arms against the new king and the potential consequences that might ensue. Hamlet famously debates (p. 995):

> To be, or not to be, that is the question.
> Whether 'tis nobler in the mind to suffer
> The slings and arrows of outrageous fortune,
> Or to take arms against a sea of troubles
> And by opposing end them. To die: to sleep.
> No more; and by a sleep to say we end
> The heart-ache and the thousand shocks
> That flesh is heir to: 'tis a consummation
> Devoutly to be wish'd. To die: to sleep.

Convinced that my training analyst was right when he said, "conflict makes the world go around," I considered applying a conflict model to my couples work. I chose to perceive each partner in a couple as if they were engaged in an unbalanced conflict of opposites and the symptoms this could produce. This is the genesis of the MCT approach. In sum, MCT borrows from Freudian theory by attempting to understand what it is that each partner truly wants and what are the internalized opposing forces preventing each from getting it; it is in the confines of these conflicts that symptoms develop, sexual and otherwise.

The authors have cited 19 master conflicts comprised of seemingly opposites that are believed to develop in the family of origin and thus merit the tracking of what Bowen (1978) referred to as each partner's "multigenerational transmission process." Again, conflicts are passed by parents to children through contradictory messages and behaviors. Bowen's concept of "differentiation," or increased autonomy from the influences of the family of origin, is employed to balance and control internalized conflicts and alleviate associated symptoms. Sexual exercises are strategically utilized to enhance conflict therapy in treating various sexual disorders. The following chapter will discuss some of the more specific characteristics of master conflicts and their development. In doing so, the similarity between them and the concepts discussed by the previously cited philosophers and scholars will become more apparent.

Summary

It makes sense that a couple with relationship problems will likely suffer from sexual problems and *vice versa*. Therefore, the value of integrating sex and couples therapy should not be underestimated. Some scholars (Betchen, 2015; Hertlein, Weeks, & Gambescia, 2015; Lief, 1977; McCarthy, 2015; Sager, 1976; Scharff & Scharff, 1991; Schnarch, 1991; Weeks & Hof, 1987) have long called for this union but with limited response. The purpose of this chapter is to acquaint the reader with an original treatment model, MCT, developed specifically to treat couples who suffer from a wide range of relationship issues, especially those of a sexual nature. The model combines certain aspects of psychoanalytic conflict theory (Freud, 1910/1957) with that of psychodynamic systems work (Bowen, 1978) and the basic principles and practice of sex therapy (Kaplan, 1974, 1983). To confirm that conflict theory has a base well-steeped in philosophy and psychoanalysis, we have traced the concept of conflict from the pre-Socratics, such as Heraclitus and Empedocles (Wheelwright, 1997), to the more contemporary philosophy of Nietzsche (Kaufman, 1974), to Freudian theory and technique (Tourney, 1965). If the reader were to track a concept back in time, that concept would likely reveal itself in many different contexts across many different professional fields. It would then be clear how the previous way in which the concept was applied has influenced its subsequent applications. We have found that the same is true for the concept of internal conflict.

References

Armstrong, J. (2015). *Nietzsche: Great thinkers of modern life*. New York, NY: Pegasus Books.
Berlin, I. (1958). *Two concepts of liberty*. Oxford, England: Clarendon.
Betchen, S. (2001a). Hypoactive sexual desire in a couple with unresolved loyalty conflicts. *Journal of Sex Education and Therapy*, 26(2), 71–81.
Betchen, S. (2001b). Premature ejaculation as symptomatic of age difference in a husband and wife with underlying power and control conflicts. *Journal of Sex Education and Therapy*, 26(1), 34–44.
Betchen, S. (2005). *Intrusive partners – elusive mates: The pursuer-distancer dynamic in couples*. New York, NY: Routledge.
Betchen, S. (2006). Husbands who use sexual dissatisfaction to balance the scales of power in their dual-career marriages. *Journal of Family Psychotherapy*, 17, 19–35. doi:10.1300/J085v17n02_02
Betchen, S. (2010). *Magnetic partners: Discover how the hidden conflict that once attracted you to each other is now driving you apart*. New York, NY: Free Press.
Betchen, S. (2015). Premature ejaculation: An integrative, intersystems approach for couples. In K. Hertlein, G.R. Weeks, & N. Gambescia (Eds.), *Systemic sex therapy* (2nd ed.) (pp. 90–107). New York, NY: Routledge.
Bowen, M. (1978). *Family therapy in clinical practice*. New York, NY: Aronson.
Brenner, C. (1982). *The mind in conflict*. Madison, CT: International Universities Press.
Brooke, T., & Crawford, J.R. (1993). The tragedy of Hamlet: Prince of Denmark. In W. Cross and T. Brooke (Eds.), *The Yale Shakespeare: The complete works* (pp. 977–1018). New York, NY: Barnes & Noble Books.
Chadwick, J., & Mann, W.N. (1983). (Trans.). *Hippocratic writings*. London, England: Penguin.
Christensen, A., Atkins, D., & Baucom, B. (2010). Marital status and satisfaction five years following a randomized clinical trial comparing traditional versus integrative

behavioral couple therapy. *Journal of Consulting and Clinical Psychology, 78,* 225–235. doi:10.1037/0018132
Cleveland Clinic. (2016). *Diseases & conditions: An overview of sexual dysfunction.* Retrieved December 13, 2016, from www. my.clevelandclinic.org/health/diseases_conditions/hic_An_Overview_of_Sexual_Dysfunction
Copleston, F. (1993). *A history of philosophy* (Vol. 1). New York, NY: Image.
Cranney, C.J. (2005). *Opposites in Plato and Aristotle.* Retrieved December 20, 2016, from: http://aporia.byu.edu/pdfs/cranney-opposites_in_plato_and_aristotle.pdf
Davidson, H., & Betchen, S. (2017, March 15). *Master conflict theory in action: A model for integrating couples and sex therapy.* Six-hour pre-conference institute. Annual American Counseling Association (ACA Conference), San Francisco, CA.
Doherty, W. (2002). Bad couples therapy: How to avoid doing it. *Psychotherapy Networker, 26,* 26–33.
Freud, S. (1910/1957). Five lectures on psycho-analysis, Leonardo da Vinci and other works. In J. Strachey (Ed. and Trans.), *The standard edition of the complete psychological works of Sigmund Freud* (Vol. 11, pp. 9–238). London, England: Hogarth Press and the Institute for Psychoanalysis.
Freud, S. (1917/1963). Introductory lectures on psycho-analysis (Part III). In J. Strachey (Ed. And Trans.), *The standard edition of the complete psychological works of Sigmund Freud* (Vol. 16, pp. 243–463). London, England: Hogarth Press and the Institute for Psychoanalysis.
Freud, S. (1921/1955). Beyond the pleasure principle, group psychology and other works. In J. Strachey (Ed. and Trans.), *The standard edition of the complete psychological works of Sigmund Freud* (Vol. 18, pp. 69–274). London, England: Hogarth Press and the Institute for Psychoanalysis.
Freud, S. (1923/1961). The ego and the id and other works. In J. Strachey (Ed. and Trans.), *The standard edition of the complete psychological works of Sigmund Freud* (Vol. 19, pp. 13–293). London, England: Hogarth Press and the Institute for Psychoanalysis.
Freud, S. (1933/1964). New introductory lectures on psycho-analysis and other works. In J. Strachey (Ed. and Trans.), *The standard edition of the complete psychological works of Sigmund Freud* (Vol. 22, pp. 7–255). London, England: Hogarth Press and the Institute for Psychoanalysis.
Freud, S. (1937/1964). Moses and monotheism, an outline of psycho-analysis and other works. In J. Strachey (Ed. and Trans.), *The standard edition of the complete psychological works of Sigmund Freud* (Vol. 23, pp. 7–301). London, England: Hogarth Press and the Institute for Psychoanalysis.
Gottman, J. (1999). *The marriage clinic: A scientifically based marital therapy.* New York, NY: Norton.
Herman, A. (2013). *The cave and the light: Plato versus Aristotle, and the struggle for the soul of western civilization.* New York, NY: Random House.
Hertlein, K., Weeks, G., & Gambescia, N. (Eds.). (2015). Systemic sex therapy (2nd ed.). New York, NY: Routledge.
Jowett, B. (Trans.). (2005). *The essential dialogues of Plato.* New York, NY: Barnes & Noble Classics.
Kaplan, H.S. (1974). *The new sex therapy: Active treatment of sexual dysfunctions.* New York, NY: Times Books.

Kaplan, H.S. (1983). *The evaluation of sexual disorders: Psychological and medical aspects*. New York, NY: Brunner/Mazel.
Kaufman, W. (1974). *Nietzsche: Philosopher, psychologist, antichrist*. Princeton, NJ: Princeton University Press.
Kleinman, P. (2013). *Philosophy 101: From Plato and Socrates to ethics and metaphysics, an essential primer on the history of thought*. Avon, MA: Adams Media.
Lehrer, R. (1995). *Nietzsche's presences in Freud's life and thought on the origins of a psychology of dynamic unconscious mental functioning*. New York, NY: State University of New York Press.
Leif, H. (1977). What's new in sex research? Inhibited sexual desire. *Medical Aspects in Human Sexuality, 2*, 94–95.
Leonard, W.E. (Trans.). (2015). *The fragments of Empedocles*. London, England. Forgotten Books.
Lloyd, G.E.R. (1995). *Polarity and analogy: Two types of argumentation in early Greek thought*. Indianapolis, IN: Hackett.
Matthews, G., & Cohen, M.S. (1968). The one and the many. *The Review of Metaphysics, 21*(4), 630–655.
McCabe, M., Sharlip, I., Lewis, R., Atalla, E., Balon, R., Fisher, A., Laumann, E., Lee, S., Segraves, R. (2016). Incidence and prevalence of sexual dysfunction in women and men: A consensus statement from the fourth international consultation of sexual medicine 2015. *The Journal of Sexual Medicine, 13*, 144–152. doi.org/10.1016/j.jsxm.2015.12.034
McCarthy, B., & McCarthy, E. (2003). *Rekindling desire: A step-by-step program to help low-sex and no-sex marriages*. New York, NY: Brunner/Routledge.
McCarthy, M. (2015). *Sex made simple: Clinical strategies for sexual issues*. Eau Claire, WI: PESI Publishing & Media. book
McKeon, R. (Ed. & Trans.). (2001). *The basic works of Aristotle*. New York, NY: The Modern Library.
Nietzsche, F. (1872/2000). *The birth of tragedy*. In D. Smith (Trans.), Oxford World Classics. Oxford, England: Oxford University Press.
Paris, B. (Ed.). (2000). *The unknown Karen Horney: Essays on gender, culture, and psychoanalysis*. New Haven, CT: Yale University Press.
Patrick, G.T.W., & Bywater, I. (Eds. & Trans.). (2006). *Heraclitus of Ephesus: The fragments of the work of Heraclitus of Ephesus on nature and Heracliti Ephesii reliquiae*. Whitefish, MT: Kessinger Publishing.
Sager, C. (1976). Sex in marital therapy. *American Journal of Psychiatry, 33*, 555–558.
Scharff, D., & Scharff, J. (1991). *Object relations couples therapy*. Northvale, NJ: Aronson.
Scharffenberger, E.W. (Trans.). (2005). *Plato: Republic*. New York, NY: Barnes & Noble Classics.
Schnarch, D. (1991). *Constructing the sexual crucible: An integration of sexual and marital therapy*. New York, NY: Norton.
Snyder, D., Wills, R., & Grady-Fletcher, A. (1991). Long-term effectiveness of behavioral versus insight-oriented marital therapy: A 4-year follow-up study. *Journal of Consulting and Clinical Psychology, 59*, 138–141. doi.org/10.1037/0022

Thompson, G.M. (2000). Review of the book *Nietzsche's presences in Freud's life and thought on the origins of a psychology of dynamic unconscious mental functioning*, by R. Lehrer. *Psychoanalytic Review, 87*, 463–467.

Tiefer, L. (1996). The medicalization of sexuality: Conceptual, normative, and professional issues. *Annual Review of Sex Research, 7*, 252–282.

Tiefer, L. (2004). *Sex is not a natural act*. Boulder, CO: Westview Press.

Toman, W. (1976). *Family constellation: Its effects on personality and social behavior*. New York, NY: Springer.

Tourney, G. (1965). Freud and the Greeks: A study of the influence of classical Greek mythology and philosophy upon the development of Freudian thought. *Journal of the History of the Behavioral Sciences, 1*, 67–85. doi: 10.1002/1520-6696(19650101)1:1<67::AID-JHBS2300010109>

Vernon, P. (April 24, 2010). The race to discover Viagra for women. *The Guardian*. Retrieved December 13, 2016, from: www.theguardian.com/society/2010/apr/25/women-viagra-polly-vernon

Waelder, R. (1960). *Basic theory of psychoanalysis*. New York, NY: International Universities Press.

Waelder, R. (1976). *Psychoanalysis: Observation, theory, application*. New York, NY: International Universities Press.

Weeks, G., Gambescia, N., & Hertlein, K. (2016). *A clinician's guide to systemic sex therapy* (2nd ed.). New York, NY: Routledge.

Weeks, G. & Hof, G. (Eds.). (1987). *Integrating sex and marital therapy: A clinical guide*. New York, NY: Brunner/Mazel.

Wheelwright, P. (Ed.). (1997). *The pre-Socratics*. Upper Saddle River, NJ: Prentice-Hall, Inc.

Chapter 2

Key Features of a Master Conflict

We have already mentioned that a master conflict unconsciously determines who we choose for a significant other, and that we pick someone with the same master conflict. Another feature of a master conflict is that it does so expeditiously ... almost magically. The unconscious conflict convinces us that: "This person understands me. Finally, I've found my soulmate."

Many people believe that they choose their mates based on physical attraction or commonality. Others look for someone with characteristics that they lacked, or their opposite: "I'm quiet and shy and I don't have a lot of friends. I wanted someone who was more assertive and outgoing," or, "I came from a small, broken home; he has a large, close-knit family." These are conscious choices. But for relationships to develop into something more significant, their underlying conflicts must match. This may or may not apply to brief encounters or short-term relationships because most can tolerate a different master conflict for a relatively short period of time. Rather, this theory pertains to those who are interested in a long-term relationship or marriage. It is in these relationships that conflicts are replicated, allowing us to live as we did as children and young adults.

Spotting someone with a similar conflict is relatively easy if consideration is given to the concept of sameness rather than opposites. An individual may reveal an underlying master conflict when speaking or telling a personal story. A male only child lamented: "I had to take care of my mother; she can be very difficult, but I'm her only child and I'd feel guilty if I neglected to look after her." This statement might reveal a conflict such as *getting one's needs met vs. caretaking*. Despite ambivalent feelings, the son fulfills an obligation to his mother. A second example: "Sadly, I attended five different colleges before I earned my degree." This individual is tenacious, but the circuitous route taken to reach a goal may reflect either an *adequacy vs. inadequacy* or a *success vs. sabotage (big vs. small)* conflict. And third: "I have always challenged authority figures. I don't like to be told what to do." This could indicate a *control vs. chaos (out-of-control)* or *conformity vs. rebellion* conflict.

Body movements and facial expressions may also reveal a master conflict: "She told me that she wanted to spend time together, but her body language conveyed that she was turned off by my presence. I actually thought that I disgusted her." This dynamic might convey a conflict such as *closeness vs. distance* or *acceptance vs. rejection*. The chapter on assessment will detail the process that leads to the discovery of a couple's master conflict.

When the master conflict senses its own kind, it compels us to home in on an individual, and our choice is made. Many of the couples we have seen in treatment can attest to the power of these conflicts. Lodged in our unconscious, they take control of our lives and flare up at the most inexplicable times. For example, we always warn our clients that once they identify their conflict to keep it in the forefront of their minds, especially when they are doing well.

It must be remembered that to achieve balance, both sides of the conflict must be operating so that a success may be closely followed by a failure: commitment must be followed by a need for freedom; or adequacy must be followed by inadequacy. Just when you think you have beaten the conflict, it strikes. For example, John was quickly climbing the academic ladder. Once he was named Dean of his university's law school, he began to act out in public—abuse of prescription drugs and a bad temper were often involved—until he was threatened by the school's board. It turned out that John was rebelling against his father's need for him to excel via the university's administration. Therefore, it was determined that John suffered from a *conformity vs. rebellion* conflict that seemed to flare up with every accolade or promotion he received. He was simply conflicted about giving his father what he wanted above all else: great success.

Master conflicts can thrive in different contexts, making them especially hard to recognize. For example, a man with a *success vs. sabotage (big vs. small)* conflict may see his conflict in one aspect of his relationship but fail to grasp its pervasiveness. That is, he may achieve great financial success but fail miserably in his personal life. A man suffering from delayed ejaculation—the symptom of his *giving vs. withholding* master conflict—neglected to consider how withholding his feelings or refusing to help colleagues in need hindered his social life as well.

Fifteen Fast Facts

There are several characteristics of a master conflict that will help the therapist to better understand what it looks like in a relational context, where it originates from, and why it is so difficult to manage (Betchen, 2010). Because "thinking conflict" is counterintuitive to most systemic practitioners, it is important for the therapist to keep these facts in the forefront when treating a couple. If they are forgotten or intentionally left out of the treatment process, a couple's behavior may appear nonsensical and at times overwhelming to the therapist. In *Thus Spoke Zarathustra*, Nietzsche (1883–1885/1966) wrote:

"There is always some madness in love. But there is also always some reason in madness" (p. 41). It is believed that a conflict perspective can explain the seemingly inexplicable better than most other models—it is the forte of this approach. All the factors to follow will be expounded upon later in the book.

1 *Master conflicts are internalized in childhood:*
   A master conflict is generally formed in youth and based on conflicts transmitted in a variety of ways (e.g., verbally, behaviorally, or both) by one's family-of-origin. By the time a person reaches young adulthood, the master conflict is usually internalized or firmly in place for life.
2 *Factors that can influence a master conflict:*
   Religious and cultural factors, as well as environmental stress, such as chronic bullying, discrimination, serious illness, and trauma, may "lead" to a master conflict or exacerbate an established one. To be the actual cause of a conflict, the experience must have occurred in one's childhood and must have been experienced as particularly intense.

   A singular traumatic event such as the Holocaust can lead to a master conflict. A female Auschwitz survivor (as a child) was referred for couple's therapy because she had difficulty trusting her husband and extended family—her behavior almost bordered on paranoia and was driving her family away. When asked in treatment if she trusted anyone, she answered: "Everyone is a German to me." Someone who was imprisoned as an adult may have experienced the concentration camp based on their pre-existing master conflict. In *Man's Search for Meaning*, Victor Frankel (1984) contended that personality was correlated with one's survival of the camps.
3 *Master conflicts are usually lodged in the unconscious:*
   Clients may be aware of one side of a conflict, but not both sides. People tend to be conscious of what they perceive as the positive side of their conflict. For example, an individual might be conscious of the wish to succeed, but not the need to fail; the latter is most often repressed to protect the individual from facing painful truths.
4 *Master conflicts are prominent:*
   Clients may have multiple conflicts, but there is only one master conflict, and it is the most powerful and influential of all conflicts. While some conflicts may appear similar, there are significant albeit subtle differences that distinguish them. An accurate assessment helps to make the treatment process and therapeutic outcome more successful. We recommend that after gathering a significant amount of data, the therapist initially choose three possible conflicts, and through a process of elimination, work with the couple to identify the true master conflict.
5 *Master conflicts are responsible for most relationship symptoms:*
   While other conflicts may cause some strife in a relationship, it is usually short-lived and less serious. An unbalanced master conflict, however, is

chronically disturbing and more responsible for relationship symptoms than any other conflict.

6 *Master conflicts may be responsible for other problems in life:*
The master conflict may be behind problems that are evident in the client's relationships with friends, coworkers, and employers. The master conflict may negatively impact the client's work, hobbies, social life, or other interests as well. In this sense, a master conflict can unconsciously control how one functions in the world.

7 *One side of a master conflict is not necessarily better than the other:*
While clients may attribute the qualities "good" or "bad" to the opposite sides of a conflict, it is important that the therapist refrains from making such a value judgment. Both sides of a master conflict have their pros and cons.

8 *Master conflicts determine your choice of partner:*
The master conflict unconsciously controls who people choose to be in serious, long-term relationships with. This concept may or may not apply to one-night stands or flings.

9 *Those in serious or long-term relationships share the same master conflict:*
The master conflict will ensure that the client chooses a partner with the same conflict. We refer to this concept as "twins-in-conflict." While partners may not be the same in every way, they will "share" the same master conflict.

10 *Master conflicts are normal:*
Even in the healthiest of relationships, master conflicts exist. These conflicts are completely normal. All of us have one.

11 *Master conflicts are hard to manage when unbalanced:*
Because master conflicts resist control with a generous tenacity, clients must understand the level of commitment and work required to manage one. Like a disease that resists antibiotics, the conflict is persistent and will present itself differently at times, or shift to unsuspecting contexts.

12 *To manage a master conflict, partners must agree on a strategy:*
For partners to successfully manage a master conflict, they must agree upon a strategy and work collaboratively to implement this strategy.

13 *There is no cure for a master conflict:*
A master conflict can never be completely eradicated. At best, a master conflict will only cause minor, intermittent "flare-ups."

14 *The master conflict goes where you go:*
No matter where a couple goes, the master conflict will always follow.

15 *Management of a master conflict is sufficient:*
While there is no cure for a master conflict, management of the conflict is good enough. If clients can learn to control their conflict, they will be able to alleviate their relationship symptoms faster and more effectively.

The Power of a Master Conflict

Understanding the power of a master conflict is crucial in helping the therapist conceptualize a symptomatic couple (Betchen, 2010). The strength of a conflict is dependent on several factors, all of which the therapist must be mindful of when assessing a couple presenting for treatment. Accurately assessing the conflict's influence will help the therapist to determine the tenacity of a couple's defenses and the couple's potential to regain control over their conflict.

The couple's tolerance for pain

The first factor that contributes to the power of the master conflict is the depth of the couple's pain. An unbalanced master conflict may inflict great pain on a couple. A more balanced conflict will exert less pain and prove more manageable. The amount of pain is determined by the amount of emotional distress both reported and observed. Some clients may express their pain via difficulty regulating emotions; others may present with a flat affect or appear emotionally closed or distant. It is important for the therapist to note the affect presented and the ability of each partner to tolerate it.

Distancing may be interpreted by partners as a form of silent suffering or as a lack of caring. The stories clients tell themselves about the meaning behind their partner's affect are often driven by their experiences in their respective families of origin. The therapist should consider whether the degree of distress reported by each partner matches their affect. If one partner has a significantly lower threshold for pain, a quick separation or divorce may not be far behind.

The length of time the master conflict has been unbalanced

The second factor to consider when examining the power of a master conflict is the length of time that the conflict has been symptomatic. Couples tend to report for treatment when their master conflict has been out of balance for some time. For example, it is not unusual for a couple to ignore a sexual disorder for several years. Oftentimes the symptom bearer will eventually be commanded by the other to attend individual sessions under the threat of divorce or separation. The longer the period of distress, the harder it is to re-balance a master conflict.

The impact of external sources

A careful examination of the power of external factors on the development and maintenance of the master conflict is recommended. It may help the couple's therapist to better understand the impact of discrimination on marginalized groups (e.g., people of color, women, immigrants, the physically disabled, the LGBTQ population), as well as how this discrimination is systemically and institutionally imbedded in our society. A partner's experience with discrimination can produce or exacerbate a master conflict.

As mentioned, a client's master conflict may have been born out of a traumatic event that occurred early in life. This experience may make it more difficult to balance a shared master conflict. A client who experiences a traumatic event in adulthood will experience the trauma via their pre-existing master conflict. The role of both discrimination and trauma on the power of the master conflict will be discussed in more detail in *Chapter 3. Assessment*.

The ability to take responsibility

Each partner's ability to take ownership and responsibility for their role in the conflict should not escape the therapist in the assessment process. Partners that blame one another or focus exclusively on their counterpart's wrongdoings will suffer a poor prognosis. To manage a master conflict, each partner must accept their individual contribution to the conflict. Some partners may be incapable of owning their roles, which in and of itself may be an indication of a specific conflict. For example, a couple with a *justice vs. injustice* conflict may consider taking ownership of any relational difficulty as unfair or unjust.

The couple's problem-solving capability

Therapists must consider the communication and problem-solving skills of each partner. Without these skills, even less intense conflicts might be impossible to gain control over. These skills are not necessarily a reflection of intellectual capacity. Sometimes the most intelligent partners may lack communication skills, while those with average or lower intelligence may be better communicators and excel at resolving interpersonal problems. Others may possess refined communication and problem-solving skills but refuse to use them, particularly if they are trying to punish their partner or have already checked out of the relationship. Because these skills are learned in the family of origin, it is important to explore this connection with each partner.

The level of relationship desire

In understanding the power of a master conflict, the therapist must also gauge how badly a couple wishes to remain together. Some couples will put up with an inordinate amount of abuse or turmoil. For example, a woman forced her husband to attend couple's therapy to stop him from carrying on his latest affair; she had no intention of divorcing him for his cumulative number of transgressions. On the contrary, others will part at the first sign of what many might consider a minor infraction. A wife contacted a lawyer and proceeded towards divorce because her husband made a habit of staring at other women, even though both partners admitted he had never engaged in any other contact.

It is important to pay attention to what each partner is self-reporting about his or her desire to stay in the relationship. In some cases, the therapist will need to see each partner alone to ascertain this information. Therapists will want to assess whether the needs to remain in the relationship are congruent with what is reported during conjoint treatment. In addition, the therapist should consider whether the stated desires to remain together actually match their actions. Sabotage and lack of follow-through could be indicative of an unbalanced master conflict. Couples can talk about staying together, but without change in their behavior, the dysfunctional dynamic will remain. Couples must also understand the amount of effort needed to manage a master conflict. Without a firm commitment to the work towards this end, a couple will likely fail.

The drive to be healthy

Some people are more comfortable in a dysfunctional environment. The therapist should therefore assess how badly a couple wants to be healthy. Without a desire to achieve success on this level, the prognosis will be a poor one. If partners are consistently resistant to the therapist's recommendations, they may be communicating that they do not want help or cannot tolerate help.

The ability to be healthy

The therapist must consider the couple's ability to achieve a healthy relationship. Those with active addictions are oftentimes unable to successfully negotiate couples therapy until they have reached a point of sobriety, and for some time. We treat these partners only after they gain significant control over their addictions. Some partners with untreated mental illness or a significant Axis-II diagnosis may be unable to maintain a healthy relationship. In these cases, each partner might need to weigh the damage that their out-of-control master conflict is inflicting on their relationship and carefully assess the cost benefit of staying together or separating.

The Development of Relationship Symptoms

Because each partner is in possession of an internalized master conflict, it is important to understand the distinction between a balanced and an unbalanced conflict. A balanced master conflict will cause few problems in the relationship. It is natural for all couples to spend their lives attempting to maintain a certain level of balance to avoid or control relationship symptoms. Problems develop in the relationship, however, when one or both partners unbalance a master conflict, or it weighs too heavily on one side of the conflict. For example, a middle-aged couple presented for treatment because the husband had no desire to have sex with his wife. The couple reported a robust sex life while they were struggling to achieve financial freedom but had taken a drastic turn when the wife's business took off and changed their entire standard of living. The couple were considered to have a *success vs. sabotage (big vs. small)* conflict. When both of their businesses achieved an equally moderate amount of success, their conflict was balanced. Once the wife had become too successful, their master conflict began to produce symptoms. Paradoxically, a master conflict may be unbalanced by good or bad experiences or events.

Traumatic life events in adulthood can also unbalance a master conflict. For example, a couple struggled with balancing their *getting your needs met vs. caretaking* master conflict after one partner was in a horrific vehicular accident. The accident shifted their once balanced master conflict (i.e., the husband did more caretaking of the wife, which the wife enjoyed) when the wife was put in position of caretaking for the husband while he was recovering. They soon found themselves in a battle over who was to take care of whom.

In *Chapter 1. Introduction*, we used a seesaw with two politicians sitting opposite one another to depict the internal battle between two sides of a master conflict. To survive and thrive, couples need to keep their seesaw balanced or agree on how much to tip it and in which direction. When the seesaw tips too far in one direction and for too long a time, serious problems can develop. For example, Figure 2.1 and Figure 2.2 illustrate a couple's *giving vs. withholding* master conflict, in and out of balance. The couple's chief complaint or their prominent symptom is of a sexual nature: one partner wants to have sex and the other refuses. In Figure 2.1, the seesaw is level or balanced, indicating that both partners agree not to have sex. It would also have been balanced if they agreed to have sex. Figure 2.2 illustrates the symptomatic couple: one side of the seesaw is tilting heavily towards the withholding end, indicating a significant imbalance. The stark imbalance is what brought the couple in for treatment. The therapist's job is to help the couple make the emotional and intellectual decisions that will rebalance their conflict, or bring their seesaw as close to a level position as tolerable.

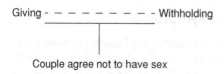

Figure 2.1 Balanced Master Conflict.

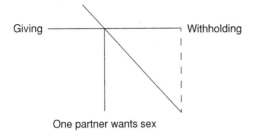

Figure 2.2 Unbalanced Master Conflict.

The master conflict model may be viewed by some as deterministic, even nihilistic. In tune with Freud (1910/1957), we concede it is deterministic in nature. But we firmly believe it to be an optimistic and realistic approach to treating couples. The MCT model accepts the reality that life is a struggle, complete with ups and downs, good times and bad. However, it also offers each couple the power to control their lives from the deepest individual and systemic levels. It may be impossible for people to achieve whatever their perception of perfection is. But they will not have to change significantly to be happier and symptom-free. People only need to be realistic and accept that they cannot have it all. This perspective helps to maintain a balanced or manageable master conflict. The subsequent chapter on treatment will expound upon this process in detail.

Summary

The term, master conflict, was originally derived from the belief that internalized conflicts were unconsciously directing a couple's thoughts and feelings and behaviors. And that these conflicts were their masters. However, after many years of specializing in treating couples with a wide array of symptoms, we came to believe that one conflict was dominant, or primarily responsible for a couple's problems. We readily admit that other conflicts exist and may in fact overlap to some degree with the master conflict, but they did not seem to be consistently responsible for a couple's relational symptoms.

Even after a couple's master conflict is brought to light, couples are skeptical of its power. Connecting the conflict to a couple's sexual issue, for example, or even an impending divorce, can be very difficult. Nevertheless, unbalanced master conflicts are very powerful forces that cannot be managed without a struggle. Couples lose sight of this fact and unwillingly offer the conflict an opportunity to strike at what often seems to be the most inopportune time: just as a person is about to receive an award or promotion, or on the eve of a nodal event such as a wedding. If the experience or event unbalances the conflict, calamity will oftentimes result.

In this chapter, we have discussed the key features of a master conflict and highlighted the influence it can wield, even over our choice of partner. While this chapter is not the most detailed, it might be one of the most important for the therapist to grasp. If the therapist understates the power of a master conflict, the couple will have little hope to regain control over their relationship and associated sexual symptoms.

References

Betchen, S. (2010). *Magnetic partners: Discover how the hidden conflict that once attracted you to each other is now driving you apart.* New York, NY: Free Press.

Frankl, V.E. (1984). *Man's search for meaning: An introduction to logotherapy.* New York, NY: Simon & Schuster.

Freud, S. (1910/1957). Five lectures on psycho-analysis, Leonardo da Vinci and other works. In J. Strachey (Ed. and Trans.), *The standard edition of the complete psychological works of Sigmund Freud* (Vol. 11, pp. 9–238). London, England: Hogarth Press and the Institute for Psychoanalysis.

Nietzsche, F. (1883–85/1966). *Thus spoke Zarathustra.* W. Kaufmann (Trans.). New York, NY: Viking Press.

Chapter 3

Master Conflicts

Listed below are 19 master conflicts that we have identified over our many years of clinical practice with couples (Betchen, 2010). For each conflict, we have included a description and three brief clinical examples. Most of these cases contain sexual content, but the immediate purpose of this chapter is to acquaint the reader with the myriad of master conflicts. We will demonstrate how we integrate sexual disorders in more detail later in the book.

For flexibility, we have allowed for a 20th conflict that we call "other (conflict adjustment)." Choosing this category allows the couple and therapist to adjust or re-name a conflict as they see fit. It is also an admittance there may be more master conflicts yet to be identified. While it is a rare occurrence, some couples prefer that the therapist create a different name for their conflict—one that they feel better resonates with them. Other couples prefer to name their own conflict for the same reason. A female client complained that she could not relate to being told that she suffered form an unbalanced *power vs. passivity* conflict. After relabeling it as a *strength vs. weakness* conflict, however, she was free to move on therapeutically. The word "power" was too pejorative for her to accept in part, because she saw her mother use her power to emasculate her father. We provide no resistance to requests such as these. The main objective is to help move the couple to a higher level of functioning, and if re-naming a conflict will accomplish that, so be it. We do, however, insist on accuracy to prevent a couple from leading themselves astray. Therefore, the name that they choose should be grounded in the couple's family of origin and life experiences. To better illustrate the power and pervasiveness of these master conflicts, we have included a diverse group of couples in the case examples.

1. Acceptance vs. Rejection: One side needs to be accepted; the other side, rejected. Clients with this conflict value pleasing others and demonstrate a desire to be accepted, especially by their partners. Many refer to themselves as "people pleasers." These individuals often have a very high threshold for difficult mates. Coupled with a need for acceptance, they paradoxically tend to reject easily and unconsciously set themselves up to be rejected.

Ex: Maria grew up feeling that she could never please her conservative, Latino parents. She claimed that they were disapproving even prior to her disclosing a lesbian sexual orientation. Maria also wished to be accepted by her beautiful girlfriend, Ally. While Maria adored Ally, she oddly showed little affection for her, even though Ally expressed a need for it numerous times. Ally also begged Maria to avoid political discussions with her family, but Maria refused to honor this request as well. Instead, Maria seemed to use these discussions as a tool to provoke Ally's family to distance from her. Having reached her threshold, Ally threatened to break up with Maria. While claiming to crave acceptance, Maria rejected Ally, and could not help but provoke Ally and her family to reject her in return.

Ex: Jamie and his wife were conservative Christians who married young and had little sexual experience prior to marriage. Jamie reported feeling loved by his wife in many ways but rejected because of their infrequent sexual encounters, which she never initiated. Despite being told numerous times by his wife that she would respond to him sexually if he approached her differently, Jamie continued to initiate sex in a way that turned her off. For example, he would use his tongue when he kissed her or pinch her nipple. For his behavior, Jamie created more opportunity to be rejected sexually.

Ex: Tammy sought treatment with her husband, Joe, because of his erectile dysfunction (ED). Tammy claimed to love Joe but believed that his ED was a result of his lack of attraction for her. Joe adamantly denied this accusation and said that he was very attracted to his wife, whom he called, "hot." Whenever the couple would attempt sex, Tammy would react negatively at the slightest sign that Joe's erection was waning. Both partners felt simultaneously accepted and rejected.

2. Adequacy vs. Inadequacy: One side needs to feel adequate; the other side needs to feel inadequate. Clients with this conflict will usually vacillate between feeling strong and confident and weak and helpless. They may underestimate the support they provide one another as well as the sabotaging behavior.

Ex: Arjun, an Indian man who immigrated to the United States to attend college, was a self-proclaimed loser. The first thing he reported in treatment was that his marriage was arranged to a woman from a lower class because he had only achieved a bachelor's degree. Arjun was skilled at his work and very bright; he excelled in college. Nevertheless, he underachieved and procrastinated in his adult life. He consistently set himself up to be criticized by his wife and parents, who expected more of him.

Ex: Mai immigrated from China with her family as a young child. Mai dreamed of becoming a professional musician. She excelled in performance arts but struggled in academics. Because she was the only Asian student in a *white, working-class neighborhood, she was targeted by her peers. Mai realized her dream by the time she reached young adulthood, yet reported never feeling "good enough" despite high praise from colleagues. Despite the lack of evidence, she also continually questioned whether she was a "good wife" and "good mother." Mai experienced low sexual desire, which she took sole blame for even though her husband's behavior contributed to the problem.*

Ex: Charlie spent his childhood overshadowed by his brother, a terrific athlete, and his sister, a scholar. Although he eventually became more than an adequate physician, Charlie turned his critical eye towards his sex life and wondered whether he was an adequate lover; this despite validation from several women in his past. Charlie's wife thought that their sexual problems stemmed from Charlie, since no former lover had ever complained. But she did wonder whether she was a good enough lover for her husband.

3. Closeness vs. Distance: One side has a need to be close; the other side feels more comfortable with distance. Couples establish levels of closeness and distance, but those who chronically vacillate between the two, producing significant symptoms, are usually suffering from an unbalanced master conflict. Some of the creative ways in which couples unbalance this master conflict may include taking on extra work obligations or domestic responsibilities, instigating fights, hyper focusing on a hobby, or consistently disappearing with friends. Because one side of a conflict is almost immediately triggered by the other side, look for distance to be inserted soon after the most intimate of moments, and *vice versa*.

Ex: Amy grew up with a mother who struggled with untreated depression. When her mother was depressed, she would neglect Amy, but when stable, she was present enough to meet her daughter's needs. The constant flux between closeness and distance represented Amy's master conflict. As a young adult, Amy always wanted to be around her boyfriend—and she enjoyed great sex with him. But when he moved into her apartment, Amy complained that he was "all over her." She soon developed low libido, which, in turn, made him think that she was having an affair.

Ex: Jim was a workaholic whose demanding job allowed him to create a comfortable distance between him and his wife. After Jim was forced into early retirement, his wife mistakenly expected to spend more time with him, but Jim quickly threw himself into golf and his many friends. In the evening, when his wife would attempt to increase their physical closeness, Jim's extreme flatulence repelled his wife, creating yet another barrier. Jim might have easily fixed this problem, but he refused to follow the order of his physician to change his diet and accept medical treatment. While Jim's wife did attempt intimacy, she failed to set appropriate limits with her husband, thus enabling distance to creep in.

Ex: Garrett said that his wife, Mara, never spent time on their relationship and left him feeling alone and lonely. In addition, the couple had infrequent sex, which they both complained about. When the couple's two children were small, Mara busied herself with raising her family, but when they got older, she decided to return to school, leaving her husband alone nearly every night of the week. Despite knowing that time would be needed to re-establish the sexual relationship with her husband, Mara continued to distance herself with activities and other plans. In therapy, Mara sat on the opposite side of the sofa and made it clear that her activities took precedence over treatment. Although her husband complained, he failed to set limits with his wife, and in doing so allowed distance to oftentimes prevail.

4. **Commitment vs. Freedom:** One side needs stability and security of commitment; the other side needs to be free of restraints. People who report jumping from relationship to relationship and those who have had multiple affairs often have this master conflict. Partners who were witness to their parent's extramarital affairs or general lack of commitment to one another may be at greater risk for developing this unruly master conflict. Look for this conflict in other aspects of the client's life, including career choices. Those who change jobs or careers relatively frequently, or choose occupations which require a great deal of travel, may have this conflict.

Ex: Carl grew up witness to his parent's numerous extramarital affairs. Upon turning 51, he claimed that he wanted to marry. But Carl always found at least one thing wrong with each partner and routinely cheated on them. He held onto a primary partner while having flings with others. Once the primary partner discovered Carl's flings, a split would occur, and Carl would promote one of his lovers to primary status. The cycle would soon repeat itself.

Ex: Erica grew up as the daughter of a young, single mother, who spent her life working multiple jobs to provide for Erica and her siblings. The family moved often, making it difficult for Erica to put down roots as a child and teen. In treatment, Erica reported that she didn't want to leave her marriage of 15 years to Dave because he provided her with financial stability. In addition, the couple had a close number of friends and family members. But Erica did have multiple, long-term affairs. Her current lover was urging her to end her marriage, leaving Erica confused: Should she choose her stable but uninspiring married life, or a potentially new and exciting life with her lover?

Ex: Harold, a traveling musician, claimed his marriage was important to him, yet he continued to ignore his wife when she expressed a desire that he curb his work travel. Harold eventually admitted in treatment that he wanted to "have it both ways": He wanted to commit to his wife, but be free to travel as he saw fit. While Harold's wife claimed to enjoy her space, she thought Harold was taking advantage of her flexibility.

5. **Conformity vs. Rebellion:** One side desires to be conservative and follow rules; the other side is compelled to rebel and be free of rules and boundaries. It is important to note that rebellious behavior may not always be blatant, such as refusing to go to work, or stereotypical, like protesting in the streets. Subtle actions, such as refusing to participate in agreed upon domestic responsibilities, or sexual behaviors that a client's partner has explicitly requested, could be construed as acts of rebellion. Clients who grew up in very restrictive households or those who benefitted by breaking the rules in youth may have this master conflict.

Ex: Aaron came across as conservative in his dress, mannerisms, and interactions with others. However, he constantly rebelled against rules and the expectations of others. Despite being at the top of his class, he dropped out of college a semester before graduating. He also refused to follow recommendations at work, which resulted in poor reviews. When his wife said that she would like to have a child, Aaron suddenly developed Delayed Ejaculation. But in treatment, when the therapist gave specific behavioral exercises, Aaron always found a way to resist completing them. Aaron's wife demonstrated her shared conflict by marrying and committing to Aaron against her father's wishes. But she also had an affair early in their marriage. She also did not push Aaron to consult a physician or sex therapist for his Delayed Ejaculation for the longest time and did not initiate any of the assigned home exercises.

Ex: Jennifer grew up in a very conservative, Christian family, but even as a young child, she rebelled. As an adult, Jennifer shuttled her kids to various activities all day and was an active participant in the Parent-Teacher Association. However, Jennifer was a chronic porn user.

Ex: Jamal married, had children, and in turn established a traditional family life just as his parents wanted for him. He also achieved professional status but consistently rebelled against the rules at work and refused to live up to his domestic responsibilities. Jamal simultaneously abided by and detested rules of any kind. For his wife's part, she wanted marriage but had a history of choosing men, like Jamal, who could never commit to her.

6. **Control vs. Chaos (Out-of-Control):** One side needs to be in control; the other side, out-of-control. People with this conflict may attempt to control their partners, and their relationships in general, yet they may choose to settle with a chaotic person. They tend to be attracted to chaos even though it may cause them a great deal of anxiety. But they enjoy the challenge of trying to regain control over the chaos. The chaos may not be obvious; it could

be represented in the form of mismanaging finances or household responsibilities. Clients who were raised in chaotic or overwhelming homes may be more likely to develop this master conflict.

Ex: James was a very controlling man and usually dominated all the women in his life—breaking up with them as soon as he heard the word "marriage." However, when he would ultimately commit to someone, she was usually uncontrollable. His latest love was a histrionic woman who fought with him and cheated routinely. Even in treatment, James would cycle through patterns of regular attendance (creating control) and then miss multiple appointments (adding to the chaos in his life).

Ex: Peter and Sarah reported feeling overwhelmed by their three young children. They said that their familial responsibilities made it difficult for them to connect sexually. Just when the couple began to better manage the daily household chaos and to have sex more frequently, they adopted a set of rambunctious puppies and became "accidently" pregnant with their fourth child.

Ex: Lanny was one of six children from a divorced household. She described her home life as chaotic and claimed that when young, she was put in charge of her mother's finances. While Lanny's controlling and concise style enabled her to become a successful businesswoman, she could not compartmentalize and soon tried to take control of her fiancé—often exhibiting jealousy of others in his life, including his mother and sisters. Lanny would also provoke fights with other female family members and friends. She also harassed her fiancé while he was away on business, often calling non-stop while he was in important meetings and accusing him of cheating or other such transgressions.

7. Getting Your Needs Met vs. Caretaking: One side wants to meet one's personal needs; the other side presents as selfless. Clients that are engaged in an addiction or have family histories of addiction, as well as those raised in families where there was a parent or sibling with an illness that demanded caretaking, may have this master conflict. Typically, one partner—the caretaker—will appear selfless and focus most of their attention and energy on the overtly troubled mate, but ironically, this partner will not allow their needs to be fulfilled. The addict claims to want help and will simultaneously do everything to avoid or sabotage its effectiveness.

Ex: Anika grew up poor and spent her childhood taking care of her mother— a drug addict. As an adult, she also struggled with setting boundaries with her extended family, almost all of whom lived in poverty and struggled with addiction. Anika gave what little money she had to family members who harassed her to support their addictions. She also adopted her cousin's disabled child. Overwhelmed by her responsibilities, Anika developed depression, low sexual desire, and inhibited orgasm. Anika's husband barely made a living yet rebuffed his wife's offer to help him to achieve economic independence. Rather, he seemed content to take advantage of her caretaking. He also proved to be a very selfish lover—which did not help Anika with her orgasm problem. Anika's husband did, however, demand that his wife set stronger limits when it came time to help her family. At times, he was right to do so.

Ex: *Kerry, who was parentified in her family of origin, had her own life goals. But she married two substance abusers who demanded her full attention. Once she realized this pattern, she attempted to choose differently but instead married a depressed, impotent man with Crohn's Disease, who required much of her energy and care. Kerry had switched context—from substance abuse to illness—but not process—the role of a caretaker.*

Ex: *Adam, a gay white male, spent his childhood watching his father battle and eventually succumb to an aggressive cancer. His family members devoted their time and energy to the care of his father before his passing. As an adult, Adam found himself drawn to partners who merited caretaking. Some of these men suffered from drug/alcohol problems, sexual addiction, or mental illness. His current partner is a man who struggles with managing his bipolar disorder.*

8. Giving vs. Withholding: One side has a desire to give; the other side withholds. Partners whose parents were conflicted about offering emotional or financial support may be more at risk for developing this conflict. Some parents might have given in one context but withheld in another.

Ex: *Tommy grew up in a very wealthy family and was showered with gifts by his distant, workaholic parents. As an adult, Tommy gave his wife all the material possessions she could ever want, but he withheld emotionally and sexually from her. Even when the couple had sex, he could not achieve orgasm.*

Ex: *Arya, a young Muslim woman, doted on her husband, a physician. Arya cooked, cleaned, and maintained contact with her extended family abroad; all of which allowed her husband to complete his medical school program more easily. However, Arya was not able to have penetrative sex due to lifelong Genito-Pelvic Pain/Penetration Disorder (GPPPD). And while she sought treatment, her resistance to dilators and physical therapy was further indicative of her sexual withholding.*

Ex: *John claimed to love his fiancé, Beth; he intended to marry her. Beth described John as very giving: always bringing flowers, cooking for her, and planning trips for the couple. But John avoided setting a wedding date despite Beth's pleas. Instead, he began to distance himself emotionally and soon developed Erectile Disorder (ED). Beth began to doubt John's true intentions and responded by withholding sex.*

9. Justice vs. Injustice: One side fervently fights for justice and fairness; the other side creates injustice. Both partners have a strong affinity for fairness and are very sensitive to what they perceive to be unjust. The injustice may be real or imagined. Nevertheless, when perceived as wronged, they may become angrily indignant and provoke retaliation, which will, in turn, serve to support their perceived victimization. Couples who have experienced significant injustice in their respective families of origin or in society are more likely to develop this master conflict. Marginalized couples are more prone to this conflict.

Ex: Claire felt that her parents favored her siblings. As an adult, she was a jealous and possessive woman: Believing that her husband was having an affair with a colleague, Claire chose to harass him despite a lack of evidence. He responded by distancing from Claire. Both husband and wife felt as if they were being treated unfairly.

Ex: Maribelle's parents immigrated illegally from Central America to the United States. Straddled between two cultures, and serving as the translator for her parents, Maribelle was subjected to many forms of discrimination. As an adult, she became an immigration lawyer, devoting her life to the underserved. Her husband, Christopher, admired her work, but was upset by Maribelle's dismissal of his concerns about the impact her work was having on their relationship. He claimed that their sex life had greatly diminished. Christopher wanted to spend more time with Maribelle; he also wanted to start a family. Maribelle accused Christopher of "not caring" about the type of the work she did. Both felt they were being treated unfairly.

Ex: Ben wanted to try an open relationship. He claimed that he felt trapped by monogamous marriage. His wife agreed, with the stipulation that he only sleep with the same partner a maximum of three times. Ben initially abided by her rule, but grew to feel that his wife's restrictions were "unfair." When Ben's wife discovered he was having an ongoing sexual relationship with another woman, she felt mistreated. When she insisted Ben end this relationship, he felt she was being unfair.

10. Legitimacy vs. Illegitimacy: One side feels authentic and valued; the other side feels like an imposter. Clients who were orphaned, adopted, or even of immigrant status may be more likely to develop this conflict. Children who felt that they were not "good enough" or that they did not "fit in" or belong in some way may also develop this master conflict. As adults, these individuals may work hard to overcompensate for their perceived lack of value. They may also sabotage their successes to unconsciously validate their illegitimacy. Many of these individuals refer to themselves as "imposters."

Ex: Kiara, an adult adoptee, married into a large, wealthy family that adored her. But she soon began to act in ways that led to alienation and divorce.

In treatment, she admitted that she had always felt like an imposter. She claimed that she did not even feel deserving of having intimate pleasure with her husband. Kiara often employed creative ways to avoid having sex with her husband. Her husband felt deceived by Kiara and threatened divorce frequently, a reaction that reinforced Kiara's imposter syndrome.

Ex: Alberto was a Puerto Rican male who grew up with a highly critical father and a passive mother. Alberto struggled in school, which he later learned was because he suffered from ADHD. As an adult, Alberto became a successful artist. Although he taught at a prestigious university, he couldn't help but feel that he didn't deserve his success. Whenever students or colleagues would praise his work, he would experience anxiety and recall the voice of his father telling him, "you'll always be a failure." Alberto admitted in treatment that he believed that someday he would be exposed for what he really was: a "fraud." Alberto developed Premature Ejaculation (PE) and saw the disorder as evidence that he was a "fraud of a man." His wife did not help matters. She said that she had lost respect for Alberto since he developed his PE.

Ex: Anita was a biracial woman who never felt as though she fit into any racial group. Growing up, Anita's family members and peers told her that she: "wasn't enough of a certain race"; was "not a real black girl"; and "didn't count as an Asian." Anita felt like an imposter, even amongst family members. As a young lawyer, Anita found herself sabotaging her professional success. She also consistently challenged her own credibility, even though she was very well-respected by her peers. Anita believed she was a lesbian but struggled with taking ownership of her identity—she claimed that her past experiences with men proved that she was an inauthentic lesbian.

11. Person vs. Object: One side has a desire to be treated humanely and with respect; the other side is comfortable with being objectified. Clients with this conflict will treat themselves and others as objects. Partners who are addicted to or obsessed with sex, for example, are more likely to have this master conflict. Clients who were abused or treated like a commodity rather than a human being with individual wants, needs, and feelings may also be more likely to develop this master conflict.

Ex: Sloane and Trevor, both artists, agreed to a cuckold-cuckoldress relationship, but Sloane soon came to believe that Trevor only desired her to fulfill his fetishistic desires. In retaliation, Sloane continued to have sex with other men, but she refused to tell Trevor about her experiences, thereby robbing him of the erotic high he normally received from hearing about her adventures. Ironically, Sloane's retaliatory behavior also enabled her own objectification.

Ex: Lola claimed that she hated her husband's sexual objectification of her and other women. However, she consistently enabled his objectification and sexual teasing by flirting back when he would engage in this behavior. She also fed his sexist treatment of other women by commenting on their physical appearances.

Ex: Cameron complained that his wife of 10 years treated him like a "checkbook" and a "sperm donor." He said that he felt "taken advantage of." Cameron held two jobs, which made it difficult for him to spend significant quality time with his family; he was also consistently exhausted. Cameron's wife countered that this arrangement was her husband's idea. She said that he agreed that she could stay home with their three children if she gave him enough sex. Cameron's wife liked the arrangement because she had been out of the workforce for so long. But she also felt Cameron treated her like a "kept woman" or sexual object.

12. **Power vs. Passivity:** One side has a need to be in control and to be in charge; the other side wants to be free of responsibility. Clients with this master conflict will battle about how much power and responsibility each of them should take on in the relationship. The partner who assumes responsibility may relish being in charge but also report feeling burned out, stressed, or overwhelmed; the passive partner may enjoy what little responsibility they have but feel powerless and pressured to perform. Clients who are from disenfranchised groups, where power is a delicacy; those individuals that may have been parentified in childhood; or those who grew up with parents who struggled with balancing power dynamics in their relationships may be more likely to develop this master conflict.

Ex: Fatema, the young wife of an African-American couple, was extremely upset because her husband wasn't working hard enough and contributing to the household chores. She likened him to her "third child," which he resented. The husband's family consisted of strong African-American women who took care of him after his father left. One side of him wanted to be respected. He repeatedly reminded his wife: "I'm the man, not you. Get off my back." The other side of the husband took little responsibility in family matters and spent much of his time on the couch or out with friends.

Ex: Price claimed that he wanted to be respected by his wife, a successful attorney. However, he worked little and changed jobs often; this prevented him from being promoted at any one company. Price also refused to help with domestic responsibilities. He spent most of his time flying his vast collection of drones and miniature helicopters, which he had purchased with his wife's earnings. In the bedroom, Price complained that his wife did not initiate sex enough, but when she would he would reject her.

Ex: Frank was an extremely successful businessman, both assertive and commanding at work. But in his personal life he was content to let his wife delegate all household responsibilities, bully him, and even berate him in front of their children. In the bedroom, Frank wished his wife would continue her more assertive role, just as she did in other aspects of her life, but his wife had little interest in sex. To fulfill his sexual needs, Frank saw a dominatrix without his wife's knowledge.

13. Resolution vs. Misery: One side wants to resolve problems; the other side blocks resolution and languishes in misery. Many people with this conflict appear hopeless and depressed. They complain about being "stuck" despite having realistic options to change their situation. Clients who grew up with depressed parents or those who were conditioned to tolerate "helplessness" may be more likely to develop this conflict.

Ex: Jerry grew up with critical parents. He described them as "whiney, chronic complainers" who never had a better idea to offer. Jerry was in a terrible marriage, and his wife agreed. He claimed that he desperately wanted a divorce, but rather than end his relationship or attempt to make it work, he did nothing other than complain—as his parents did—and languish in it for years. Jerry also hated his job but made no effort to improve his situation at work or find new employment. In treatment, Jerry complained about his appointment time, but when offered an alternative, he would decline.

Ex: Cynthia said that she desperately wanted to have a child. Although her physician told her that she would be a candidate for fertility treatments, she continued to try to get pregnant without medical intervention; she also refused to consider adoption or surrogacy. Eventually, infertility took its toll on Cynthia's marriage, but neither she nor her husband could seem to find a solution to their family dilemma.

Ex: Barry reported that he was never sexually attracted to his wife. In addition, he found her to be overbearing. But rather than deal with the consequences of a divorce, Barry spent much of his time complaining about her and his situation. He was clearly stuck. His wife knew how Barry felt about her but did nothing about the situation either.

14. Satisfaction vs. Disappointment: One side feels comfortable and satisfied; the other side remains in a chronic state of disappointment. Clients with this master conflict may be described as "complainers" or "nitpickers." They will often vacillate between feeling satisfied to being dissatisfied with whatever context they are in. These individuals may have grown up in families where they felt incapable of pleasing their parents.

Ex: Katherine wanted to be happy. She said that she had led a charmed life and was very attracted to her husband, Patrick. Nevertheless, Katherine could not let go of even the smallest disappointments in her life. Even in bed, no matter how hard Patrick tried to please her, she seemed dissatisfied.

Ex: Despite a job and a luxurious lifestyle, Jing, a lesbian, could not help but focus on life's little disappointments, such as meals not being prepared to her liking or her bed sheets not being soft enough. Jing always seemed to find something to complain about, which in turn pushed most of her friends and family away. In addition, Jing was upset because she was unable to find a long-term partner, but likewise, she seemed to find something wrong with each of her prospects.

Ex: Victor constantly strove for "more" and "better" in his life, which made him extremely successful in his career as a professor. He eventually secured a tenure-track position at a prestigious university, but even this did not prevent him from feeling that he might be missing out on other professional opportunities abroad. Victor experienced a similar pattern with dating. After seeing a partner for approximately six months to a year, he questioned whether there was someone "better" for him; he would then end the relationship.

15. Security vs. Risk: One side fears risk and prefers security; the other side likes to take chances. Clients with this conflict may be cautious in some ways and adventurous in others. Clients who grew up in unstable families—or to the contrary—anxious, rigid, controlled families may be more likely to develop this master conflict. In its extreme form, clients may appear to be "adrenaline junkies" on the outside but crave structure on the inside.

Ex: Sydney grew up in a very unstable family and spent most of her childhood living just above the poverty level. As an adult, Sydney feared being poor, but ironically, she had trouble staying within her financial means; she perceived this as a "boring experience." Sydney craved the security of her marriage and adoring husband, but when bored, she would become involved with men at her place of employment.

Ex: Jared claimed that he loved his wife and could not envision a life without her. The couple had met in middle school and got married soon after completing high school. Jared sadly described his childhood as chaotic. But throughout his marriage, he admitted that he replicated this chaos by having countless affairs with unstable women. A couple of Jared's lovers threatened to tell his wife. In a panic, Jared considered moving his family and bribing his lovers with money. Jared's need for risk was also evident in his career choice as flight paramedic—a career which enabled him to participate in risky medical evacuation missions. Jared's wife was a self-contained, organized individual who preferred stability. But she also was admittedly enamored of her husband's adventurous side.

Ex: Marianne, a single, divorced mother of three, grew up in poverty. In her first marriage, she struggled with reining in her husband's spending, which eventually bankrupted the family. In her second marriage—to a financially stable man—she found herself creating contingency plans for leaving him.

These included stealing groceries and toiletries in case she needed to make a quick getaway.

16. Self vs. Loyalty (Others): One side makes independent life choices; the other side is compelled to live the life their family-of-origin prefers. Clients who were pressured to adhere to the cultural or religious norms or general values of their families of origin may be more likely to develop this conflict. This is especially true if the cost of breaking from these values was met by significant punishment, such as being emotionally or financially cut off from them.

Ex: Keeley was raised in a very conservative family; her father was a judge. While she came out to her close friends, she struggled to tell her parents and husband that she was gay. Keeley ultimately wanted to leave her husband for a woman she had met at work, but as a compromise she convinced her husband to participate in a polyamorous threesome with her lover. Her husband was ambivalent about marriage but agreed to Keeley's offer for fear that if he rejected it, he might have to tell his conservative parents that his marriage was in trouble and might end.

Ex: Jaya was a young Pakistani woman who moved to the United States for medical school. She was in an arranged marriage to a Pakistani man who was also studying in the states. While in school, Jaya met and fell in love with a Pakistani-American student. Fearful of disappointing her parents, Jaya struggled with ending the arranged marriage to be with the man she truly loved.

Ex: Sun knew as a youngster that he was sexually attracted to other males. But because he grew up in a traditional Chinese family, he suspected that he would never be accepted if he were to come out. Rather than risk alienation, Sun chose to live in a platonic relationship with a female roommate while pursuing a graduate degree, a decision that gave his parents the impression that he was straight. This façade was easy to maintain until Sun met and fell in love with Ben. Once he and Ben began to plan their future, Sun experienced an existential crisis: Should he risk losing his family of origin to be with Ben?

17. Specialness vs. Ordinariness (Less than Ordinary): One side has a strong need to feel special—apart from the crowd; the other side feels ordinary or less than ordinary. People with this conflict will often build themselves up while simultaneously tearing themselves down. On the one hand, they tend to seek constant validation, both inward and outward. They may shower themselves with material possessions or experiences that they believe set them apart from others. They may be interested in music or films that few know about, or travel to remote destinations. They may also be prone to affairs, giving themselves a false feeling that they are truly special. The pursuit of specialness may at times be subtle, such as simply dyeing one's hair purple or driving a fancy sports car. Knowing that others desire them, and the secret it takes to maintain this type of relationship, may make them feel special. On the other hand, because they often feel a lack of authenticity in their accomplishments, and in this sense they consider themselves to something less-than.

Ex: Laurel, an attorney, did everything she could to set herself apart from the crowd. She got the best education, bought the most expensive clothes, and even drove fancy cars. But she never saw herself as anything but ordinary, which only fueled her need to impress. Laurel also had a long-term affair with a neighbor, which she felt set her apart from the average woman. Ironically, her husband knew of her transgression and saw himself as special for tolerating it—a Saint, if you will.

Ex: Addison was the youngest of five. As the only girl, she was treated special by all her family members. She also was put on a pedestal by her family for her talent as a singer and was often the star of the high school and college theater productions. As an adult, Addison constantly sought the attention of her coworkers, family, and friends—without this, she felt ordinary. Addison became infuriated when her fiancé wanted a long engagement, explaining that she would be an "old bride that no one cares about." If she and her fiancé missed a week of sexual contact, she would become irate, comparing her relationship to the national statistics on the frequency of sexual relations. Without the validation of sex, she believed that her fiancé did not view her as special. Her fiancé did see Addison as special and considered himself as such because she was his. But he also did not feel that he deserved her.

Ex: Miguel grew up an only male child in a large Mexican-American family. As a child, he was diagnosed with a seizure disorder and was constantly looked after and doted on by his sisters and adoring mother. Overly sheltered, Miguel soon found himself behind his peers socially, and with a longing to fit in. To achieve parity, however, he was required to distance himself from his family and sacrifice some of the special treatment they gave him. As an adult, Miguel demanded that his wife treat him special—like a prince, but at the same time he felt as if it detracted from his ability to be the kind of independent man that part of him longed to be.

18. Success vs. Sabotage (Big vs. Small): One side wants to be successful or big; the other side is compelled to fail or be small. Each partner with this conflict demonstrates the potential to succeed professionally but tends to find ways to prevent this or make sure it is fleeting. This conflict differs from *adequacy vs. inadequacy* in that each partner has usually achieved a modicum of success—well beyond relative adequacy. With success, there is, however, the potential for significant failure. Therefore, anyone at the near top of their field who possess this conflict may be at risk for sabotage.

Ex: Kyle had it all: a beautiful wife, a nice family, and a great law practice. He also built quite an academic reputation for himself. Soon, however, he was caught practicing voyeurism. He admitted in treatment that he was uncomfortable with his accomplishments and had a history of sabotaging significant accomplishments. His wife, a socialite from a wealthy conservative family, knew of her husband's past but married him anyway, vicariously sabotaging her own reputation.

Ex: Vera was a successful fashion designer who worked for some of the top global brands. However, she soon tarnished her reputation by failing to meet deadlines and by not responding to client calls. Her long-term boyfriend accused her of being irresponsible and was hesitant to ask her to marry.

Ex: Derek was a professional athlete who was particularly admired by those in the professional sports community for his charity work. Nevertheless, Derek eventually admitted that he used some of his charitable funds for lavish dates and to buy gifts for women he was having extramarital affairs with. In treatment, he expressed how he did not know how to handle the fame that came with his success. Derek's wife loved being married to a celebrity and had known that he had a roving eye since their dating years.

19. Trust vs. Distrust: One side wants to trust others and to be trusted; the other side distrusts others and often creates distrust. Clients with this conflict are compelled to maintain a sense of distrust in their relationships. They may lie about insignificant things but also be prone to chronic cheating. Some keep secret bank accounts, travel places without telling their partner of their true whereabouts, and even have second families. Clients who grew up in families in which they were witness to (or were a part of keeping) secrets may be more likely to develop this conflict. In the extreme, clients with this master conflict may be perceived as "pathological liars" or "sociopaths."

Ex: As a little boy, Joe was expected to keep his father's secrets: His father had several affairs and an array of shady business dealings. When married, Joe wanted to gain his wife's unquestionable trust but chronically lied to her about relatively insignificant things. For example, he would tell her that he was going out to get a gallon of milk and he would stop to see a friend and return home hours later with no milk. Joe's wife had her own trust issues, but this kind of behavior exacerbated them, and she developed into what Joe called "an investigative nag." This, of course, enabled Joe to lie even more to his wife.

Ex: Brittney claimed that she wanted to be loyal to her husband. However, she maintained at least three different online dating-site profiles, and regularly met with various male suitors. Some of these meetings escalated into full blown affairs. When her suspicious husband would confront her about the time spent away from home, she created an elaborate set of lies centered around the hobbies and activities she was involved in. Brittney even engaged in tennis lessons, cooking classes, and joined a charity board just to cover her tracks.

Ex: Isabelle struggled with low sexual desire for most of her life. But any time her partner Abby would question her about it, Isabelle would present a different excuse. Isabelle first claimed to be overworked; she then blamed it on a hormonal imbalance. Abby knew prior to the couple moving in that Isabelle did not act as if she desired her sexually, but she allowed Isabelle to move in with her nonetheless.

20. **Others (Conflict Adjustment)**: There are probably more master conflicts out there than those identified in this chapter. Allowing a couple to label their own conflict, if they wish to do so, may prove to be most useful if it better resonates with them and is deemed accurate by both therapist and couple. In some cases, however, the client's decision to develop a personal master conflict will reflect the conflict itself. The first example will illustrate this point.

Ex: Bailey could not relate to having a "specialness vs. ordinariness (less than ordinary)" conflict. But what did resonate with her was a "different vs. ordinary" master conflict. Having the same conflict as others apparently did not separate her enough from the crowd.

Ex: Andy and Clark suffered from a shared, unbalanced "success vs. sabotage (big vs. small)" master conflict. But the couple felt that "achievement vs. fear of achievement" better reflected their dynamic. The couple believed a fear of achievement paralyzed them, rather than owning that they were neurotic enough to engage in specific acts of sabotage.

Ex: Robert and Anne seemed to suffer from a "security vs. risk" master conflict. However, they preferred to call their conflict "safety vs. excitement," because it was their belief that it better captured their individual and relational patterns and reflected more accurately what took place in their respective families of origin.

Now that the master conflict has been defined and described in detail, and the many conflicts presented, the remainder of the book will address the assessment and treatment of unbalanced master conflicts and the specific sexual symptoms they produce in greater detail. In doing so, a smooth and seamless model for integrating couples and sex therapy will be revealed.

Summary

It took many years and many hours of treating couples to determine which master conflicts were worthy of attention. We did find that some showed up more in treatment than others. For example, *adequacy vs. inadequacy, justice vs. injustice*, and *success vs. sabotage (big vs. small)* proved to be very common. Other conflicts were considered but seemed to overlap too closely with those we had already identified.

We have listed the master conflicts that we thought were closely tied to our couple's problems and the ones we believed would resonate better with the couples. We acknowledge that other conflicts may exist, hence the reason we have included a 20th conflict entitled, *others*. We wanted to avoid forcing couples into one of our readymade conflicts, especially if it was deemed inappropriate.

Reference

Betchen, S. (2010). *Magnetic partners: Discover how the hidden conflict that once attracted you to each other is now driving you apart.* New York, NY: Free Press.

Section II

Assessment and Treatment

Chapter 4
Assessment

Structuring the Therapy

When a couple presents for treatment, each partner tends to blame the other for any relationship problems. This dynamic allows both to avoid taking individual responsibility for contributing to their symptoms. Some partners take turns playing offense and defense; one attacks and the other defends. Rabin (2014) wrote: "In most cases the blame is squarely on the partner. The partner is at fault and the partner is supposed to change" (p. 110). For example, a wife might scold her husband for failing to initiate sex with her; she might proceed to accuse him of having lost physical attraction for her, having an affair, or even being gay. Her husband might deny every accusation yet claim to be at a loss for his low libido. If he has enough courage, he might confront her about her spending habits. The point being that couples bring the fight that they experience at home into the session and show it to the therapist. This may be demonstrated even before the therapist asks what the chief complaint is.

Partners may waste hours complaining about one another, thus preventing the therapist from intervening appropriately. In this sense, it might be a diversion to keep the therapist from succeeding in helping them change. Therefore, the first step in the assessment process is to structure the treatment (Gurman, 2010; Weeks & Fife, 2014). When supervisees first present cases to us, we always ask questions about the couple; and oftentimes the supervisees do not have the answers, in part because they claim the couple wouldn't allow them to take a history. The supervisees are allowing the couple to overwhelm them with interactional dynamics and endless symptoms. One intervention we use with a couple is to point out that we appreciate their pain, but to help them, we must carry out our assessment. We believe that the sooner an understanding of the couple's conflict is obtained, the more quickly the therapist will be able to intervene appropriately.

Many couples therapists have countered that they prefer to take several sessions to "join" (Weeks & Fife, 2014) with a couple before asking probing questions, especially those regarding sex (Gambescia, personal communication,

November 9, 2016). We believe that it is more difficult to collect personal information in the middle of treatment, when the therapist and couple are fully engaged in the interactional dynamic. This is considered a regression, even though we acknowledge that some data gathering takes place throughout the treatment process. We have witnessed therapists of all developmental levels focus so intently on joining that they know little about the couple after several months of treatment. While this is to be expected for those following an ahistorical bent, we also see this phenomenon in psychodynamic approaches.

If the therapist expects both partners for a conjoint session and one is much earlier than the other, it is best to wait for the tardy partner before beginning the therapeutic process. This shows a commitment to the partners as a couple and prevents the perception of favoritism. For couples that are on the verge of separating, or for those in which one partner is highly anxious, jealous, or paranoid, it is safer if the therapist were perceived as balanced. Reluctantly, Howie allowed the couples therapist to see he and his wife, Jana, in separate individual sessions following their initial conjoint evaluation. Even though Jana made it clear that she was considering divorce, Howie expressed the belief that in her individual session, the therapist convinced Jana to leave him.

In MCT, the "couple" is to present for treatment unless extraordinary circumstances make it impossible. For example, some clients have been suddenly called away on business or are needed to care for a sick child. In other cases, one partner may have taken ill. Nevertheless, the evaluation will go on even with one party present—to be followed by an individual session with the other mate. They are then brought back together for the third session, so the therapist can begin to observe the couple's interactional style.

Not exclusively, but perhaps more exceptional to couples with sexual difficulty, we have noticed that one partner may force the other to begin treatment alone. It seems to be particularly convenient to blame the sexual-symptom-bearer for the relationship problems, in part because sex is tied to one's self-worth. McCarthy (1999) wrote: "When sexuality is dysfunctional or nonexistent, it plays an inordinately powerful role, 50 to 75%, draining the marriage of intimacy and vitality" (p. 297). One woman claimed that she had prodded her husband to attend couples therapy with her for years to address his low libido, but to no avail. Under the threat of divorce, his punishment was to go alone for a time to be decided by his wife.

The absent partner may have no intention of attending treatment. Some of these individuals are hoping that their partner will do the work; others are biding time until they can divorce. Doherty and Harris (2017) refers to couples in which one partner is "leaning out" and the other is "leaning in" as *mixed-agenda couples* (p. 3). For example, Bart came to therapy at the behest of his wife for the treatment of his premature ejaculation (PE). He was very cooperative and said that he would do anything to save his marriage. While his wife, Jane, claimed that she wanted her husband to "fix his problem," she was uncooperative in the treatment process and flatly refused to attend sessions. With the help of psychotherapy, solo stop-start exercises (Kaplan, 1989), and medication for anxiety, Bart was ready to have sex with Jane. To his dismay, however, Jane refused all sexual contact. It was soon discovered that while Bart was in treatment, Jane was having an affair and preparing to leave him. When Bart discovered this, he was devastated. He said that he felt duped.

It is the job of the couple's therapist to discern whether a couple's sexual dynamics mimic their relational dynamics and to what extent. If one partner relentlessly pursues a procrastinating partner to seek treatment for a sexual disorder, we do not consider it a stretch if they pursued and distanced in other contexts as well. For example, the pursuing partner may seek affection or time spent together, while the distancing partner may move further away (Betchen, 2005).

In MCT, we follow the initial session by holding one individual session with each partner. We tell the couple that we reserve the right to incorporate individual sessions as we see fit. In tune with Weeks and Fife (2014), individual sessions, if balanced between partners, can be useful in the context of couples therapy. We find these particularly helpful in dealing with therapeutic blocks such as: (1) Secrets (e.g., affair) that one or both partners may be keeping; (2) A sexual issue that neither partner wants to address out of embarrassment; (3) When countertransference issues need to be processed; and (4) When internalized conflicts result in a rigid system.

It is deemed important that the therapist charge the couple for missed sessions unless a valid reason for the failure to attend is presented. There are more cancellations in couple's therapy because of the nature of the work: two people must show for treatment, and then the odds of something going wrong are far greater, especially if they have careers and children. After years of practicing, it is not hard to make an educated guess as to who will show for the first session and who will appreciate the structure of the treatment process. When it takes weeks to schedule a couple because they fail to make an appointment or because they keep changing their appointment time—there is a good chance further trouble is awaiting the therapist. Others make trouble from the very first contact. If there is too much resistance, we do not take the case but remain polite and offer a referral. The therapist must show the couple that they must take the couple's therapy and the outcome of the treatment very seriously. If the therapist fails to maintain therapeutic structure, the integrity of the treatment process will suffer, and with it, the couple.

Using the Genogram as an Assessment Tool

The formal assessment commences once the proper paperwork is filled out, the rules of treatment discussed, and a few pleasantries exchanged.

The therapist then takes charge by asking the couple why they saw fit to seek treatment. It is recommended that the therapist begin to pay close attention to the couple's interactional dynamic, including where they choose to sit in the office. Those partners that sit relatively close may not be in as much trouble as those that sit farther away. But in our experience, those that choose to sit on top of one another or hold each other throughout the therapeutic process may be experiencing quite a bit of anxiety and may be in much deeper trouble than it appears. Attention should be given to eye rolling, sighing, or any other expressions of frustration or pain, which may help the therapist to better decipher the relational dynamic.

The question regarding the chief complaint is not aimed at any one partner. We do not decide who will speak first; that is decided by the couple, and it may convey something about their dynamic, such as: Who is the dominant partner? Who is most anxious? Who is the initiator in the therapeutic process? Who is most invested in the treatment? It is usually the initiator of the treatment or the most dominant mate that speaks first. Once the first speaker is finished, the therapist turns to the other mate for their version. Most of the time, the couple agree on the problem. What they disagree on is who is at fault. For example, they may each agree that they have communication issues but not necessarily who is responsible. By giving each partner a say, the couple's therapist is beginning to put the couple on notice that balance is important. As mentioned earlier, it is important not to let the couple take up the therapist's assessment time with fighting or long-winded answers. The primary complainer may attempt to take over the treatment, but the therapist must stop this immediately. To calm initiators, we often tell them that while we have the same therapeutic goals in mind, we may have another way of reaching them.

Once the couple's therapist understands the presenting problem or chief complaint, the therapist tells the couple that it is important to take a history of each partner. While rare, a partner may balk at this and claim that they wish to focus on the present. Others will resist out of concern that the therapist will blame or bash their parents. These individuals are generally anxious and vying for control of the treatment process. We make it clear that this is the way we work. If a couple do not like our model, we offer them the option of terminating with a referral.

We use the genogram as a tool to gather data from each partner (Bowen, 1978, 1980; DeMaria, Weeks, & Twist, 2017; McGoldrick, Gerson, & Petry, 2008). Berman and Hof (1987) originally recommended the use of the genogram to record and "explore issues of sexuality in the structure and belief system of the client's family of origin" (p. 45). They believed that the sexual life of an adult is greatly influenced by family history and that "sexuality is a central and binding force in the life of a couple" (p. 37). Most sexually-oriented questions used in our assessment were based on the work of Berman and Hof (1987); DeMaria, Weeks, and Hof (1999); and Kaplan (1983).

The formal assessment begins with asking one partner as many questions as it takes to understand who they are and the influences that have shaped them. Unlike Bowen (1978, 1980), who assigned this task to partners as homework, we simply draw a genogram for each partner in our notes and fill it in as our questions are answered. We do not move from one client to the other. Rather, we may spend almost an entire session questioning one partner. We believe that it is important for partners to listen to the experiences of their mates. It may help them to better understand their dynamic and develop some empathy in the process.

The partner who is not the focus of the questioning is encouraged to contribute to their mate's interview. Given that most know one another's parents and family members, they may have a different, or perhaps more accurate, perspective to offer. Ginny abruptly interrupted the near end of her husband's interview: "Gary, why didn't you mention that your twin brother committed suicide?" Another client exclaimed: "How could you leave out the fact that your mother was sick and dying for years?" In each of these examples, a partner provided information that would help the therapist to better understand their cases. Of course, the information doesn't have to be traumatic to be helpful. Consider the following: "Now, Faith, you're not giving an accurate picture of your mother. She's abusive, and you know it." Another example is: "You know that your father was never around when you were growing up. He was too focused on his job to be there for you."

Once the therapist has completed interviewing one partner, it is the other's turn to be questioned. Many of the same questions are posed to the next partner, but follow-up questions will most likely reflect a difference based on variations in the couple's respective families of origin. The therapist does not have to collect every piece of information to develop an adequate framework from which to proceed—in most cases, this would be an impossible task. But because data gathering continues throughout the therapeutic process, information missed should eventually reveal itself to the therapist. We stress that without immediate direction in couple's therapy, the therapist is at risk of becoming bogged down and overwhelmed by the simultaneous deluge of the couple's content and process.

Some have asserted that our style of interviewing unbalances a couple. On the contrary, we see that our insistence on interviewing each partner sends the message that both partners are considered factors in the couple's relationship difficulty and will be held accountable for their contributions. We also view couples treatment as a "process" that does not have to be balanced at every moment, and in each session. If time does not allow for both partners to be interviewed, a second consecutive session will be conducted to complete the evaluation. If a partner complains about our style, we explain that balance is very important to us and that we plan to make every effort to treat each partner equally in the therapeutic process.

In most cases, we complete the entire assessment—both genograms—in one to two sessions, depending on the complexity of the case. This can be accomplished if the therapist knows what questions to ask. The therapist will want to complete a sexual history if a couple present with a sexual symptom, but we highly recommend that both a general and a sexual evaluation be conducted regardless of the chief complaint, because a sexual issue may eventually emerge—a philosophy in tune with an integrational approach such as MCT.

Because the remembrances of clients are subjective, validation of their claims helps the therapist to more accurately identify their master conflicts. We therefore recommend that the therapist routinely ask each partner to give examples to validate their assertions when conducting the assessment. For example, if a partner describes a mate as emasculating, we would request specific examples of this. If a partner says that a parent often made off-color jokes about sex, once again, we would want examples of these jokes. Consider the following case of a 27-year-old woman, Tina, who was suffering from inhibited orgasm.

Tina: My father used to say weird things to me about sex.
Therapist: Like what?
Tina: One time I was wearing a short skirt, and he said that I was covering my skirt up with my ass. It was his way of saying that my skirt was too short.
Therapist: How did that make you feel?
Tina: Gross. I thought it was perverted for a father to look at his daughter's ass, let alone comment on it. All the girls were wearing short skirts at the time, and none of their fathers said that kind of stuff to them.
Therapist: Do you have any other examples of this behavior?
Tina: He made jokes about sex at the dinner table sometimes. Just stuff he would pick up at work. I never thought they were funny, but it got to the point that I didn't want to bring any of my girlfriends home.
Therapist: Would he say anything of this nature to your mother?
Tina: Yeah. He was always commenting on her breasts. I know it made my brother uncomfortable.

Because this book is primarily concerned with the "clinical integration" of couples and sex therapy, we refrain from burdening the reader with a myriad of medical facts and details about specific sexual dysfunctions. To aid the therapist in the assessment process, however, we offer a table describing the most common sexual disorders (see Table 4.1) and a second table linking the most common sexual disorders with their associated master conflicts (see Table 4.2). We also provide what we think is an appropriate amount of

Table 4.1 Common Sexual Disorders

Disorder	Description	Common Treatments	Recommended Resources
Erectile Dysfunction	Difficulty getting or maintaining an erection	PDE5 Inhibitors Focus on pleasure and fantasy	Levine (2016). Rosen, Miner, & Wincze (2014).
Premature Ejaculation	Ejaculation within a minute of penetration or before the client desires	Off-label use of SSRIs Stop-Start Technique Finding point of ejaculatory inevitability	Jannini, McMahon, & Waldinger (Eds.) (2013). Althof (2014).
Delayed (Early) Ejaculation	Delayed or absence of ejaculation	Increased stimulation to let go	Foley, & Gambescia (2015). Perelman (2014).
Male Hypoactive Sexual Desire Disorder	Low or absent sexual desire and sexual fantasies	Increase fantasy and stimulation Underlying causes	Althof (2016). Meana & Steiner (2014).
Female Sexual Interest/Arousal Disorder	Delay or absence of orgasm	Increase fantasy and stimulation	Weeks, & Gambescia (2015). Basson (2016).
Genito-Pelvic Pain/ Penetration Disorder	Pain with penetration or the fear of pain with penetration	Dilator Therapy Anxiety reduction	Bergeron, Rosen, & Pukall (2014). Meana, Maykut, & Fertel (2015). ter Kuile & Reissing (2014).
Female Orgasmic Disorder	Delay, infrequency, or the inability to achieve orgasm	Increase fantasy and stimulation for letting go	Graham (2014). McCabe (2015).

detail on a variety of sexual disorders in the case study sections at the end of the book. The following questions are offered as a guideline for the couples therapist that will prove useful in the integration of couples and sexual issues and in uncovering a couple's master conflict:

Questions for the Genogram

Why are the two of you seeking treatment?

It is important that each partner give their perspective on their problem or chief complaint. Oftentimes this is when the mutual blame game begins. Nevertheless, it is important that the therapist begin to "think conflict" immediately. For example, Corinne complained that her husband, Joel, never "initiated" communication or sexual contact with her during their marriage. But when Joel was asked to give his version of the problem and

Table 4.2 Sexual Issues and Their Possible Master Conflicts

Sexual Issue	Possible Master Conflicts
Erectile Dysfunction	Adequacy vs. Inadequacy
Premature Ejaculation	Satisfaction vs. Disappointment
Genito-Pelvic Pain/Penetration Disorder	Control vs. Chaos
	Giving vs. Withholding
Male Hypoactive Sexual Desire Disorder or Female Sexual Interest/Arousal Disorder	Control vs. Chaos
	Giving vs. Withholding
	Specialness vs. Ordinariness
	Resolution vs. Misery
Out-of-Control Sexual Behavior	Person vs. Object
	Getting Your Needs Met vs. Caretaking
	Control vs. Chaos
Infidelity	Specialness vs. Ordinariness
	Justice vs. Injustice
	Conformity vs. Rebellion
	Commitment vs. Freedom
	Closeness vs. Distance
	Trust vs. Distrust
Delayed Ejaculation	Giving vs. Withholding
	Resolution vs. Misery
	Satisfaction vs. Disappointment
Female Orgasmic Disorder	Giving vs. Withholding
	Adequacy vs. Inadequacy

he began to speak, Corinne immediately interrupted him with a barrage of criticisms—behavior which reflected a conflict in wanting to engage him. In turn, Joel accommodated Corinne and shut down—behavior which exhibited a similar conflict.

If a couple present with a specific sexual problem, the therapist should ask for details to help diagnose it properly (Kaplan, personal communication, September 30, 1987). Kaplan (1983) wrote:

> A detailed description of the patient's current sexual experience and an analysis of his sexual behavior and of the couple's erotic interaction is the best method for ruling out organic causes and for identifying the immediate and currently operating psychological antecedents of the sexual disorder.
>
> (p. 78)

This is especially important for disorders such as PE. For example, does the client ejaculate prior to, or during intercourse? The answer to this question can give an indication as to whether there is something specific about intercourse that is significant and not sex per se. How long does the client last before ejaculating? This can tell the therapist if the client truly has PE. A young man reported for treatment with his girlfriend claiming he had PE, but he was having uninterrupted intercourse for 45 minutes. It was soon determined that the couple was engaged in a competitive control struggle with sex as the vehicle. A man in his late 60s reported with ED, but when asked to rate his erection in terms of firmness on a scale of 1 to 10 (Kaplan, personal communication, September 30, 1987), he rated it an 8: firm enough for penetration. The gentleman did not suffer from ED, as he thought; education regarding sex and the aging process sufficed.

The therapist should consider asking the couple for a step-by-step or "video" picture of their most recent sexual experience (Kaplan, 1995, p. 96). The therapist may also want to ask each partner how they felt or what they thought during the experience. This description may reveal any sabotaging behavior that the therapist can use to determine a couple's master conflict. For example, one woman jumped up from her bed right before intercourse to ask her boyfriend a business-related question. Her boyfriend reported that this behavior almost destroyed the passionate mood he was in—he found it very distracting. Another woman complained that her boyfriend's touch was "harsh" during foreplay. And no matter how often she complained about this, he never made any adjustments. She said that she could not wait to have intercourse because her boyfriend's foreplay was physically painful.

It is particularly important to determine the non-symptom bearer's reaction to the sexual symptom. Partners often take sexual disorders personally and express feelings ranging from sadness and disappointment to rage. Angry partners may exert even greater pressure on the symptom-bearer to perform, exacerbating symptoms. Because these individuals often feel victimized, and justified in their anger, they should be empathized with but also warned of the consequences their reactions may bring.

How long have you had the problem?

In most cases, the couple has lived with their symptom(s) for many months or even years. This is useful evidence that the therapist can use to challenge the couple's defenses to show them that some part of each of them has a need to maintain their conflict. The couple may not like their symptoms, but they are not uncomfortable enough to try and adjust their conflict. This is especially pertinent to couples with sexual difficulty when the symptoms are obvious, such as PE and ED. In less obvious disorders, such as female inhibited orgasm, one partner may have hidden a symptom from the other for some time, but the fact that it was hidden still may convey that something is blocking the couple from getting what they say they want—usually the need to preserve their master conflict.

Knowing how long a couple has been suffering from a sexual disorder and the progression of it can help the therapist to distinguish between a "lifelong" and an "acquired" problem. Lifelong problems are harder to treat and may have a biological base (Kaplan, 1974). Tracing the acquired disorder to a specific point in time may offer the therapist significant information on the couple's master conflict. For example, a woman's low drive may have commenced soon after she had children, suffered the death of a family member, discovered her husband's extramarital affair, or experienced another significant or traumatic event. It is not unusual for an individual to have a sexual problem with one partner but not another. And it is not uncommon to experience a sexual disorder soon after moving closer to, or marrying someone—a sign of a conflict regarding intimacy or closeness (Betchen, 2005).

Did either of you experience this symptom in previous relationships?

Aside from differentiating between an acquired and lifelong disorder, the answer to this question can help the therapist to determine whether either partner is replicating a specific sexual symptom in their relationships. This is useful to the therapist because master conflicts may change context, but they do not go away. The more alike past and present symptoms are, and the timing and conditions under which they appeared, the easier it will be to identify a master conflict. For example, a woman claimed that her husband had lost sexual desire for her soon after they moved in together—and the problem worsened following marriage. The same thing occurred in his two previous marriages, indicating the possibility that they were struggling with a *commitment vs. freedom* master conflict.

Did your parents discuss sex when you were a child?

If one or both partners were raised in a home environment that considered sex a taboo subject, they may have developed some guilt-related inhibitions that may be contributing to their sexual disorder. For example, a woman who came from a strict religious background was told that if she masturbated, she might go to hell. If the therapist therefore wishes to assign any sexual exercises as homework for this woman, he or she should consider that she may not be able to use masturbation as a vehicle. In treating a case of Genito-Pelvic Pain/Penetration Disorder (GPPPD), specifically vaginismus, the woman could not insert the dilators into her vagina but was fine if her husband did so with her instruction.

On the other hand, some parents talk about sex too much, and in inappropriate ways, thereby turning their children off or scaring them. We've experienced some parents who routinely told off-color jokes that embarrassed their children; others made sexually seductive comments to their children. Some of this was done under the influence of alcohol, but not always. For example, a woman claimed that nearly every time she was preparing to go out on a date as a teenager, her mother told her "not to do anything she wouldn't do." The client said that her mother's remarks made her feel like a "slut."

Did your parents show affection towards one another when you were a child?

The answer to this question can help the therapist to gauge the level of closeness and intimacy in each client's family of origin and to determine whether a conflict around these issues may have been passed down.

When did you lose your virginity and how was the experience?

Most clients report having had an awkward experience the first time they attempted intercourse; others claim that their experiences were embarrassing or somewhat painful—data that doesn't necessarily indicate what conflict may be operating. But if consummation comes at an unusually late stage of life, or many months or even years after the start of a relationship, this should be investigated. For some highly religious couples, this may not signal a red flag, but it certainly will for others, particularly if the partners were at odds over this issue.

Sometimes the therapist will discover that the relationship is still unconsummated, but this would usually be the chief complaint—most likely in the form of vaginismus. And because "control" is usually a key factor in this disorder, the therapist may want to consider a *giving vs. withholding* or *control vs. chaos (out-of-control)* master conflict.

Were you ever sexually abused?

Many partners are open when it comes to discussing sexual abuse, but we always consider it a sensitive topic. Therefore, we generally consider it safer to ask this question in individual sessions. As previously mentioned, a traumatic experience that occurs early enough in one's life may lead to a master conflict, and sexual abuse would qualify. For example, a male client reported that as a child he was molested by an adult female neighbor. In adulthood, he presented with a *success vs. sabotage (big vs. small)* master conflict. He said that he felt very inadequate during sex with this woman and did so with girlfriends thereafter. It was clear that his inadequacy followed him into marriage—he chose someone who was nearly impossible to please—someone who eventually had left him for another man.

Were you ever exposed to something sexually provocative?

We ask this question because some clients have a different definition of abuse than we do. For example, a man reported that from the ages of 8–10, his teenage sister and her friends would strip in front of him and tease him by rubbing up against him, but he never saw this experience as abusive. Boundaries are at a premium in some large families, and many clients have reported that they have repeatedly been spied upon while dressing, or were witness to their parents dressing and behaving in a seductive manner. Some have witnessed their parents having sex. As mentioned, some family members choose to make sexually provocative remarks that can have a lasting effect, especially if the remarks were found to be embarrassing or disgusting.

Have you ever had, or considered having sex, with someone of the same sex?

This is another question that might be better asked in an individual session. But it should not be overlooked, because it may lead the therapist to a master conflict. For example, a 35-year-old married man presented as confused and disturbed. The client claimed that although he disliked gays, he had a "crush" on an openly gay male colleague. He believed that he held these feelings for his colleague because he was molested by a man when he was a child. While the trauma did complicate matters, the client eventually accepted that he was gay before the abuse, and that the incident only made it more difficult for him to own his identity. It was eventually revealed that he had suffered from a *legitimacy vs. illegitimacy* conflict for many years.

Are you attracted to your partner?

We consider this a vital question to ask each partner—preferably in individual sessions. The answer can help lead the therapist to a master conflict and help to determine a couple's prognosis. But it is a question that many couples therapists seem afraid to ask, in part because it can get to the bottom of things very fast and the news might not be good. For example, we believe that if one partner was "never" physically attracted to the other, the relationship will eventually experience severe difficulty or end. A modicum of attraction can be increased, especially if there is an emotional connection; but if one or both partners started at zero, we believe that they will never reach a satisfactory level of attraction. This will not necessarily result in a separation or divorce; there are many couples who have maintained a sexless relationship for many years. But it may leave a gap between partners and in some cases a longing that can evolve into one or both having extramarital affairs (Betchen, 2015, 2013).

Do you masturbate, and if so, how often?

Some individuals choose to masturbate rather than have sexual relations with their mates (Betchen, 1991). Others self-pleasure so often that they have little energy left to engage their partners. Masturbation in and of itself is usually not the issue, but making it a priority over one's sexual relationship often points to a conflict: *giving vs. withholding* comes to mind.

Do you fantasize?

Not all individuals can fantasize, and not all use fantasy when they masturbate; some are excited enough by the pure physical sensations that self-pleasuring can generate. Barring organic issues, we have found that individuals who cannot fantasize may be in conflict about allowing themselves to become aroused. Nevertheless, it is common to use one's favorite fantasy to enhance masturbation that can lead to orgasm. A client's fantasies can tell the therapist what turns the client on and whether these sexual needs are being met in the relationship. Master conflicts are at risk of becoming unbalanced when each partner's fantasies are incongruent, and neither will negotiate a compromise. For example, a male client admitted to being turned on by female prostitutes. When his wife dressed as one, he couldn't wait to have sex with her, but when she refused, he could not function. His only recourse was to employ his prostitution fantasy while having sex with her.

Some partners can function if they look at porn before sex; some need to look at it during sex, and others prefer to visualize what turns them on. Nevertheless, if partners share similar or compatible fantasies, they can prosper. An exhibitionist may do well with someone who is somewhat voyeuristic; or a sadistic individual might fare well with someone who is somewhat masochistic.

We highly recommend the therapist use individual sessions to inquire about fantasies and only reveal them with permission from the partner who holds them. Perhaps the best avenue to take is to encourage this partner to reveal the fantasy. If a fantasy is exposed prematurely, it can evoke guilt, shame, distrust, or a relationship crisis. For example, when her husband finally revealed his fantasy that women infantilize him during sex, the wife was both shocked and angered: "I had no idea this is what really turned him on," she said. "Apparently, our whole sexual life has been a fraud. I don't think I can, or want, to meet his needs."

Can you achieve orgasm? If so, under what conditions?

Some individuals can achieve orgasm via solo masturbation—either with their hand, vibrator, or by some other means—but not with a partner. Some can only achieve an orgasm under specific circumstances and with a specific partner. Sorting out under which circumstances and with what type of partner an individual can achieve orgasm may lead the therapist to a master conflict. For example, a young woman longed to marry but felt guilty abandoning her father, to whom she was very close her entire life. Consequently, she could only achieve orgasms with men that she did not consider serious contenders for a long-term relationship, not those that she could conceivably marry. It was determined that this woman suffered from an unbalanced *self vs. loyalty (others)* master conflict.

Do you excessively engage in any sexual activities—with or without your partner—such as masturbation, porn, prostitution, sadism/masochism, exhibitionism/voyeurism, or any others? If so, when did you first experience this type of behavior? How often do you indulge in it? And what is it about the behavior that turns you on?

It would be helpful to the therapist to get as much detail as possible if a client admits to relying on some of the behaviors mentioned. To avoid shaming, we recommend asking: What is your delicacy? Clients may offer short shrift to this question, but we believe that sexual symptoms and their conflicts may be better explained if there is too big a disparity between the real and the imagined. For example, if a client prefers bondage/domination/sadism/masochism (BDSM) activities, but his or her partner abhors them, low sexual drive might develop on the part of the partner that is excited by BDSM. It is important for the therapist to consider that some individuals with a fetish may only be able to function if that fetish is incorporated into their relationship; to others, it may be employed as an erotic enhancer, but the client can function sexually without it.

Some would argue that excessive engagement to the detriment of the client's personal and professional life would constitute an addiction on par with alcoholism and drug addiction (Carnes, 2001, 2015). These individuals base their treatment on the addiction's 12-step program made popular by Alcoholics Anonymous (AA). Others (Krause, Voon, & Potenza, 2016; Prause, Steele, Staley, Sabatinelli, & Hajcak, 2015) argue that there is no such thing as sexual addiction. These individuals consider those who act out sexually as having an impulse control issue. They base this assertion, in part, on their findings that the neural response of sex addicts does not demonstrate the same level of enhanced sexual cue responsiveness to sexual images as other addicts do to their substances of choice.

Regardless of what stance the therapist takes on this matter, we find that these types of symptoms are often linked to a *person vs. object* master conflict. The symptomatic partner tends to treat his or her mate as a sexual object, and the mate enables this behavior by playing the role. For example, a woman complained in therapy that her husband treated her like a sex object; sometimes she would say, "like a piece of meat." But it was found that she intermittently reinforced his objectification of her by responding with something flirtatious.

Objectification is a common dynamic in couples with addictions (Betchen, 2010). And individuals often suffer from more than one addiction (Botelho, 2012). We therefore recommend that the therapist ask each partner whether they or any members of their respective families of origin have addictions of any kind.

Are you married or in a committed relationship? If so, for how long?

The answer to this question can give the therapist an idea as to whether the partners can sustain a long-term relationship; it is also an indication of how long the couple have been in their dysfunctional dynamic. The longer and more entrenched the couple have been dysfunctional, the more in crisis they will be.

How long did you date before you decided to fully commit to one another?

The answer to this question might reveal if either partner was ambivalent about committing to the relationship. Although some couples have dated many years, their relationships were inconsistent or on and off. Determining the timing of breakups and who initiated them may help the therapist home in on a master conflict. Some of these same couples maintained long-distance relationships—a relationship style we generally frown upon because there is less opportunity to know one another on an intimate level.

How did you decide to commit to one another?

The sad truth is that some partners put enormous pressure on their counterparts to commit. While this may work in the short-run, the pressured partner may eventually resort to a passive-aggressive style of interaction—one that demonstrates ambivalence. For example, a couple reported to treatment because the husband was having an affair with his law partner. In an individual session, he admitted that he had had several affairs over the years because he was not attracted to his wife and never wanted to marry her. When asked why he did so, he said that he always did what he was told to do, and was pressured by his girlfriend and his parents.

Have either of you ever been in any committed relationships before? If so, can you describe them? How did they end?

Some individuals have never been in a long-term relationship prior to their current one, and this is often a sign of a conflict. But if they have, it is important to determine whether there are any relationship patterns that may be related to the couple's chief complaint. How a partner's past relationships ended—if there is consistency—can sometimes tell you what danger lies ahead for the couple. For example, a woman tended to end all her significant relationships after six years; it was as if she had an internal alarm clock that went off at the six-year mark telling her it was time to move on. Her father had died when she was 6 years old, and it was suspected that she was unconsciously replicating abandonment.

If you had a honeymoon, how did each of you experience it?

This is another question that can reveal conflict on the part of one or both partners. While this will be discussed later, the therapist might be surprised to find just how many couples failed to have sexual relations on their honeymoons. One woman reported that her husband took this time to tell her that he didn't find her smart or attractive enough. When asked why she stayed with him, she said that his comment was too strange to believe. She preferred to think that he was simply in a bad mood that day. She never followed up on his assertion.

Have you and your partner agreed to be sexually exclusive? If so, from the time of your agreement have you committed infidelity, emotional or physical? Is there any remaining contact with this person(s), such as, email, texting, or telephone conversations?

We pose the first question to the couple. We have found couples who fail to clearly define the parameters of their relationships (e.g., sexual exclusivity) may unconsciously enable future sabotage—an indication of a shared master conflict at work. We assess a couple's level of consciousness regarding this issue.

The second and third questions—better asked of each partner in their respective individual sessions—are important follow-ups to consider in part, because sexual infidelity may traumatize a relationship, rendering it irreparable (Doherty & Harris, 2017). Allen and Atkins (2012) examined the association between divorce and "extramarital sex" (EMS) in a study of 16,090 individuals assessed between 1991 and 2008 as part of the General Social Survey (GSS). The authors found that approximately half of the individuals who engaged in EMS ended up divorced or separated. They suspected the percentage might have been larger if other forms of infidelity were considered, such as emotional and technological infidelity.

Because few people admit to having cheated, it is difficult to obtain accurate figures on infidelity. Analyzing data from the GSS, the Institute for Family Studies reported that the affair rates have been rising over the past 30 years, especially in adults in their 50s and 60s (Wolfinger, 2017). This is believed to be in part because of women entering the work force and the availability that modern technology affords both genders. While approximately three out of every four Americans see it as morally wrong to have an affair (Wolfinger, 2017), the AAMFT (American Association for Marriage and Family Therapy, 2017) reported that approximately 25% of married men and 15% of married women have cheated at least once during their marriage.

There is evidence that women have affairs to get their emotional needs met and men do so to have their sexual needs met (Fisher, 2004). We acknowledge that emotional involvement with someone outside of one's primary relationship is a form of infidelity. But we have found that having sex, particularly some form of intercourse, often takes the affair to a new level for both genders. This, in turn, makes it difficult for lovers to distinguish between fantasy and reality. We prefer the general term "sex" rather than rely on the penis-driven heterosexual model of "intercourse." We do not wish to exclude the lesbian population or others that do not subscribe to such a model (Iasenza, 2000, 2010).

Couples who seek treatment because of infidelity tend to do so under two circumstances: (1) If one partner has had an affair in the past and the couple are struggling to get over the indiscretion and save their relationship. The "affairing" partner may want the "non-affairing" partner (Doherty & Harris, 2017, pp. 143–144) to forgive and forget the experience, but the non-affairing partner may be struggling to get past the trauma; and (2) One partner is engaged in an active affair and is having difficulty choosing between the lover and the primary relationship. The affairing partner may be having trouble choosing one partner over the over, or is trying to hold onto both relationships. The non-affairing partner may be desperately trying to save the relationship or trying to decide whether the relationship is worth saving. The affair might be exposed or only known to the affairing partner.

In MCT, when a couple present with a past indiscretion, the therapist should consider both the symptom and the difficulty alleviating it as a sign that the couple are fueling their shared master conflict. For example, infidelity can feed several master conflicts, especially a *trust vs. distrust* conflict. When an affair is exposed, the non-affairing partner may gain enough ammunition to fuel a master conflict indefinitely. That is, a lack of trust can go a long way. The affairing partner can reinforce the conflict by vacillating between his lover and the primary relationship.

If a couple report for treatment having experienced a recent affair, it is understandable that both partners will have to work to uncover the meaning of the infidelity (Levine, 2010) or what we refer to as the underlying conflict that may have sparked the symptom. But a more blatant sign of an unbalanced conflict is when the partners are having difficulty resolving a transgression that took place several years ago, especially after the couple have had several bouts of professional treatment. Here, we assume that the very dynamic that caused the affair is now being unconsciously used by the couple to maintain the unbalanced conflict and to keep the associated symptom alive; in this case, the pain of the affair. The therapist should be most interested in the question: Why is the couple's symptom still thriving after all this time and treatment?

Therapists differ on how to handle an active affair in treatment: some will maintain an affairing partner's confidentiality and some will not. In "Discernment Counseling," Doherty and Harris (2017) maintain the confidentiality of the affairing partner to help the partner to discern whether to stay in the affair or to work on their primary relationship. If during the discernment process the affair is terminated, the authors will then encourage the affairing partner to expose the affair to the non-affairing partner. They feel that if the affair is not exposed, it will undermine subsequent couples therapy.

In MCT, if both parties are aware of the affair, we tend to proceed with treating the couple (Doherty & Harris, 2017; Gordon, Khaddouma, Baucom, & Snyder, 2015). Individual therapy may be recommended for each partner if it proves that the affairing partner cannot terminate contact with the lover (Wachtel, 2017) or make any progress towards reconciling residual feelings for the individual—a reflection of the affairing partner's conflict. The affairing partner will need to decide which partner to pursue, and the non-affairing mate will need to consider how much longer he or she wishes to invest in the relationship.

If an affair is exposed in an individual session, the authors suggest that couples therapy be terminated unless the initiator of the affair ends the indiscretion or confesses to the significant other. The therapist takes no other stance on the matter other than couples therapy cannot proceed successfully while the secret is being kept. How this issue is dealt with is up to the initiator of the affair, but the therapist will not reveal the secret. Because it is believed that affairs are hard to terminate, especially once sex has taken place, the therapist should hold a skeptical position as to whether the affair has been terminated unless proven otherwise in treatment. In many cases, an affair has been terminated only to start up again when the relationship crisis is over or when the initiator feels the therapist has forgotten about it. A major sign that the affair has truly ended is if the affairing partner's behavior towards the non-affairing partner and the treatment has changed for the better and it appears that the initiator is fully invested in the therapeutic process.

Can you describe each of your parent's personalities?

This is a key question. The answer can expose abuse, mental illness, conflicting messages, and various significant relational dynamics. For example, a male client described his mother as completely unpredictable, unruly, and volatile. It was determined that she may have suffered from a form of untreated bipolar disorder. While the client's wife seemed logical and stable, the client often behaved in ways that would provoke strong reactions from his wife. In this sense, it was determined that the client was unconsciously trying to recreate his family of origin by baiting his wife to act like his mother.

What did each of your parents do for a living?

We find the answer to this question useful because we believe that there is some truth in the concept that people choose their professions based on their personalities and not *vice versa*.

If, for example, the client's father was an engineer, perhaps the expression of emotions was not reinforced. If a parent was a traveling salesman, a professional athlete, a musician, or an airline pilot, perhaps the parent was rarely home. While we acknowledge that these are stereotypes, we do have many years of clinical data to support them. And we have seen the correlation between having distant parents and the transmission of a *closeness vs. distance* master conflict.

What was your perception of your parents' marriage?

We ask this question because we have found that too many individuals have a skewed perspective of their family of origin, which can help to create or exacerbate a master conflict (Betchen, 1992). For example, a male client reported that he felt sorry for his father and hated his mother, in part because he saw his mother as blocking her husband from fulfilling his dream of becoming an actor. When his father died suddenly, the client attributed his death to heart break. It wasn't until the client entered therapy that he gained a more balanced perspective. The client's mother was very demanding, but his father had reservations about his own ability to make it in the entertainment field. In many ways, he sabotaged his own career. Armed with this insight, the client was better able to improve his relationship with his mother, whom he had cut off for many years since his father's death. It was eventually determined that the client suffered from an unbalanced *adequacy vs. inadequacy* master conflict that was transmitted to him by his parents, particularly his father.

Did your parents fight a lot? If so, was there a common issue that they fought over?

Growing up in what we often refer to as a "war zone" can have a lasting effect on an individual. But we are most interested in what the parents fought about and their fighting styles. Sometimes individuals mimic their parents' fighting styles and the context they repeatedly fought about; both of which can provide evidence of a master conflict. For example, if parents fought about secrets such as extramarital affairs, mishandling of money, or chronic lying, and this manifested in one parent continuously pursuing and battering the other, a *trust vs. distrust* master conflict may have been transmitted to the client. If the client empathized with or felt sorry for one of the parents, or developed a grudge towards one, a *justice vs. injustice* conflict may have been passed on.

Did your parents ever separate or divorce? If so, what was the chief reason?

Divorce often traumatizes all those involved. The more volatile the divorce, the greater the trauma. Having experienced the divorce of one's parents can shake a child's confidence about relationships, particularly if the post-divorce process was mishandled (e.g., if a parent fails to maintain contact with a child). This kind of experience can later lead to those conflicts more closely associated with intimacy and commitment, such as a *closeness vs. distance*, *commitment vs. freedom*, or *trust vs. distrust* conflict. The specific reason for the divorce and the client's perception of who was at fault may help to refine the therapist's search. For example, if the client felt that one parent was being unfairly treated by the other, perhaps a *justice vs. injustice* conflict might have been transmitted.

If a client's parents separated but did not divorce, we recommend that the therapist ask if there was more than one separation, how long the separation(s) lasted, and who initiated the breakup(s) and reconciliation(s). On and off again relationships can be particularly indicative of a *misery vs. resolution* conflict.

How did your parents feel about your relationship?

Oftentimes, the pressure from disgruntled parents can strain a couple's relationship and, in turn, create great internal conflict in each mate; in extreme cases, this strain can lead to the relationship's demise. The best examples of this are when parents take a rigid stance against their children entering interracial (Karis, 2009; Killian, 2013), interreligious (Killian, 2013), or cross-class relationships (Streib, 2015). We have had several experiences where, in protest, parents have refused to attend their children's weddings. The therapist should gauge the pressure exerted by parents and other significant family members and determine whether the pressure is splitting the couple. An in-depth examination of cross-cultural, minority, and marginalized couples is addressed later in this chapter.

Do you have any children? If so, what are their ages and genders?

While children are usually not the focus of our model, it may be good to get basic information about them in case they turn out to play a significant role in the couple's dynamics.

What roles do your children play in your family?

Children who play a special role in their families of origin can shed some light on their parents' master conflict. For example, parentified children (Boszormenyi-Nagy, 1965) may have been enlisted to take on age-inappropriate duties by the couple, such as assuming parental duties like taking care of younger siblings, paying bills, or making many of the major decisions in the household. This dynamic may reflect the parents' conflict about assuming responsibility.

Some couples have children with special needs that may burden the couple and place great strain on the relationship. Oftentimes, couples fail to strike a balance between living their lives and caretaking their children, which may be reflective of a *getting one's needs met vs. caretaking* master conflict.

Are either of you taking any medication? If so, what kind and for what problem?

When you're treating couples with sexual problems, it is important to ask about medication because certain drugs can cause or exacerbate sexual problems, such as thiazides, beta-blockers, and anti-androgens. Selective serotonin reuptake inhibitor (SSRI) antidepressants such as sertraline (Zoloft) and fluoxetine (Prozac) may lower libido; other medications, such as bupropion (Wellbutrin) might raise it (Phelps, Jones, & Payne, 2015; Seretti & Chiesa, 2009). It is important to note whether the symptom bearer of a sexual disorder has any medical problems and if he or she consulted a physician before seeking therapy. One way that couples collude to maintain their symptoms and underlying conflict is to not seek proper medical attention. We recommend that the therapist inquire about medical conditions and medications taken and consider making the appropriate referral, preferably to a gynecologist or urologist. As mentioned, our stance, while considered by some to be somewhat rigid, is to require a physical examination for all those presenting with a sexual disorder.

But seeking medical attention is not a guarantee that the couple are ready to adjust their unbalanced master conflict. Many couples have been prescribed medicine to help with their disorders only to never fill these prescriptions; others fail to use them properly. One man who suffered from ED claimed that he would jump at the chance to cure his ED if there was a pill for it. However, when sildenafil citrate (Viagra) was available, he obtained a script from his doctor but failed to fill it. Many men we have treated for ED have taken the medication, but in a way that all but guarantees failure; they then tell us that the medication didn't work and give up. Some men take these medications only a few minutes before intercourse rather than the prescribed hour, or they take it knowing their partners are not in the mood or are unable to have sex. One man would take it in the morning as his wife was getting ready for work.

Have you ever been in therapy before? If so, for what reason? Why did the therapy terminate?

Couples who have sought treatment in the past may have an authentic desire to work through their problems, but this alone is not a guarantee that a couple wants to change. Many couples come to therapy so they can tell themselves that they have tried to save their relationships; some partners attend to get their way; and others come seeking validation from the therapist: "See, even the doctor thinks I am right and you are wrong."

Knowing why prior treatment was terminated might be important because it may give the therapist an indication of what may or may not work with a couple and the strength of their defenses. Knowing which partner terminated prior treatment and how the other partner reacted can provide the therapist with an indication of a couple's collusive powers or reveal control struggles. For example, a female client reported that she had made the decision to terminate prior couples therapy because she felt that the therapist did not understand why she chose to stay in her marriage with no guarantee that her philandering husband would remain faithful. The client explained that she had two special needs children and she was sure that her husband would be very difficult in a divorce process. She said that she felt "judged" by the therapist. The client's husband agreed with his wife's decision to terminate the prior treatment, but he was not happy about being in treatment again. Despite being warned of the risks involved, the client allowed her husband to stop attending couples sessions, thereby colluding in his inability to control himself with other women. It was determined that the couple suffered from a shared *security vs. risk* master conflict.

Do you have any siblings? If so, what role did each play in your family of origin?

We pay limited attention to sibling dynamics, giving most of the credit for these dynamics to the parent-couple. For example, a woman claimed to have hatred for her brother because he apparently tortured her when they were children. Upon investigation, the parents were reluctant to set any limits with their son—who had mental health issues—for fear of upsetting him. Much of the client's anger needed to be re-directed to her passive parents, who, in a sense, sacrificed her to their son.

Nevertheless, sibling constellation can contribute to the therapist's search for a couple's master conflict. For example, several scholars (Betchen, 1996; Boszormenyi-Nagy, 1965; Toman, 1976) have contended that oldest children are often burdened with age-inappropriate responsibilities or parentified in their families of origin, such as caring for elderly or sickly parents or a sick or special needs sibling. One client claimed that because his Italian parents refused to assimilate while living in America, he was pressed to serve as their interpreter for most of his life.

We have found that individuals who were parentified in childhood may be more prone to developing a *getting your needs met vs. caretaking, justice vs. injustice,* or *self vs. loyalty (others)* master conflict. They have their own needs, but they have been trained primarily to meet the needs of others. Middle siblings are often lost or ignored in their families of origin and may be more prone to a *closeness vs. distance* conflict. Some middle siblings told us that they used distance to hide from family dysfunction. And youngest siblings are sometimes infantilized, which can lead to *adequacy vs. inadequacy, power vs. passivity,* or *specialness vs. ordinariness (less than ordinary)* master conflicts. These individuals are often treated special, but their development may have been be hampered.

Starting with the oldest sibling, can you tell a little about their personalities?

We like to know a little about each sibling to determine whether there are any significant distinctions between them and our clients that can help us to home in on a master conflict. We look for advantages that one may have had over another (e.g., Was one supported to go to college over others?), parental favoritism, differences in temperament, sexual identity issues and how they were handled, and whether any cutoffs exist. We also look for coalitions in which siblings took sides against one another, and for what reasons. Some of this information may have manifested in *justice vs. injustice* or *giving vs. withholding* conflicts.

In your opinion, do any of your siblings have any mental or physical problems?

The answer to this question can reveal whether any serious disorders run in the family. It can also help the therapist to determine whether the client had any special responsibilities as previously mentioned, like taking care of a sick sibling. We have treated numerous families where our clients were charged with the role of caretaking siblings with substance abuse issues. This can lead to a *getting your needs met vs. caretaking* conflict. A female client claimed that her terminally ill mother made her promise to always take care of her heroin-addicted sister. Although a loyal daughter, the client admitted that she felt as if her mother had just handed her a prison sentence.

What is the relationship status of each of your siblings?

The answer to this question may help the therapist to establish a relationship pattern among siblings that could be relative to the client. For example, in some families all siblings have experienced at least one divorce; in others, all or most were married to addictive partners. A female client reported that she and her siblings married individuals their parents did not approve of: the client married interracially; another married interreligiously; and a third chose someone from a lower socioeconomic background. It was no surprise when it was determined that the client turned out to have a *conformity vs. rebellion* master conflict.

Content and Process

It is important in couples work that the therapist distinguish between *content* and *process*. Content is the subject matter that troubles the couple—it is usually presented to the therapist as the chief complaint. Sex, money, and work-related issues are some of the most common types of content. In this book, the concern is primarily with sexual content.

Process is a couple's interactional style or the way in which a couple deal with their content issues. Content is therefore considered the baggage, and the process is the vehicle by which it is carried. The master conflict drives the process, which in turn produces the sexual symptoms. Because the process rarely changes, a couple can fit any content into their process. For example, Kenneth and Ruth were a couple in their 40s who had been married for 12 years. The one thing that remained constant in their relationship was the tendency to lie (i.e., process) to one another; but what they lied about (i.e., content) often changed. Ruth insisted that Kenneth attend therapy with her primarily because she found that he lied to her when he told her that he had made an appointment with his urologist to seek medication to combat his erection difficulty. Before they married, Ruth told Kenneth that she had given up smoking cigarettes, but he soon found out otherwise.

It is important that the therapist begin observing the couple's process from day one. Because the process is most representative of the couple's master conflict, it can better lead a therapist to the conflict. For example, Paula claimed that Josh was having less sex with her in the past couple of months. She first thought Josh was having an affair, but she eventually realized that he was heavily into Internet porn. Paula grew to distrust Josh and, in turn, kept a close eye on his use of the couple's computer. Although Josh claimed that Paula exaggerated his porn usage, he continued to hide it from her for fear of her punitive reactions: Paula would scold him and attempt to tighten her control over his behavior. The content in this case was sexual: porn and sexual frequency. The process: Josh's secretive use of the computer for added sexual stimulation and Paula's punishing reaction and investigative behavior. The couple's process represented a *trust vs. distrust* master conflict. Josh wanted to be trusted. But although he complained bitterly about Paula's distrust of him, he enabled her distrust by reducing his sex with her and hiding his porn usage. Paula claimed that she wanted to trust Josh, but her anxiety about his porn usage and her punishing reactions to his deceitful behavior made it less likely that he would be honest with her. "I can't tell Paula when I want to add porn to our sex life because I'm afraid of her reaction. It just seems easier to look at it myself and to hide it from her."

Another example is that of Rose and Ed. Rose, who suffered from inhibited orgasm, was raised to be "perfect" by highly critical parents who were obsessed with neatness and orderliness. Ed had difficulty with a controlling and manipulative father. "When it came to my father, the punishment never seemed to fit the crime," he said. Following in her parents' footsteps, whenever Rose saw anything out of place in the house, she would nag Ed for his sloppiness. Feeling these attacks were petty and unjustified, Ed would trivialize his behavior. In response, Rose increased her nagging and withheld sex. "I'm not going to stop picking on him until he recognizes what's important to me," she said. It was determined that the couple had a shared *justice vs. injustice* master conflict.

While most couples firmly believe that the content they present in treatment is the major problem, we find a faulty process to be the biggest impediment to restoring balance and harmony to a relationship. If a couple's process is relatively functional, they can usually resolve most of their content issues. But if their process is dysfunctional, they can fight over the most insignificant things. Tom and his wife, Lois, fought viciously over sexual frequency—but not in the usual sense. Lois liked to have sex in the morning. She said it was only then that she could relax. Tom preferred sex in the evening. He didn't want to get up any earlier than he had to on a work day. While the content issue (i.e., when to have sex) seemed relatively benign, the couple's chronic struggle for control (i.e., process) was so pervasive and entrenched that they were considering divorce rather than negotiating a compromise.

In some cases, the content issue is significant enough to take precedence over a couple's process. If so, ironically, the prognosis might prove fatal. Couples who fight over how often to have sex, or how many children to have, might not be able or willing to negotiate a compromise. For example, Jen, a 37-year-old interior designer, was born and raised in a big family and longed for a second child. She believed that her daughter would be lonely without a sibling; Jen also wanted her daughter to have someone to possibly rely on when she and her husband, Seth, passed.

Although never committed to having more than one child prior to marriage, Seth decided against the idea, and with that, the couple were locked into a potentially fatal disagreement. Each partner took terms politely expressing their points of view and were never critical of one another. While it would have been better to have processed this issue more definitively prior to marriage, they nevertheless had what appeared to be a very healthy process by the time they reported to treatment. But their dilemma over content proved to be insurmountable, and they ended their relationship.

Identifying a "process pattern" and a "content pattern" in each partner's prior intimate relationships may help the therapist to uncover a couple's shared master conflict. For example, Jim was on his third marriage, all of which began and ended the same, and over the same issue: Jim would usually pick very sexy and sexual women who he initially couldn't keep his hands off of. He loved these women to dress up so that he could show all his buddies just how attractive they were. But within a year of marriage, Jim would lose interest and develop a low libido (i.e., content). No matter how hard these women tried to turn him on, nothing worked. Although Jim would continue to lavish them with gifts, he would withhold sex until they would end the relationship in frustration (i.e., process)—the circular process would then regenerate. All three women had a history of never getting what they wanted out of their relationships. Eventually, it was determined that Jim and his third wife had a shared *giving vs. withholding* master conflict.

As mentioned, the process usually remains the same, but the content can change. For example, Jim's behavior would have qualified as a process pattern of giving and withholding and led the therapist to a *giving vs. withholding* master conflict even if he had withheld from his previous wives in nonsexual contexts. The wife's previous lovers may have also failed to meet her needs in a variety of ways. This is an important assessment tenet of MCT to remember, because couples sometimes may not present sexual content as the chief complaint. Rather, they may attribute their need for therapy to poor communication or chronic fighting; sexual symptoms may only be mentioned or even develop later in the therapeutic process. This is another reason that the therapist should always conduct a complete relational and sexual assessment with the help of an extensive genogram.

Identifying Incongruent Feelings and Behaviors

We tell our students to follow anything that they might experience in treatment that "confuses them" or seems to "defy logic," because it may take them straight to a couple's master conflict. To the psychoanalyst or psychodynamic therapist, such signs may be interpreted as mechanisms of defense, which are employed by the client's ego to help from being overwhelmed by the demands of the id and superego—demands which are considered "painful or unendurable" (Freud, 1936/1966, p. 42). There are many defense mechanisms, but the most common, *repression,* serves to exclude any unpleasant thoughts or feelings from consciousness. Freud referred to repression as the "most primitive and thorough-going" defense (Freud, 1936/1964, p. 245).

In MCT, we simplify certain complex concepts from psychoanalysis and recommend the therapist look for incongruence between thoughts, feelings, and behaviors; the seemingly irrational; and most of all, any contradictions that would be indicative of an internal conflict. Because MCT is constructed to relentlessly challenge a couple, identifying a couple's incongruence will aid the assessment process. It most certainly will give the therapist an idea of how hard it will be to utilize MCT to help a couple alleviate their symptoms.

Considering the Irrational

The therapist's "common sense" is a useful assessment tool for uncovering a master conflict. If the therapist perceives anything odd, out of character, or out of the ordinary, it is important that it be investigated. It could be something a client may have said, or a certain behavior; it could be something that took place many years prior to therapy, or something that happened to only one partner. It could also be something that the client is unconsciously building towards. Because conflicts are counterintuitive, what the therapist will pick up may appear to have little to do with the couple's presenting problem, or seem totally out of context. That is, if the couple present with a sexual problem, the provocative behavior which can lead the therapist to the couple's master conflict might be nonsexual in nature, and *vice versa*. Here are some examples:

Fred, a 55-year-old man, was having a long-term extramarital affair. He was very unhappy in his marriage and claimed that he had difficulty finding work. He said that he needed to think about ending his relationship and making a career change, but he could not seem to make a move. Fred was experiencing external stress that could manifest in depression, but what struck the therapist as odd was that as a singer/songwriter, he had turned down a major recording contract as a singer in his 20s. Prompted by this information, the therapist continued to investigate and soon discovered that Fred had also turned down several opportunities in different contexts that might have changed the course of his life for the better. It was found that Fred had great difficulty making decisions—as if he were perpetually paralyzed. He grew up feeling trapped by two drug-addicted parents and with little hope of escape. His wife was equally unhappy. It was later discovered that she was also having an affair but could not manage to leave her husband. It was determined that Fred suffered from an unbalanced *misery vs. resolution* conflict.

Rand, a married physician, presented with ED. Rand said that he preferred to try a course of couples therapy rather than settle on medication. What struck the therapist was that although Rand had excellent medical credentials, he barely made a living. Part of the reason for this oddity was that his office was in disarray and Rand could not seem to organize it enough to bill patients and insurance companies for his services. The therapist insisted on following up on this issue and discovered that Rand had sabotaged many opportunities in a variety of different contexts of his life. When the couple were assigned sex therapy exercises for Rand's erection problems, true to form, he would find a way to sabotage them ... but not necessarily in the moment. Rather, he would build towards it over the course of the day by intermittently agitating his wife until she refused to participate in the exercises later that evening. Rand's history revealed that he was criticized by his highly competitive father and a demanding mother. His wife was raised in a similar background. Her parents were perfectionists who gave her the message that she was never good enough. Consequentially, she had dated a bevy of men who rejected her for a variety of reasons: attraction, personality flaws, income potential, to name a few. It was eventually determined that this couple suffered from a shared *success vs. sabotage (big vs. small)* conflict.

Brandi, a very attractive woman in her 30s, looked as if she stepped out of a modeling magazine. She presented for therapy because she had lost sexual desire for her husband, Phoenix. In turn, he gradually developed ED. What struck the therapist was that although Brandi was a very beautiful woman, her hygiene was awful. How could someone so beautiful and well-dressed be so unclean? Using this mystery as a springboard, the therapist discovered that Brandi was in conflict about her station in life: She had come from a poor, blue-collar family and felt guilty marrying a wealthy executive—a conflict that manifested in a lack of sexual interest in her husband. Brandi turned out to have a *self vs. loyalty (others)* conflict. By choosing a mate outside her socioeconomic class and status, she unconsciously perceived herself as disloyal to her family of origin. Phoenix initially blamed his ED on Brandi's lack of sexual interest, but it turned out that his erectile problem was secondary to an acquired low libido that was determined to be correlated with his social and financial success. The son of a poor, abusive father, Phoenix could not allow himself to have a nice life and a beautiful wife. He would cry when he spoke of his successes.

And our last example of significant irrational behavior is that of Shane. A geologist by training, Shane was wealthy enough to purchase several expensive drums sets yet he barely knew how to play. Shane would walk into a music store, pull out a wad of bills, and pay cash for any set he desired. The store employees—all of whom were drummers—were quite impressed. When asked about his musical goals, Shane said he would love to play in some local bars. This seemed reasonable enough, but when I suggested that he take a few lessons, he declined. His wife, Gail, a physician and the breadwinner of the family, found Shane's fascination with drums a bit "weird." But she also believed that the therapist's attention paid to her husband's obsessive interest in drums was a waste of the couple's session time; Gail wanted to talk sex.

The couple's presenting problem was Shane's low sexual interest, which Gail blamed herself for—she did not believe that she was attractive. Shane's interest in drums became more instrumental, if you will, in helping the couple resolve their sexual issues than either partner initially thought. Shane's irrational behavior was the pathway to a shared *adequacy vs. inadequacy* master conflict. The ability to do what many drummers cannot: purchase any drum set at any given time, made Shane feel adequate. But his inability to play, by his own admittance, made him feel inadequate. Shane's low libido and the pressure Gail put on him to resolve his sexual issue did not help him feel any better about himself. Although Gail was professionally accomplished and the breadwinner of the family, she saw herself as unattractive and unwanted by her husband.

Considering Contradictions

Because conflict theory is based on the concept of opposites, it would benefit the therapist to pay close attention to "contradictions" in the therapeutic process. Contradictions may present in verbal or behavioral form and are the most important indicator of a master conflict—they are the heart of master conflict therapy. Partners are unaware that they contradict themselves on a consistent basis—their defenses block them from seeing this so that they can continue to mask their master conflicts. It is up to the therapist to call attention to any contradictions and use them as an assessment tool to help uncover a couple's master conflict. The following are some examples of contradictions with sexual content. We also offer some of the master conflicts that "may" be associated with these contradictions, but the therapist will need much more data from each partner's family of origin, life experiences, and current interactional process to accurately pinpoint a couple's shared conflict.

- Jane complained that for years her husband failed to initiate sex with her. When he did approach her, however, she rejected him with the non-specific excuse that she was not feeling well. This could be a sign of an *acceptance vs. rejection* master conflict.
- Ted claimed that he was very attracted to his wife, Sarah, but he rarely touched her or made sexual advances towards her. He said he was not necessarily as afraid of rejection as he was of upsetting her. Sarah agreed that she could be unpredictable. This could be a sign of a *power vs. passivity* conflict.
- Jim said that he craved sex with his wife, Jill, but only initiated it at the most inopportune moments, like when she was getting ready to go to work or a doctor's appointment. Jill was therefore often placed in a position to reject him. This could indicate an *acceptance vs. rejection* or *closeness vs. distance* master conflict.
- Tim loved the sexy way his wife, Marie, dressed before marriage, but was highly critical of it after marriage. This could also be a sign of an *acceptance vs. rejection* conflict.
- Tom said that if a pill was invented for ED, he would jump at the chance to take it. But after a medication emerged, Tom never filled the script his doctor gave him. His wife, Lori, never confronted him about this. This could be a sign of an *adequacy vs. inadequacy* or *success vs. sabotage (big vs. small)* conflict.
- Renee claimed that she wanted to have sex with her husband, Josh, but she always seemed to initiate it at the most inopportune times. She might even start a fight with her husband just prior to sexual intimacy. Josh never offered other, more convenient times for the couple to engage. This might have indicated a *closeness vs. distance* conflict.
- Tyrone said that he enjoyed fulfilling his wife, Tasha's, sexual needs. Nevertheless, he did insist she participate in a sexual act that he knew she disliked. Tasha complained but honored Tyrone's requests. This could indicate a *power vs. passivity* or *justice vs. injustice* conflict.
- Peter said that his wife, Joan, would turn him on if she wore a French maid's outfit just prior to having sex. But when she presented herself

to him in uniform, she claimed that he demonstrated little to no reaction. This could be indicative of a *satisfaction vs. disappointment* master conflict.
- Bill, a man with a conservative religious background, engaged in kinky behavior with his equally conservative wife, Alice. This could be an indication of a *conformity vs. rebellion* conflict.

Again, even nonsexual contradictions can lead the therapist to a master conflict and its associated sexual symptoms:

- Kristen regularly told her husband, Todd, that she thought he was "very smart." But as soon as Todd made the tiniest of mistakes, Kristen called him an "idiot" or "moron." This could be a sign of an *adequacy vs. inadequacy* master conflict.
- Sally complained that she could not afford an expensive home. However, she lost the equivalent of a monthly mortgage by being chronically late for work. This could lead to a *success vs. sabotage (big vs. small)* conflict.
- Hannah complained that her husband, Ari, never engaged her in conversation. But the minute Ari opened his mouth, Hannah cut him off with criticism. This could indicate a *power vs. passivity* conflict.
- James bragged how great his wife, Natasha, was at handling money. Nevertheless, James insisted on taking sole charge of the couple's finances. This dynamic might suggest an *adequacy vs. inadequacy* or *satisfaction vs. disappointment* conflict.
- With effort and sacrifice, Steve, a man in his 40s, completed a master's degree in business administration from an Ivy League graduate school. But while his classmates all took city jobs in big firms, he returned to state employment with no raise. His wife, Chris, was extremely upset, having helped him earn his degree. This might indicate a *success vs. sabotage (big vs. small)* or *adequacy vs. inadequacy* conflict.
- Sam, a man in his 50s, claimed that he desperately wanted to marry. But every time Sam got close, he found a way to sabotage his relationship. He was engaged a total of five times. This might be a sign of a *success vs. sabotage (big vs. small)* or *commitment vs. freedom* conflict.

When faced with a blatant contradiction in the assessment phase, it is hard to refrain from prematurely treating a couple. We do, however, gently point out the contradiction. It is our way of planting a seed in each partner's mind that a conflict is at play.

Incongruent feelings and behaviors

Another form of assessment the therapist can use to evaluate a couple and help to uncover their shared master conflict is to determine whether each partner's feelings match their experiences. We split reactions into three categories: underreactions, overreactions, and inverse reactions.

Underreactions

People who underreact exhibit little to no reaction to an experience that would otherwise merit one. For example, Becky claimed to love her husband but watched on coldly as he sobbed about losing his beloved mother. When asked how she felt seeing her husband in such pain, she tersely responded that his mother was "old," and that he should get over it and get back to work. Not surprisingly, a *person vs. object* conflict turned out to be at play. Another example is that of Ray, a mild-mannered man with a dominant, free-spending wife and two sickly children. Following the loss of his job, one might expect Ray to have been devastated, but he had little reaction. It was eventually revealed that he had a *power vs. passivity* master conflict.

Consider Drew, who reacted too calmly and somewhat indifferently to his wife Jan's recent affair and her request for a separation. His reaction could have easily led one to believe that he was glad that his wife was about to leave him. On the contrary, however, Drew admitted that he was madly in love with his wife, and equally enraged and saddened by the situation. He said that he could not believe that someone so "hot" would marry him in the first place. The following is a brief example of the couple's dynamic:

Therapist: Jan, you've agreed to be here but under the condition that you and Drew separate.
Jan: Yes. I just need my space. I am willing to give this a try, but it is just too tense living with Drew right now.
Therapist: You sound as if you are under pressure.
Jan: Everybody wants a piece of me: my mother, the kids, and my boss. Drew is always up my ass. I can't take it. I've never been good at juggling responsibilities.
Therapist: How is Drew up your ass?
Jan: He always wants to be near me. He always wants to talk. And he's always trying to hug or kiss me.
Therapist: Is that true, Drew?
Drew: Yup. I'm the obnoxious type. I love her, and I find her very attractive. I like to be around her.
Therapist: Jan, you've had a reasonably long-term affair. Did you ever think of leaving Drew?
Jan: Yes.
Therapist: What has kept you in the relationship?
Jan: I couldn't handle my kids and my mother on my own. I'm not good with stress, and Drew is a help.

82 Assessment and Treatment

Therapist: So that's what they mean by "true love"?
Drew: (No reaction).
Therapist: Drew, you've clearly stated that you are in love with your wife. But she has had a long-term affair and asked for a separation. Yet you seem to be taking this rather well.
Drew: What can I do? I hope she turns things around.

The therapist helped to uncover an *adequacy vs. inadequacy* conflict. It is important to note that Jan was by all standards extremely attractive and Drew average. Drew was quick to point out this disparity. Their incomes were comparable. This was a clear sign of Drew's inadequacy; his adequacy showed in his career as a chemist. Jan possessed more than adequate looks but little confidence in her ability to handle the stress of being a wife, mother, and caretaker for her mother. She was overwhelmed without the help of her husband.

We also categorize a partner who fails to reveal something that may be of importance as an underreaction. For example, if a prior trauma is not mentioned or is exposed in a session by accident, a master conflict might be operating. Consider the following example of John and Carol:

Therapist: John, your wife seems very worried that you will spend all your family's resources on your mother by caring for her at home. She feels you're being unfair to the rest of the family.
John: I realize taking care of her is expensive, but she has Alzheimer's. What else can I do?
Carol: She's 83 years old with no hope of improvement. You can do what everyone else does in this situation: use her insurance and social security and put her in a home with proper medical care. Having her around is also depressing the children and makes it difficult for all of us to have friends over.
John: I can't do it. I wouldn't do it to you. Asking me to put her away is unfair.
Therapist: You seem to be very obligated to your mother. How did your father die?
John: He had a heart attack. He was gone in a minute. It wasn't like this.
Therapist: Where did he have his attack?
John: In our den.
Therapist: Was it known that he had a bad heart?
John: I didn't know.
Therapist: Were you close to him?
Carol: They were very close. They even worked together.
Therapist: Were you in another room when he collapsed?
John: No, I was in the den.

Therapist: So, you were just talking, and he collapsed? What were you talking about?
John: I don't remember. Is it important?
Therapist: I don't know ... maybe.
Carol: They sometimes fought over work-related issues.
Therapist: Did you have a fight in the den?
John: (Tearing up). We had a fight about the direction of the business, and he dropped. I tried to save him: I gave him mouth-to-mouth resuscitation and I called 911. But he died in my arms. I felt so guilty. I kept trying to save him. I forgot all about this.
Carol: I didn't know this. You never told me about the fight.
Therapist: You did not want to give up on your dad, did you?
John: No. But by the time the paramedics came, he was already dead.
Therapist: That might make it especially hard to give up on your mother.

Shame and guilt were painful factors in John and Carol's case. We noted the blockage and traced it to an *adequacy vs. inadequacy* conflict. While this example was reflective of a trauma, we have also experienced couples who withhold information such as previous affairs or bankruptcies, even if these events were closely connected to the couple's presenting problem.

Overreactions

Overreacting to an experience is considered by many to be much more common than underreacting. For example, Janice intermittently scolded her long-time, live-in boyfriend, Wally, for several days because he left some facial hairs in the bathroom sink after he had shaved. Janice explained that she felt Wally was taking advantage of her by refusing to honor her wishes to keep her house clean. Janice would also become angry with Wally if he failed to perform sexually, no matter the circumstances. For example, when he failed to achieve an erection the morning he was to give a major presentation, she threatened to leave him. When Wally tried to tell her that he was under pressure and that his lack of interest in sex at the time had little to do with her, she did not believe him. Wally felt "picked on" for what he considered minor infractions and normal reactions under difficult circumstances. It was determined that this couple shared a *justice vs. injustice* master conflict.

A female client, Kathy, always seemed to be angry about some injustice in the world. She was frequently involved in many causes and participated in several protests. Her anger was not typical, however, there was a self-righteous quality to it, as if she were being tortured. When her husband, Brad, would challenge her stance on an issue, she would perceive him as disloyal. Brad, in turn, felt mistreated. It was no surprise that this couple also suffered from an unbalanced *justice vs. injustice* master conflict.

Inverse Reactions

Inverse reactions will probably be perceived by the therapist as most incongruent. Both underreactions and overreactions exist on the same continuum: an individual overreacts or underreacts to a behavioral stimulus. But inverse reactions are not continuum-dependent. Rather, they are represented by a counterintuitive reaction or a reaction opposite to one that would normally be expected. In extreme cases, the client's reaction tends to be equally startling. For example, several individuals have experienced depression and even committed suicide after winning the lottery. Researchers (Bitette, 2016; Chan, 2016; Doll, 2012) have attributed this to drug use, gambling, legal issues, loss of friends, family squabbles over money, and discrimination. Edelman (2016) found that many lottery winners go broke. Other studies have shown that while people who win the lottery are initially happy, they will eventually settle into the state of mind they were in prior to winning (Griffiths, 2009, 2010). In a classic study, Brickman, Coates, and Janoff-Bulman (1978) found lottery winners to be only as happy as their control group. We believe that these findings may signify that the winner's internal master conflict may have been unbalanced by the win itself. Other studies, however, have found that many lottery winners fared quite well (Ariyabuddhiphongs, 2011; Kaplan, 1987). It might be said that these individuals were more prepared to cope with such change, in part because they were less conflicted about their good fortune.

While we have yet to see a lottery winner in treatment, we have witnessed several inverse reactions on a much smaller scale. One example is that of Kurt, a professional athlete, who presented with a depressed mood directly related to his successful performance in a soccer game in which he scored several goals. Kurt confessed in treatment that his parents routinely downplayed his accomplishments as a child and even went as far as to reprimand him if he celebrated his achievements. Kurt clearly wanted to be successful, but he also exhibited guilt and shame admitting it. He suffered from an unbalanced *success vs. sabotage (big vs. small)* master conflict. A second example is that of Tricia, who complained vociferously for many years about her husband's lack of sexual interest; the couple had not had sex in four years. With a few months of treatment under their belt, Tricia's husband decided to approach her to make love, but was surreptitiously rejected. The husband proposed sexual intimacy at an appropriate time and was astonished that his wife offered little in the way of an excuse or counterproposal. An *adequacy vs. inadequacy* conflict was found to be at play.

MCT proposes that the unexpected be expected, and that the couple's words should not wholly be taken at face value. The therapist must gather sufficient evidence by observing the couple's interaction and identifying their individual and conjoint patterns before accepting their assertions and perceptions. While this theoretical stance may be considered somewhat skeptical by some therapists, it is well in line with a theory that is based on internal conflict. Reactions that seem counterintuitive are part and parcel of this model and should therefore be welcomed as important indicators of a couple's true conflict. The MCT practitioner should keep in mind that no matter how absurd a client's behavior, it is designed to avoid the anxiety that accompanies making a choice. At the very least, the loss of a "primary gain" is at stake.

Assessing Sociocultural Factors

We cannot address every population that we believe MCT can be applied to—that would merit a book of its own. And then there are groups that we do not feel qualified to comment on because we do not have enough treatment experience with them, such as genderqueer and transgender couples (Dworkin & Pope, 2012; Pfeffer, 2017). We do, however, include the types of couples that we see most often in treatment. And we offer what we consider to be some of their unique struggles and associated master conflicts. Because we are still in the formal phase of clinical assessment, all case vignettes to follow have taken place in the first few sessions. We do, however, recognize that assessment informally continues throughout the treatment process. We realize that the therapist might have initially forgotten to ask something significant, or the couple may have failed to reveal something of similar importance.

Culture

According to Lee and Park (2013), the values inherent in therapy often come into direct conflict with the values of a multicultural population. The authors defined a culturally-competent therapist as one with the "awareness, knowledge, and skills to intervene effectively in the lives of culturally diverse backgrounds" (p. 6). Lee (2013) referred to this individual as someone who "simultaneously acknowledges human similarity and celebrates human difference" (p. 17). Some of the author's specific guidelines for therapists included: (1) Considering cultural factors in the therapeutic interaction; (2) Being aware of one's own cultural baggage; (3) Looking at one's own cultural privilege; (4) Considering the relevance of one's own theory; (5) Avoiding stereotyping; (6) Being open-minded and willing to learn from clients; and (7) Advocating for diverse clients.

Because all couples have conflicts, MCT is a widely applicable therapeutic model. Nevertheless, we agree with Lee (2013) and the many others (Lee & Park, 2013; Moodley, Lengyell, Wu, & Gielen, 2015; Sue & Sue, 2015) who contend that understanding the role of factors such as culture, ethnicity, race, religion, sexual orientation, and experience with discrimination is necessary to join with and accurately assess couples.

86 Assessment and Treatment

Studies have found that because therapists can miss culturally-related cues and values in the therapeutic setting (Lee & Bhuyan, 2013; Lee & Horvath, 2013, 2014), it is important for them to develop their "eyes and ears to tease out implicit cultural meanings" (Lee, 2015, p. 9). In the initial session, the meaning of a Hindu man's behavior was initially misinterpreted by the therapist even though the behavior was directly related to the man's presenting problem with ED. Here is his story: A male client, Mandip, reported for treatment without his wife because they were currently separated and in crisis; he was hoping to include her at some point. Mandip refused to take an office seat before the therapist did. The therapist initially misinterpreted the client's behavior. He thought Mandip was looking over the therapist's book collection, or chose to stand because of back problems. When the therapist finally did realize that the man was waiting for him to sit, he then assumed that the man was being polite. But it was more complicated than that. Consider the exchange between this man—who suffered from an underlying *adequacy vs. inadequacy* conflict—and his therapist:

Therapist: I notice that you do not sit until I do. You do not have to wait for me.
Mandip: Yes, I do.
Therapist: Well, that is very polite of you, but there is no need.
Mandip: I am not doing it for the reason you may think. In India, we have respect for people with higher education, particularly those few with doctorates. My father and my professors always taught me to allow for the doctor to sit first ... out of respect for his accomplishment.
Therapist: I understand. Well, thank you for educating me. When you first called for an appointment, you gave me an idea as to why you are seeking treatment. Might this have something to do with why you are here? You told me that because you did not have better academic credentials you were arranged—in India—to marry a woman of a lower socioeconomic level. You sounded very disappointed.
Mandip: Yes, I feel I should have worked harder to achieve more. I sense my wife is disappointed in me as well. I have been upset and unable to function sexually.

Lee (2015) made the point that a client's culture is too often considered an external factor rather than something internalized or psychological—a misconception that may lead the therapist to mistakenly believe that an understanding of the client's cultural background will automatically offer insight into the client. In tune with Lee, Ho (1995) presented culture as a psychological construct rather than an anthropological one. He is credited with the concept "internalized culture," which he referred to as: "the cultural influences operating inside the individual that share (not determine) personality formation and various aspects of psychological functioning" (p. 5). This would include how emotions are expressed, independence/dependence issues, and most germane to MCT, relationship customs or norms such as arranged marriages.

Consider the case of a highly combative Hindu couple in their middle 30s—both engineers—in an arranged marriage. While 85% of the people in India still favor arranged marriages (Cultural India, 2017), and the majority believe that a woman's place is in the home, Devi, an engineer, disagreed. Devi was rebelling against tradition. She wanted children but insisted on speaking up against what she perceived as a sexist culture. Her husband, Ajay, a computer programmer and a man loyal to the traditions of his culture, was angry with his wife's stance and withheld sex. This, in turn, enabled his parents to nag and threaten Devi to succumb to tradition so that she could give them grandchildren. The following dialogue revealed rather quickly that the couple's cultural heritage and individual personalities played a role in their marital troubles. The couple was determined to have struggled with a shared *self vs. loyalty (others)* conflict—a conflict that is commonly seen in couples with backgrounds steeped in various traditions. The *conformity vs. rebellion* master conflict would be also considered in these types of cases.

Therapist: Were you attracted to your wife when you first met and married her?
Ajay: Yes, I found her attractive. I still think she is a beautiful woman. But all we do is fight. She has turned me off.
Devi: We fight because he wants me to obey him. I'm a professional woman, and I have a right to my own opinion. We are in the United States. His parents control him and tell him he must get me under control.
Therapist: Do you agree, Ajay?
Ajay: My parents are old and set in their ways. Devi fights with them all the time, and then they put pressure on me to do something about it. They are not bad people. I like my Hindu culture, but Devi is rebellious.
Therapist: Apparently, Devi did agree to an arranged marriage.
Ajay: I think she wants children.
Therapist: Devi, when did you decide that you didn't approve of some of the aspects of your cultural background?
Ajay: Now that I know more about her, I can say that she was always rebellious. She can fight about anything.
Devi: This is true. I've never been a follower. But I did go along with an arranged marriage.
Ajay: She is not in love with me. She is just stubborn. I would like to divorce, but it is frowned upon in my culture, and my parents would be very upset with me. I do not want to disgrace them.

Devi: See, he doesn't care about me. But he will give in just to avoid angering or disgracing his family. We both have had to achieve and to succumb to please our families and our community. Ajay far more so than I.

Therapist: So, Devi, am I clear that you have always been a rebellious sort, and you, Ajay, a compliant one?

The research supports Devi's assertion regarding achievement and conformity. Southeast Asian Americans, specifically East Indians, are among the hardest working, most financially successful people in the United States. They have also been found to be among the highest educated: approximately 70% of Indian Americans aged 25 and older hold a college degree or more (Pew Research Center, 2017).

Cross Culture

As of 2015, there were 43.3 million immigrants in the United States, or 4.7% of the total population (Zong & Batalova, 2016). We have had the opportunity to treat several cross-cultural couples (i.e., foreign born and raised individuals married to Americans) and to assess how cultural difference plays a significant role in their conflicts and symptoms. For example, we have seen numerous Israeli men married to American Jewish women. Most of the women were in Israel working on a kibbutz when they met their Israeli counterparts. The Israeli men seemed eager to come to the United States to pursue the American Dream. Soon thereafter, many started their own businesses or were set up in business by their new in-laws. All worked exceedingly long hours and achieved moderate to large degrees of success. The American Jewish women saw these men as manly, and it pleased their parents that they had married within their faith. The presenting problems, however, were similar: The Israeli husbands felt as if their wives were "entitled" and "spoiled"; they soon lost respect for them. Some of these men resorted to affairs, while others developed sexual symptoms. The women saw their husbands as "bossy, controlling workaholics" who cared more about achieving success than their families; the women felt more like a meal ticket than they did loved. Many of them presented angry and depressed. Notice how cultural differences played a part in Ari and Rivka's *person vs. object* master conflict, and Ari's symptomatic low sexual desire with secondary ED:

Ari: I work hard every day to provide for the family. You could at least dust.

Rivka: That's all you think about is money. You never loved me. Since you've come to the U.S., all you ever do is obsess about work.

Ari: You don't seem to mind using my hard-earned money to buy fancy clothes and cars.

Rivka:	I had these things before I met you. I didn't need you to get them for me. You saw dollar signs and knew my father would help you out.
Ari:	And you needed me because I was Israeli, and it pleased your parents to marry me. They were concerned you would marry a Christian.
Therapist:	It sounds as if you are accusing one another of having ulterior motives to marry.
Ari:	I just want her to work a little. My mother in Israel works very hard. It's a hard life, and she don't complain.
Therapist:	Your voice softens when you mention her, as if you feel sorry for her.
Ari:	I didn't when I was in Israel. But now that I see the way some of these American Jews live, especially my pampered wife, it makes me sick.
Rivka:	This isn't Israel. And you knew I was raised in a wealthy family with a maid. If you want an Israeli woman, go back to Israel. And now you can't even get it up … and you won't even take a pill.
Ari:	Maybe if you did the dishes or dusted the furniture now and then I would get it up.

Ollivier (2009) addressed the differences between the French and Americans when it came to love and sex, contending that they are steeped in their respective cultures. The French, she believed, were far more open and accepting about sex, and separate sex and love more easily. The author also said that French women respect men, and that their battle for equality was more of a respectful protest, in part because French women do not wish to live without men and *vice versa*. The author also pointed out that the French take pleasure in living life, whereas Americans are goal-oriented.

We believe it is helpful in the assessment process to understand what piece of culture each partner brings to their relationship and to the clinical setting. Adelais and Saul met in Paris, where Saul, an American, was transferred for a five-year stint by his New York-based company. Adelais was born and raised in Nice before moving to Paris to pursue a career in fashion. The couple saw each other for a little over a year and married in France. Notice the role culture (i.e., work and sexual differences) played in their marriage. The presenting problem was Adelais's fling with a co-worker, about which Saul was threatening to divorce. It was determined that the couple were experiencing an unbalanced *security vs. risk* master conflict.

Adelais:	Saul is very upset that I had sex with this man at work. I told him that I found this man attractive, but I am not in love with him. I understand that Saul is distraught, but threatening divorce is an overreaction.

Saul:	I guess it's the French in her, but she is not taking this seriously. She thinks it's okay to screw anybody she wants.
Therapist:	Adelais, is there any other reason you had the fling?
Adelais:	Saul is never around. He works so many hours. I think you Americans are crazy. He doesn't even take a lunch break. And if I call him in the middle of the day, he gets annoyed with me. I'm not used to this.
Saul:	France never gets anywhere because you people have two-hour lunch breaks. Anyway, that's no excuse to casually have sex with some guy and then expect me to live with it. Do you really think I want a divorce?
Adelais:	Oh, you Americans are so hung up on sex.
Therapist:	I assume each of you knew where the other stood on this issue, yet you both took a risk with one another.

The final example is that of a Guatemalan man and his American wife. Luis and Joan presented for therapy because Joan was emotionally distancing and refusing to have sex with Luis. Studies (Beaulieu, 2004) have shown that Anglo Saxons favor the largest zones of personal space, whereas Latinos adopt a face-to-face position that requires much less personal space. According to Provasi (2012), Americans consider personal space 1.5 to 4 feet, with 3 feet being the most comfortable. Latinos prefer a personal space zone of 1.5 feet. In the Latino culture, it may even be thought of as rude to step away from someone when they are stepping closer. Consider the cultural factors that revealed themselves in the assessment phase. The couple were determined to have a problematic *closeness vs. distance* master conflict:

Therapist:	How long has it been since you last had sex?
Luis:	Six months. I don't know what I did. How can she treat me this way?
Joan:	I just feel suffocated. Luis is all over me. If he's not trying to get me in bed, he's constantly groping me or trying to kiss me. I can't take it. I can't breathe.
Luis:	I love my wife. I find her attractive and I desire her. What's wrong with that?
Joan:	Even when he talks to me, I can feel his breath on me. I need a break. He's also very jealous. If I talk to another man, even a colleague, he gives me the third degree.
Luis:	Most women would die to be desired by their husbands. My wife can't wait to get away from me. She didn't seem to mind it that much when we dated.
Joan:	I was always a little uncomfortable, but it's gotten a lot worse.

Race

African American couples experience many of the same struggles and relational similarities as do couples from other racial and ethnic backgrounds (Allen & Helm, 2013); we also believe that they share the same master conflicts (Betchen, 2010). However, like other oppressed groups, African Americans are vulnerable to outside forces of prejudice and discrimination that can yield a host of individual (e.g., anger, depression, emasculation, self-esteem), interpersonal (e.g., commitment, intimacy), and financial problems (e.g., challenges associated with being a provider, poverty) that negatively affect their romantic relationships (Bethea & Allen, 2013; Dixon, 2007).

Benton-Goodley (2014) found that African American couples are more susceptible to economic downturn due to intergenerational wealth inequity, discriminatory hiring practices, and lower income. According to the U.S. Bureau of the Census (2014), 26.2% of African Americans live in poverty, compared to 12.7% of White Americans. To expect all African Americans to exude the confidence to easily compete successfully in a predominantly white society without some conflict is unrealistic.

Joseph, a 42-year-old African American man, was under pressure to succeed in his career as an engineer. His father, a maintenance man, constantly cajoled him to work harder. In the interim, Joseph developed high blood pressure and ED. In the initial session, Joseph and his wife, Tisha, discuss their chief complaint with the therapist:

Tisha: Joe is working 80 hours a week. I think he's going to have a stroke. It's his dad: He keeps telling Joe that a black man must work harder to get ahead. But Joe's not going to be good to anybody if he's dead. It's already in our bed.

Therapist: Meaning the ED?

Tisha: Yeah. He can't think of anything but work.

Joseph: She doesn't understand. I'm under a lot of pressure. I have projects due all the time and I need great reviews to get promoted and to keep getting those raises. Tisha complains about my work, but she sure doesn't mind spending the money it brings in.

Therapist: I understand your father's position. In his day, times were no doubt worse for a black man. But where is the ceiling? How do you know when you've made it? With no end in sight, you might never feel successful.

Tisha: Maybe he'll hit the ceiling when he's dead.

Therapist: And then there are types of success. You're doing well at work, but having trouble at home. In that case, success and failure are operating at the same time.

In our experience, racism—both systemic and institutional—makes it even more difficult for African American couples to balance or rebalance the master conflicts they seem most susceptible to, such as: *adequacy vs. inadequacy, justice vs. injustice, success vs. sabotage (big vs. small)*, and *trust vs. distrust*. Being born into discrimination can produce master conflicts, let alone exacerbate them. For an accurate assessment, the therapist will need to empathize with the African American couple's plight but differentiate any racially-driven limitations from those produced solely by their master conflicts or determine how they might be intertwined.

Consider the case of Thad and Genecia: The driving force in their therapy was Genecia's affair with an old boyfriend she found on the Internet. Thad, a tall, muscular man with a tough exterior, said that he felt humiliated by his wife's behavior, which he attributed to retaliation for his difficulty making a good living. Genecia denied this. She claimed that Thad felt sorry for himself and was frustrated with his difficulty supporting the family. She said Thad grew financially stingy, controlling, and jealous of other men. She also said that he became more easily agitated, critical, and quick to anger.

Thad did not admit it at first, but he saw Genecia's behavior as an attack on his masculinity, which he had worked long and hard to prove. He tied his inability to get over her transgression in part to his hyper-masculine upbringing in the Chicago projects. "I've always prided myself on being tough. I grew up without a father. I'm lucky to still be alive, and then she goes and does this to me," he said.

Therapist: How long did the affair last, Genecia?
Genecia: About six months. I stopped it after Thad found some texts.
Therapist: Do you know why you had the affair?
Genecia: I know I was unhappy. Thad isn't a bad man, but things haven't turned out the way he thought they would, and he's been bitter. All he thinks about is money.
Thad: I'm bitter about your affair.
Genecia: Don't play with the doctor. You know you thought you were going to the NFL. Thad played football in college and was on his way to making it big until he wrecked his knee. He then lost his scholarship and had to quit college.
Therapist: You were close. Most people can't say that.
Thad: I had a shot. I was raised by my mom, and we had nothing. The only way I could get an education was to play football. I was good enough to get a scholarship, but I hurt myself in practice, and they took it back. It was the only thing I was good at.
Therapist: I'm sorry, Thad. Tough luck. So, your father is out of the picture.
Thad: Yeah, he left before I was born. I don't even know where he is.
Genecia: And he always keeps getting passed over for promotions at his agency, even though he works hard [Thad is an insurance

	agent]. I'm sure it's because of his attitude. I think he feels like a loser, and every year he seems to be more and more miserable. You act like a loser, they'll treat you like a loser.
Thad:	I had a chance to get out of the hood and be somebody. I wanted to help my mother and brother get off welfare. Now I'm selling insurance. Then Genecia has an affair on me. I guess I wasn't down enough.
Genecia:	My behavior was weak. But you're not the man I married. You treat me and the kids like you wish we weren't even there.

In this case, the ravages of racism and the couple's master conflict are closely connected. Thad was a man who tried to rise above his past, but he suffered a fatal blow to his dream when he hurt his knee and could no longer play football at the level he was accustomed to. Thad was raised fatherless by his mother in a single-parent household. He and his family were poor and on welfare, and the neighborhood they lived in was dangerous. Thad saw football as the only way to improve his life. This is an all-too-familiar situation in the lives of African Americans. But Thad also revealed that he never really thought very highly of himself and was having difficulty making a comeback. He needed help for years, but his machismo pride and the fear of exhibiting weakness—not uncommon in African American males—kept him from admitting this and enabled the displacement of his anger and disappointment onto his wife and children (Bethea & Allen, 2013; Shelton-Wheeler, 2013). It turned out to be helpful for Thad and Genecia to see themselves as suffering from the symptoms of an unbalanced *adequacy vs. inadequacy* conflict in the context of discriminating limitations.

We have found that the master conflict *trust vs. distrust* is relatively common in African American couples. This coincides with the research that indicates that another casualty of oppression and prejudice is a high degree of distrust in African American couples compared to white couples (Allen & Helm, 2013; Harknett & McLanahan, 2004; Hill, 2009). Consider the case of a couple in their late 30s, Terrance and his wife, Tamicka. Terrance had an affair with a single neighbor, he claimed, because Tamicka tricked him into marrying her: she used to give him sex everyday but cut it down to approximately once a month soon after marriage. Both claim that they cannot trust one another. Here is a brief vignette from their first session:

Terrance:	I feel I was played for a fool. When we were dating we had sex all the time and Tamicka seemed liked she was really into it. But as soon as we got married, she acted like it was a bother. No more oral or manual sex and just one position.
Tamicka:	I'd still be into it if you didn't flirt with every ho with a dress. Go ahead, tell the doctor this isn't your first affair. Go ahead.
Therapist:	So, you've had others?

Terrance: Yeah, two years ago.
Therapist: So, they took place before marriage.
Terrance: Yeah, whatever.
Therapist: When the sex was plentiful.
Terrance: Yeah, but I was young and stupid.
Tamicka: You still are. I just can't trust this man.
Therapist: He cheated on you twice, but you still married him.
Tamicka: I'm a fool.
Therapist: Did you ever trust him?
Tamicka: For about the first month we met. But who knows what he was doing behind my back.
Therapist: Terrance, you said you feel as if Tamicka tricked you. Did you ever trust her?
Terrance: Nah, I always thought she only cared about money and not me. Like I said, she just wanted to get married, so she played the ho and pulled it back the day after we married.
Therapist: Tamicka, you said that you were once into sex.
Terrance: Tell the truth.
Tamicka: For the most part, but I guess I never liked oral sex.
Therapist: But you did it frequently before marriage.
Tamicka: Yeah. Got to keep the customer satisfied.

There are many other characteristics unique to African American couples that are beyond the scope of this book, and the ones that were presented have been expressed by others in greater detail (Helm & Carlson, 2013). There are also related areas that we wished we had more clinical experience with, such as interracial couples (Killian, 2013; Thomas, Karis, & Wetchler, 2014). Our main objective was far less ambitious: to show the therapist the importance of assessing an African American couple from a clinical as well as an environmental perspective in relation to their associated master conflicts.

Sexual Orientation

In 2011, Americans opposed same-sex marriage by a margin of 57% to 35%. But as of 2016, they supported it 55% to 37% (Pew Research Center, 2016). In a study conducted by Badgett and Herman (2011), nearly 150,000 same-sex couples have either married or registered civil unions or domestic partnerships. About 1% of the total number of currently married or registered same-sex couples get divorced each year, compared to 2% of the total of straight marriages.

There is no doubt that gays have made great strides in the social, political, and legal arenas of our society (Lev & Nichols, 2015). And although the therapist should not assume that sexual orientation is always in some way responsible for the gay couple's chief complaint, it remains important—especially for the heterosexual therapist—to factor in the institutional and systemic discrimination gays face (Connolly, 2012). Dworkin and Pope (2012) recommended that the therapist be aware of: (1) Societal discrimination that has contributed to internalized negative attitudes toward their sexual orientation; (2) Heterosexism that pervades the social and cultural foundations of many institutions and traditions that may foster negative attitudes toward lesbians and gay males; and (3) Biological, familial, and psychosocial factors that influence the course of development of gay orientations.

In our clinical experience, lesbian and gay male couples may be prone to the *self vs. loyalty (others)* master conflict—a conflict that is born out of, or exacerbated by, a disapproving family. According to Merrill (2016):

> Coming out not only alters relationships between the lesbian or gay individual and family members but also has the potential to change relationships between additional members of the family who will often react differently to the news. It can worsen preexisting tensions and conflicts and result in placing blame on one another.
>
> (p. 15)

William, a 55-year-old perfectionistic attorney from an overachieving family, had a very difficult time coming out, and for good reason. Once he confronted his family, the micro-aggressive attacks ensued, and William was no longer considered the perfect son. William's desire to be the perfect son versus accepting himself as a gay man was believed to contribute to his internal homophobia and low libido.

Therapist: At what age did you come out, William?
William: Very late. I think I was in my early 40s.
Therapist: How did your parents respond?
William: At first, they tried to ignore it. I think they hoped it would all go away. But I wouldn't let that happen. Anyway, once they got to know Thomas, they were pretty accepting. They love Thomas, and all is good.
Thomas: I think William has more of a problem with being gay than his parents do.
William: No, I don't.
Thomas: Then how come you have never told anybody at work? And why can't we go to parties together?
William: You know why. Politics!
Therapist: William, aren't all your siblings professionals?
William: Yes.
Therapist: And aren't they all quite successful.
Thomas: They're maniacs.

Therapist: Explain.
Thomas: They can't just be successful. They want to be superstars. They even compete against each other.
Therapist: Something in the water?
William: No, my parents were demanding.
Thomas: He didn't even want to be a lawyer.
Therapist: Is that true, William?
William: Yeah. I'm glad I am, but there was a lot of pressure on us to succeed.
Therapist: And if you didn't?
Thomas: Disgrace!
Therapist: So being yourself wasn't the desired objective.
Thomas: And being gay is being himself. And being himself means having sex with another man.
Therapist: Something like that.

The therapist must take care not to assess a gay couple based on a heterosexual model.

Inflicting such values may only serve to pathologize the gay couple's relational system (Connolly, 2012). Research, for example, has shown that gay men do not favor monogamy in long-term relationships (Green & Mitchell, 2008; Peplau & Fingerhut, 2004). Badgett (2010) argued that "gay men in married and nonmarried couples were not monogamous, suggesting that the meaning of marriage for gay male couples is different than it is for heterosexual couples" (p. 91). Consider Jon and Michael and their *closeness vs. distance* conflict. Jon insisted that Michael, his partner of seven years, attend couples therapy because he felt Michael was distancing from him.

Jon: Michael and I have always protected our primary relationship. But we do allow one other man in our relationship at a time. I know that you are heterosexual, but we do not want you to try and change that. We do not have a problem with it.
Michael: I agree.
Therapist: Got it. So, what brought you two here?
Jon: Michael and I have always been close, even with a third party in our lives. But in the last couple of months, he has been distant. He hasn't been as talkative, and he's cut back on initiating sex with me. I believe that he's spending more time with this other man, Christopher. But he swears that he's not in love with him or anyone else.
Michael: There's no need for me to cheat. And I'm not in love with Christopher. It's just that Jon requires more connection than I do, and sometimes I need space. If he won't give it to me, I take

it. Christopher has his own life and he doesn't require much from me. He's just someone I can run to for a breather.

Gay couples may request help with something or set certain treatment parameters that a couple's therapist with traditional values may view as odd or potentially damaging to the long-term health of a relationship. Jon and Michael's request that the therapist avoid challenging their open relationship was supported by the literature. For example, LaSala (2004) reported that non-monogamy in gay male relationships was not associated with lower levels of relational satisfaction or commitment.

Lesbian couples have long been viewed as the least sexual of all couples. Whitman (2012) wrote: "lesbians have historically been characterized as losing a desire for sex and decreasing the initiation and frequency of sex more quickly than women in heterosexual couples" (p. 249). It was in this vein that Blumstein and Schwartz (1983) coined the controversial term "lesbian bed death," or the relatively fast decline of sexual activity in lesbian couples.

While no one doubts that some lesbians suffer from low sexual desire, many scholars have challenged the lesbian bed death concept, believing that it was propagated by evaluating the sexual life of lesbians from a heteronormative perspective (Iasenza, 2000; Nichols, 2011; Whitman, 2012). Iasenza wrote: "Asking lesbian couples about frequency is problematic because sexuality between women is not defined by discreet genital acts in the way that sex often is when a penis is involved" (p. 61). Whitman (2012) contended that lesbians express their sexuality in a variety of ways, such as cuddling, kissing, romantic touches or glances, holding, and sex play. Leslie and Pat, a married lesbian couple, were not having sex. But an assessment revealed that the couple's symptom had little to do with lesbian bed death and more to do with unresolved loyalty issues courtesy of Pat's family of origin and a *self vs. loyalty (others)* master conflict.

Therapist: So, what brings you here?
Leslie: I have a great sex drive, but Pat hasn't been interested in having sex with me for the last couple of years. I've finally got her to see somebody with me.
Therapist: Are you affectionate with one another?
Leslie: Somewhat. But I can say we get along great in all other areas: We think the same, like the same things, and have similar values. My parents love Pat and they've accepted our lifestyle.
Therapist: What say you, Pat?
Pat: I agree with Leslie. I love her, and we have a wonderful time together. I'm just not interested in having sex with her or anyone else. I wish I felt differently. I know Leslie is a great person, and I wouldn't want to be married to anyone else. Maybe it's my depression. I've suffered from it for years.

Therapist: Do you take medication, Pat?
Pat: No. I'm trying to deal with it myself. My mother suffered from it.
Therapist: Did she take medication?
Pat: No. I've tried to convince her to be evaluated.
Leslie: Her mother is the ultimate martyr. She's always depressed or in pain about something. And she won't go for help. She even has bad knees but won't get them checked out.
Therapist: And you had to drag Pat here.
Leslie: Yeah, I've been trying to get her help for years.
Therapist: So, Pat pushes her mom to get help, and you push Pat.
Leslie: I never thought of the connection.
Therapist: Pat, did you feel sorry for your mother?
Pat: (Starts to cry). Yes, all the time. I tried to help her, but nothing seemed to make her happy.
Therapist: Did your dad try and help?
Pat: No, he was never around. I think he kept away as best he could.
Therapist: It sounds as if you had a serious childhood.
Pat: Yeah.
Therapist: And you're still serious ... out of loyalty to your mother, of course.

And last, when assessing gay male and lesbian couples, the heterosexual therapist should not be surprised to find that the level of egalitarianism is greater than that of heterosexual couples (Gotta *et al.*, 2011; Lev & Nichols, 2015). According to Lev and Nichols (2015), gay couples "do not have the inherent imbalance that comes when two partners have been socialized differently and have unequal access to power in the world outside the marriage" (p. 223). The authors contended that gay couples are, for the most part, "free of gender stereotyping and power imbalances in the still-sexist culture in which we live" (p. 222). They are therefore less likely to separate relationship responsibilities such as financial obligations, household chores, and childcare the way many heterosexual couples do. There exists a greater emphasis on the concepts of reciprocity and fairness. Merrill (2016) found that:

> Same-sex couples tend to divide labor equally out of a desire for egalitarian relationships and to spend time together. They create equity by doing tasks together, complementing one another's preferred tasks, with similar tasks, taking on projects together, and dividing undesirable tasks equally. Rather than re-creating a traditional division of labor or assigning one person with 'pink tasks' and the other with 'blue tasks,' they have redefined how couples run their households and families.
>
> (p. 69)

While gay male couples and lesbians have made great strides in dispelling some of the stereotypes inflicted upon them by a predominantly heterosexual society, many heterosexual therapists still look for gay couples to fall along heterosexual lines and exhibit a butch/femme dynamic. We surmise that these therapists feel more comfortable fitting the gay couple into something that they might more readily know and understand. But they may be disappointed with the results. Apparently, the butch/femme is not as prevalent in the gay community as one might think (Chernin & Johnson, 2003).

Summary

It is not unusual for a couples therapist to feel overwhelmed by the symptoms a couple might present for treatment and the mutual blaming dynamic that often accompanies them. We believe, however, that every couple has but one master conflict that is responsible for all symptoms, and if unveiled and controlled, these symptoms will dissipate. This is not an attempt to minimize any pain associated with a couple's problems or to simplify the complexity of couples work. It is to make the point that much of what the couples therapist will hear in treatment serves as a cloak to hide a couple's deeper issue—their master conflict—from themselves and the treating therapist.

In this chapter, we presented our assessment process—a process that includes using the genogram to examine each partner's family of origin and the couple's interactional style. We firmly believe that because every couple has a master conflict, MCT can be applied to couples of every race, religion, ethnicity, and orientation. We have also made it clear that despite MCT's general appeal, knowledge about a couple's sociocultural background, particularly as it relates to relationships and sex, is a key component for adequate treatment. We have not demonstrated how we assess every couple type, but this was not our objective. Rather, it was to offer the reader a clear indication as to how we assess couples and their master conflicts and to show how these conflicts are intricately connected to a couple's sexual symptoms. We began the process of encouraging the therapist to "think conflict."

Assessment is an ongoing process. But we feel it is important that the therapist develop a framework or direction for treatment as quickly as possible so that interventions may be utilized and pain alleviated. We have found that too many therapists wander through treatment under the guise of joining with a couple, only to find that they have been sucked into the couple's chaos. We have tried to show how it is possible to develop a framework within the first two sessions and the value of this endeavor. With added information, a therapist may decide that they were initially in error, and that a different master conflict is, in fact, the culprit behind a couple's symptoms. But we find that a detailed assessment, carried out in the beginning of the treatment process, will often reduce the likelihood of a need for change in a master conflict.

References

Allen, E., & Atkins, D. (2012). The association of divorce and extramarital sex in a representative U.S. sample. *Journal of Family Issues, 33*(11), 1477–1493.
Allen, T., & Helm, K. (2013). Threats to intimacy for African American couples. In K. Helm & J. Carlson (Eds.), *Love, intimacy, and the African American couple* (pp. 85–116). New York, NY: Routledge.
Althof, S. (2014). Treatment of premature ejaculation: psychotherapy, pharmacotherapy and combined therapy. In Y. Binik & K. Hall (Eds.), *Principles and practice of sex therapy* (5th ed., pp. 112–137). New York, NY: The Guilford Press.
Althof, S. (2016). Low Sexual Desire in Men. In S.B. Levine, C. Risen, & S. Althof (Eds.), *Handbook of clinical sexuality for mental health professionals* (3rd ed., pp. 97–110). New York, NY: Routledge.
American Association of Marriage and Family Therapy (2017). Infidelity. Retrieved from http://www.aamft.org/iMIS15/Content/Consumer_Updates/Infidelity.aspx - 68k
Ariyabuddhiphongs, V. (2011). Lottery gambling: A review. *Journal of Gambling Studies, 27*, 15–33. doi:10.1007/s10899-010-9194-0
Badgett, L.M.V. (2010). *When gay people get married: What happens when societies legalize same-sex marriage.* New York, NY: NYU Press.
Badgett, L.M.V., & Herman, J. (2011). *Patterns of relationship recognition by same-sex couples in the United States.* Los Angeles, CA: The Williams Institute.
Basson, R. (2016). Clinical Challenges of Sexual Desire in Younger Women. In S.B. Levine, C. Risen, & S. Althof (Eds.), *Handbook of clinical sexuality for mental health professionals* (3rd ed., pp. 43–59). New York, NY: Routledge.
Beaulieu, C. (2004). Intercultural study of personal: A case study. *Journal of Applied Social Psychology, 34*, pp. 794–805. doi:10.1111/j.1559-1816.2004.tb02571.x
Bent-Goodley, T.B. (2014). *By Grace: The Challenges, strengths, and promise of African American marriages.* Washington, DC: NASW Press.
Bergeron, S., Rosen, N., & Pukall, C. (2014). Genital pain in women and men: It can hurt more than your sex life. In Y. Binik & K. Hall (Eds.), *Principles and practice of sex therapy* (5th ed., pp. 159–176). New York, NY: The Guilford Press.
Berman, E., & Hof, L. (1987). The sexual genogram: Assessing family-of-origin factors in the treatment of sexual dysfunctions. In G. Weeks & L. Hof (Eds.), *Integrating sex and marital therapy: A clinical guide.* (pp. 37–56). New York, NY: Brunner/Mazel.
Betchen, S. (1991). Male masturbation as a vehicle for the pursuer/distancer relationship in marriage. *Journal of Sex & Marital Therapy, 17*(4), 269–278.
Betchen, S. (1992). Short term psychodynamic therapy with a divorced single mother. *Families in Society: The Journal of Contemporary Human Services, 73*(2), 116–121.
Betchen, S. (1996). Parentified pursuers and childlike distances in marital therapy. *The Family Journal, 4*(2), 100–108.
Betchen, S. (2005). *Intrusive partners, elusive mates: The pursuer distancer dynamic in couples.* New York, NY: Routledge.
Betchen, S. (2010). *Magnetic partners: Discover how the hidden conflict that once attracted you to each other is now driving you apart.* New York, NY: Free Press.

Betchen, S. (2013, November). The role of physical attraction in your relationship: Can you get it if you've never had it? Retrieved from www.psychologytoday.com/blog/magnetic-partners/201311/the-role-physical- attraction-in-your-relationship

Betchen, S. (2015, September). Why we marry people we aren't physically attracted to: The importance of laying a good relational foundation. Retrieved from www.psychologytoday.com/blog/magnetic-partners/201509/why-we-marry-people-we-arent-physicallyattracted

Bethea, S., & Allen, T. (2013). (Eds.). Past and present societal influences on African American couples that impact love and intimacy. In K. Helm & J. Carlson (Eds.), *Love, intimacy, and the African American couple* (pp. 20–59). New York, NY: Routledge.

Bitette, N. (2016). Curse of the lottery: Tragic stories of big jackpot winners. Retrieved May 15, 2017 from www.nydailynews.com/life-style/tragic-stories-lottery-winners-article-1.2492941

Blumstein, & P., Schwartz, P. (1983). *American couples: Money, work, sex*. New York, NY: William Morrow & Co.

Boszormenyi-Nagy, I. (1965). A theory of relationships: Experiences and transactions. In I. Boszormenyi-Nagy & J. Framo (Eds.), *Intensive family therapy: Theoretical and practical aspects* (pp. 33–86). New York, NY: Harper & Row.

Botelho, B. (2012, May 15). Many addicts have more than one addiction. Retrieved from www.butlerfirststep.org/2012/05/many-addicts-have-more-than-one-addiction

Bowen, M. (1978). *Family therapy in clinical practice*. New York, NY: Aronson.

Bowen, M. (1980). Key to the use of the genogram. In E.A. Carter & M. McGoldrick (Eds.), *The family life cycle: A framework for family therapy* (p. XXIII). New York, NY: Gardner Press.

Brickman, P., Coates, D., & Janoff-Bulman, R. (1978). Lottery winners and accident victims: Is happiness relative? *Journal of Personality and Social Psychology, 36*, 917–927. doi:10.1037/0022-3514.36.8.917

Carnes, P. (2001). *Out of the shadows: Understanding sexual addiction*. Center City MN: Hazelden Publishing.

Carnes, P. (2015). *Facing the shadows: Starting sexual and relationship recovery*. Forest Lake, MN. Gentle Path Press.

Chan, M. (2016, May 15). Here's how winning the lottery makes you miserable. Retrieved from http://time.com/4176128/powerball-jackpot-lottery-winners/time.com

Chernin, J., & Johnson, M. (2003). *Affirmative psychotherapy and counseling for lesbians and gay men*. Thousand Oaks, CA: Sage Publications.

Connolly, C. (2012). *Lesbian couples and marriage counseling*. Alexandria, VA: American Counseling Association.

Cultural India (2017, June 5). Arranged marriage. Retrieved from www.culturalindia.net/weddings/arranged-marriage.html

DeMaria, R., Weeks, G., & Hof, L. (1999). *Focused genograms: Intergenerational assessment of individuals, couples, and families* (1st ed.). Philadelphia, PA: Brunner/Mazel.

DeMaria, R., Weeks, G., & Twist, M. (2017). *Focused genograms: Intergenerational assessment of individuals, couples, and families* (2nd ed.). New York, NY: Routledge.

Dixon, P. (2007). *African American relationships, marriages, and families*. New York, NY: Routledge.

Doherty, W., & Harris, S. (2017). *Helping couples on the brink of divorce*. Washington, DC: American Psychological Association.

Doll, J. (2012, May 15). A treasury of terribly sad stories of lotto winners. Retrieved from www.yahoo.com/news/terribly-sad-true-stories-lotto-winners-164423531.html

Dworkin, S. & Pope, M. (2012). (Eds.). *Casebook for counseling for lesbian, gay, bisexual, and transgender persons and their families*. Alexandria, VA: American Counseling Association.

Edelman, R. (2016, May 15). Why so many lottery winners go broke. Retrieved from http://fortune.com/2016/01/15/powerball-lottery-winners/

Fisher, H. (2004). *Why we love: The nature and chemistry of romantic love*. New York, NY: Henry Holt.

Foley, S., & Gambescia, N. (2015). The complex etiology of delayed ejaculation: Assessment and treatment implication. In K.M. Hertlein, G.R., Weeks, & N. Gambescia (Eds.), *Systemic sex therapy* (pp. 107–122). New York, NY: Routledge.

Freud, S. (1936/1964). New introductory lectures on psycho-analysis and other works. In J. Strachey (Ed. and Trans.), *The standard edition of the complete psychological works of Sigmund Freud* (Vol. 22, pp. 7–255). London, England: Hogarth Press and the Institute of Psychoanalysis.

Freud, A. (1936/1966). The ego and the mechanisms of defense. In C. Baines (Ed. and Trans.), *The writings of Anna Freud* (Vol. 2). New York, NY: International Universities Press.

Gordon, K., Khaddouma, A., Baucom, D., & Snyder, D. (2015). In A. Gurman (Ed.), Couple therapy and the treatment of affairs. *Clinical handbook of couple therapy* (5th ed., pp. 412–444).

Gotta, G., Green, R., Rothblum, E., Solomon, S., Balsam, K., & Schwartz, P. (2011). Heterosexual, lesbian, and gay male relationships: A comparison of couples in 1975 and 2000. *Family Process, 50*, 353–376.

Graham, C. (2014). Orgasm Disorders in Women. In Y.M. Binik & K.S. Hall (Eds.), *Principles and practice of sex therapy* (pp. 89–111). New York, NY: Guilford Press.

Green, R.-J., & Mitchell, V. (2008). Gay and lesbian couples in therapy: Minority stress, relationship ambiguity, and families of choice. In A.S. Gurman (Ed.), *Clinical handbook of couple therapy* (4th ed., pp. 662–680). New York, NY: Guilford Press.

Griffiths, M.D. (2009, November 11). The lottery of life after a jackpot win. *Western Mail*, p. 16.

Griffiths, M.D. (2010). The effect of winning large jackpots on human behavior. *Casino and Gambling International, 6*(4), 77–80.

Gurman, A. (2010). (Ed.). *Clinical handbook of couple therapy* (pp. 1–20). New York, NY: Guilford.

Harknett, K., & McLanahan, S. (2004). Racial and ethnic differences in marriage after the birth of a child. *American Sociological Review, 69*(6), 790–811.

Helm, K., & Carlson, J. (2013). (Eds.). *Love, intimacy, and the African American couple*. New York, NY: Routledge.

Hill, S.A. (2009). Why won't African Americans get (and stay) married? Why should they? In H.E. Peters and C.M. Camp Dush (Eds.), *Marriage and family: Perplexities and perspective* (pp. 345–364). New York, NY: Columbia University Press.

Ho, D.Y.F. (1995). Internalized culture, culturocentrism, and transcendence. *The Counseling Psychologist, 23*(1), 4–24.

Iasenza, S. (2000). Lesbian sexuality post-Stonewall to post-modernism: Putting the 'lesbian bed death' concept to bed. *Journal of Sex Education and Therapy, 25*(1), 59–69.

Iasenza, S. (2010). What is queer about sex?: Expanding sexual frames in theory and practice. *Family Process, 49*(3), 291–308.

Jannini, E., McMahon, C., & Waldinger, M. (2013). (Eds.). *Premature ejaculation: From etiology to diagnosis and treatment.* Milan, Italy: Springer-Verlag Italia.

Kaplan, H.S. (1974). *The new sex therapy: Active treatment of sexual dysfunctions.* New York, NY: Brunner/Mazel.

Kaplan, H.S. (1983). *The evaluation of sexual disorders: Psychological and medical aspects.* New York, NY: Brunner/Mazel.

Kaplan, H.S. (1989). *PE: How to overcome premature ejaculation.* New York, NY: Brunner/Mazel.

Kaplan, H.S. (1995). *The sexual desire disorders: Dysfunction regulation of sexual motivation.* New York, NY: Brunner/Mazel.

Kaplan, H.R. (1987). Lottery winners: The myth and reality. *Journal of Gambling, 3,* 168–178. doi:10.1007/BF01367438

Karis, T. (2009). We're just a couple of people: An exploration of why some black-white couples reject the terms cross-cultural and interracial. In T. Karis & K. Killian (Eds.), *Intercultural couples: Exploring diversity in intimate relationships* (pp. 89–110). New York, NY: Routledge.

Killian, K. (2013). *Interracial couples: Intimacy & therapy.* New York, NY: Columbia University Press.

Krause, S., Voon, V., & Potenza, M. (2016). Should compulsive sexual behavior be considered an addiction? *Addiction, 12,* 2097–2106. doi:10.1111/add.13297

LaSala, M. (2004). Monogamy of the heart: Extradyadic sex and gay male couples. *Journal of Gay and Lesbian Social Services, 17*(3), 1–24.

Lee, C. (2013). The cross-cultural encounter: Meeting the challenge of culturally competent counseling In C. Lee (Ed.), *Multicultural issues in counseling: New approaches to diversity* (4th ed.) (pp. 13–19). Alexandria, VA: American Counseling Association.

Lee, E. (2015). How to critically use globally discerned case studies in local contexts. In R. Moodley, M. Lengyell, R. Wu, & U. Gielen (Eds.), *International counseling: Case studies handbook* (pp. 3–11). Alexandria, VA: American Counseling Association.

Lee, E., & Bhuyan, R. (2013). Negotiating within whiteness in cross-cultural clinical encounter. *Social Service Review, 87,* 98–103. doi: 10.1084669919

Lee, E., & Horvath, A.O. (2013). Early cultural dialogues in cross-cultural clinical practice. *Smith College Studies in Social Work, 83,* 185–212. doi:10.1080/00377317.2013.802639

Lee, E., & Horvath, A.O. (2014). How a therapist responds to cultural versus non-cultural dialogues in cross-cultural clinical practice. *Journal of Social Work Practice, 28*, 193–217. doi: 10/1080/02650533.2013.821104

Lee, C., & Park, D. (2013). A conceptual framework for counseling across cultures. In C. Lee and D. Park (Eds.), *Multicultural issues in counseling: New approaches to diversity* (4th ed., pp. 3–12). Alexandria, VA: American Counseling Association.

Lev, A., & Nichols, M. (2015). Sex therapy with lesbian and gay male couples. In K. Hertlein, G. Weeks, & N. Gambescia (Eds.), *Systemic sex therapy* (2nd ed., pp. 213–234). New York, NY: Routledge.

Levine, S. (2010). Infidelity. In S. Levine, C. Risen, & S. Althof (Eds.), *Handbook of clinical sexuality for mental health professionals* (2nd ed., pp. 87–102). New York, NY: Routledge.

Levine, S. (2016). The mental health professional's treatment of erection problems. In S. Levine, C. Risen, & S. Althof (Eds.), *Handbook of clinical sexuality for mental health professionals* (3rd ed., pp. 123–133). New York, NY: Routledge.

McCabe, M. (2015). Female Orgasmic Disorder. In K.M. Hertlein, G.R. Weeks, & N. Gambescia (Eds.), *Systemic sex therapy* (pp. 171–186). New York, NY: Routledge.

McCarthy, B. (1999). Relapse strategies and techniques for inhibited sexual desire. *Journal of Sex & Marital Therapy, 25*, 297–303.

McGoldrick, M., Gerson, R., & Petry, S. (2008). *Genograms: Assessment and intervention* (3rd ed.), New York, NY: W.W. Norton.

Meana, M., Maykut, C., & Fertel, E. (2015). Painful intercourse: Genito-Pelvic pain/penetration disorder. In K.M. Hertlein, G.R. Weeks, & N. Gambescia (Eds.), *Systemic sex therapy* (pp. 191–215). New York, NY: Routledge.

Meana, M., & Steiner, E. (2014). Hidden Disorder/Hidden Desire: Presentations of Low Sexual Desire in Men. In Y. Binik & K. Hall (Eds.), *Principles and practice of sex therapy* (5th ed., pp. 42–60). New York, NY: The Guilford Press.

Merrill, D. (2016). *When your gay or lesbian child marries*. Lanham, MD: Rowman & Littlefield.

Moodley, R., Lengyell, M., Wu, R., & Gielen, U. (2015). (Eds.), *International counseling: Case studies handbook*. Alexandria, VA: American Counseling Association.

Nichols, M. (2011). Variations on gender and orientation in a first interview. In C. Silverstein (Ed.), *The initial psychotherapy interview: A gay man seeks treatment* (pp. 71–91). New York, NY: Elsevier.

Ollivier, D. (2009). *What French women know: About love, sex, and other matters of the heart*. New York, NY: Berkley.

Peplau, L., & Fingerhut, A. (2004). The paradox of the lesbian worker. *Journal of Social Issues, 60*(4), 719–735.

Perelman, M. (2014). Delayed ejaculation. In Y.M. Binik & K.S. Hall (Eds.), *Principles and practice of sex therapy* (pp. 138–155). New York, NY: Guilford Press.

Pew Research Center (2016, June 5). Changing attitudes on gay marriage: Public opinion on same-sex marriage. Retrieved from www.pewforum.org/fact-sheet/changingattitudes-ongay-marriage/

Pew Research Center (2017, June 5). The rise of Asian Americans. Retrieved from www.pewtrends.org/asianamericans-graphics_12-06-17_aa-higher-education-2

Pfeffer C. (2017). *Queering families: The postmodern partnerships of cisgender women and transgender men*. New York, NY: Oxford University Press.

Phelps, K.W., Jones, A.B., & Payne, R.A. (2015). The interplay between mental and sexual health. In K. Hertlein, G.R. Weeks, & N. Gambescia (Eds.), *Systemic sex therapy* (2nd ed., pp. 255–275). New York, NY: Routledge.

Prause, N., Steele, V., Sabatinelli, D., Hajcak, G. (2015). Modulation of late positive potentials by several images in problem users and controls inconsistent with "porn addiction." *Biological Psychology, 109,* 192–199. doi:10.1016/j.biopsycho.2015.06005

Provasi, L. (2012, June 8). Cultural connections: Exploring a world full of diverse cultures and People. Retrieved from http://lizprovasi.wordpress.com/2012/04/01/personal-space

Rabin, C. (2014). *Winnicott and 'good enough' couple therapy*. New York, NY: Routledge.

Rosen, R., Miner, M., & Wincze, J. (2014). Erectile dysfunction: Integration of medical and psychological approaches. In Y. Binik & K. Hall (Eds.), *Principles and practice of sex therapy* (5th ed., pp. 61–88). New York, NY: The Guilford Press.

Serretti, A., & Chiesa, A. (2009). Treatment-emergent sexual dysfunction related to antidepressants: A meta-analysis. *Journal of Clinical Pharmacology, 29,* 259–266. doi:10.1097/JCP.0b013e3181a5233f

Shelton-Wheeler, F. (2013). African American male-female romantic relationships. In K. Helm, & J. Carlson (Eds.), *Love, intimacy, and the African American couple* (pp. 63–84). New York, NY: Routledge.

Streib, J. (2015). *The power of the past: Understanding cross-class marriage*. Oxford, England: Oxford University Press.

Sue, D.W. & Sue, D. (2015). *Counseling the culturally diverse: Theory and practice* (7th ed.). Hoboken, NJ: John Wiley & Sons, Inc.

ter Kuile, M., & Reissing, E. (2014). Lifelong vaginismus. In Y. Binik & K. Hall (Eds.), *Principles and Practice of Sex Therapy* (5th ed., pp. 177–194). New York, NY: The Guilford Press.

Thomas, V., Karis, T., & Wetchler, J. (2014). *Clinical issues with interracial couples: Theories and research*. New York, NY: Routledge.

Toman, W. (1976). *Family constellation: Its effects on personality and social behavior*. New York, NY: Springer.

U.S. Census Bureau News (2014). *Income, poverty and health insurance coverage in the United States: 2014*. Retrieved from www.census.gov/newsroom/press-releases/2015/cb15-157.html

Wachtel, E. (2017). *The heart of couple therapy: Knowing what to do and how to do it*. New York, NY: Guilford.

Weeks, G., & Fife, S. (2014). *Couples in treatment: Techniques and approaches for effective Practice* (3rd ed.), New York, NY: Routledge.

Weeks, G., & Gambescia, N. (2015). Definition, etiology and treatment of absent/low desire in women. In K.M. Hertlein, G.R. Weeks, & N. Gambescia (Eds.), *Systemic sex therapy* (pp. 125–147). New York, NY: Routledge.

Whitman, J. (2012). Sex and lesbian women. In S. Dworkin and M. Pope (Eds.), *Casebook for counseling: Lesbian, gay, bisexual, and transgender persons and their families* (pp. 249–267). Alexandria, VA: American Counseling Association.

Wolfinger, N. (2017). Institute for family studies. *America's generation gap in extramarital sex*. Retrieved from www.ifstudies.org

Zong, J., & Batalova, J. (2016). *Frequently requested statistics on immigrants and immigration in the United States*. Retrieved from http://discuss.i/w.com/content.php?6229-Article-Frequently-Requested-Statistics-on-Immigrants-and-Immigration-in-the-United-States-By-Jie-Jong-andJeanne-Batalova

Chapter 5
Treatment

Following the assessment phase, the couples therapist should have a good indication of which master conflict is producing a couple's problems. There are times when a little education or a few exercises will alleviate a couple's sexual symptom; in some cases, medication will work. This is particularly true if certain aspects of the aging process, anxiety, or a lack of knowledge and skill are the culprits. But in most cases, the couples who choose to see us are referred by a physician: a urologist or a gynecologist. These couples were found to be free of a significant organic malady, and a significant emotional or relational issue was suspected to be behind their sexual issues. This is where MCT becomes a valuable part of the overall treatment plan.

The 5-Stage Treatment Process

The treatment phase consists of four objectives: (1) To help the couple to uncover their shared master conflict; (2) To help the couple to determine the origin of their master conflict; (3) To aid the couple to decide which side of the conflict to choose, or to integrate both sides of the conflict to a tolerable, balanced state; and (4) To alleviate the couple's sexual symptoms. To accomplish these objectives, a 5-stage process is offered. Two cases will illustrate the stages.

In the 5-stage process, the therapist is to ask a myriad of questions that are meant to weaken the couple's defenses and to set them up for an intervention that will help to expose their contradictions and their shared conflict. A prominent attorney once commented that the model reminded her of trial work: "It's like the litigation process: gathering as much evidence as possible to build a successful case against the opposition," she said. To us, the treatment resembles a game of chess between the therapist and the couple's defenses. The therapist utilizes each partner's past experiences and present interactions to corner the couple into acknowledging their conflict and the way they have unconsciously employed it to service their sexual symptom. In this sense, MCT has a more confronting style than other models, such as Emotionally Focused Therapy (EFT) (Greenberg & Johnson, 2010).

It can also be said that MCT treats each partner individually in the context of couples work.

The first case example presented in the 5-stage process is that of Mark and Marcy, a married couple in their early 40s suffering from an unbalanced *specialness vs. ordinariness (less than ordinary)* master conflict. Mark, an accountant, has low sexual desire, and has avoided having sex with Marcy, a model, for approximately two years. Although the stages are listed as 1 through 5, the therapist can move from one to another in any order throughout treatment. In this sense, the therapist follows the flow of the treatment process.

Stage 1: Exposing Contradictions and Conflict on the Interactional Level

The therapist can immediately begin the process of exposing a couple's master conflict by noticing and challenging any verbal or behavioral contradictions in their interactional dynamic. This will not be too difficult if the therapist is "thinking conflict." The contradiction should be between what the partners say they want and what they are blocking themselves from achieving.

Therapist: Marcy, how was your vacation?
Marcy: Well, Italy was great, but we still didn't have sex. If Mark couldn't do it in Venice, he'll never be able to do it in New Jersey.
Mark: I tried to have sex. I was beginning to feel in the mood for the first time in a couple of years, so I took a pill. I got a surprisingly good erection. But when I tried to have sex with Marcy, she screamed at me. (Sarcastic) That really helped my erection.
Marcy: (Angry) Mark came out of the bathroom with a big erection, and I just knew he took some medication.
Therapist: That's interesting, Marcy. You've been desperately pursuing Mark to attend therapy with you for a couple of years because of his low libido, yet now that he feels some desire, you reject him. Do you know that it usually takes some desire for an ED medication to work?
Marcy: I heard that somewhere. But I want Mark to want me for me.
Therapist: So, I guess you didn't believe what I just told you about ED medications. By the way, Mark, why didn't you discuss taking the medication with Marcy ahead of time? It seems to me that after two years of sexual difficulty, she would be suspicious of your newfound functioning.
Mark: You heard her. It wouldn't have mattered.
Marcy: It would have helped. It would have shown that you cared about me rather than just trying to screw me to get me off your back.

Stage 2: Examining the Origin of the Conflict on a Psychodynamic Level

In this stage, the therapist's objective is to help each partner connect the conflict they are exhibiting in real time to that which they have experienced in their respective families of origin. For support, the therapist can use each partner's prior relationship experiences to illustrate the power of the conflict. When each partner can see that the process has been with them most of their lives and in prior relationships, it helps to reduce *self* and *other* blame. It gives the couple the message that while neither were the cause on one another's problems, they do exacerbate them and must be held responsible for doing so.

Therapist: Marcy, I do think that if Mark discussed taking medication, it would have helped, but I do not think it would have been completely satisfactory. In fact, I'm not so sure you want Mark to want you. I know that men are physically attracted to you, but judging from your history, they never seem to give you everything that you want. They always seem to fall short in some way. I believe that your first husband disappointed you, didn't he?
Marcy: My first husband worshipped me.
Therapist: And what happened to the marriage?
Marcy: I left him because he was "too nice." I became bored with him. Too bad; he was a sweetheart.
Therapist: Well, that's what I mean. Apparently, he failed you because he worshipped you. Even *he* let you down in some way.
Marcy: That's weird.
Therapist: It's not that unusual. I suspect you're in conflict about being wanted. Your father treated you special, didn't he?
Marcy: I was daddy's little girl.
Mark: (Sarcastic) She still is.
Therapist: How did mom feel about that?
Marcy: She hated it. I used to feel sorry for her. But hey, who wouldn't want their daddy to love them? Sometimes, I got angry at her for acting like such a baby.
Therapist: So, in exchange for special treatment from your father, you suffered alienation from your mother.
Marcy: We still don't get along.
Mark: (Sarcastic) Your dad still treats you like a princess.
Marcy: (Angry and Sarcastic) Shut up. You're not the doctor.
Therapist: Mark, you say you want Marcy to ease up on you, but you continue to take pot-shots at her. Is this some new way of pleasing a woman I don't know about?

Mark: (Chuckles).
Marcy: This is the way he and his father treat his mother—it's disgusting.
Therapist: We'll get to that in a minute. Marcy, all I'm suggesting is that your specialness is not without conflict. And, maybe it was a conflict about being special that reflected what happened in Venice.

Stage 3: Examining the Options on a Behavioral Level

This stage merits a concrete discussion aimed at helping the couple to decide whether they wish to remain in their current state or to do the work it will take to tackle their master conflict. As will be discussed later, some couples cannot or will not do the work to change. The MCT practitioner empathizes with this dilemma but clearly points out the pros and cons of the couple's decision.

Therapist: Mark, it seems as if you have shut down after your experience in Venice. What's going on?
Mark: What's the use? You know how Marcy reacted. I'm damned if I do and damned if I don't.
Therapist: Are you planning to divorce?
Mark: No, I don't want a divorce.
Therapist: So, are you planning to live without sex indefinitely?
Mark: I don't know. I don't want to.
Marcy: I don't want to live like this. If my sex life is like this now in my 40s, it will be even worse in my 60s.
Mark: (Sarcastic) That's the good news. It can't get much worse.
Marcy: This isn't funny.
Therapist: Well, folks, let's examine your options. What do you see them as?
Marcy: If Mark won't change, divorce is one option.
Mark: I wouldn't be here if I didn't want to fix this.
Therapist: Plenty of people come here but don't put the work in to change. Others simply can't change.
Marcy: Staying the same might be an option, but not one that I'll accept.
Therapist: Well, another option is that you both do the work to change your situation.

Stage 4: Examining the Options on a Psychodynamic Level

This stage evokes the most emotional reaction of all stages because it encourages each partner to examine what they will need to give up to successfully control their master conflict. Most often, it is something deep and meaningful, or the couple would not fight so ferociously to hold onto it. If a couple achieve insight, it will be in this stage, but there will be a price. And the battle to regain control of the master conflict will take time.

Marcy: (Proud of herself) I've been nice to Mark this past week.
Mark: (Smiling) She has.
Therapist: Was it easy or hard?
Marcy: Very hard. I'm afraid he will distance even further if I let him off the hook. I think he wants marriage without having to do anything in return. He learned this growing up. His mother is a "sweetie pie," but all the males in her family treat her like a slave.
Mark: (Nervous laugh).
Therapist: Is that true, Mark?
Mark: Kind of.
Therapist: What do you think about that?
Mark: It's been going on for so long.
Therapist: Maybe it's too good to give up. After all, you have your own personal slave.
Mark: That sounds horrible.
Marcy: (Tearful) That's the way you treat me.
Therapist: Think about it. If you begin to treat the women in your life better, you will lose your slaves. If you keep them, however, you'll have to live with enabling them.
Marcy: What about me? I can't get my mother to treat me better.
Therapist: You may or may not be able to do something about that depending on what you're willing to try. Attempting to limit the specialness from your father to get more from your mother might be risky. You probably have more control over balancing things out with Mark.

Stage 5: Moving Toward the Resolution of the Underlying Conflict and Increased Differentiation

This is another potentially emotional stage. If treatment is working, it is in this stage that the couple are better able to see the influences of their families of origin on their conflict and on their current relationship. It is here that the process of differentiation is most prominent, and the couple are seriously challenged to reach for and maintain a certain autonomy from their internalized conflict. In this stage, the therapist expects to see symptom relief.

Mark: When I'm around my parents now, I get upset more easily.
Therapist: What do you see?
Mark: Like Marcy said, my dad really takes advantage of my mom. If he wants a drink, he bugs her to get it for him. The telephone

rang, and he was closer to it, but he growled at her to pick it up. It's worse than I ever thought. He never has anything good to say to or about her. And she's so passive.

Therapist: I imagine on some level your mother has her own agenda.
Mark: It's sick.
Therapist: Well, you didn't come here to fix your family of origin. But, maybe you can avoid replicating the process in your marriage.
Mark: (Sadly) Yeah.
Therapist: Of course, Marcy will have to cooperate.

Mark decided to exchange the "princely" position he held as a male in his family of origin (specialness). He chose to do the work required to please his wife sexually and to gain her respect (ordinariness). Marcy gave up the coveted position of "princess" bestowed upon her by her father (specialness). She learned to accept her less than perfect mother and husband (ordinariness). Only then was she able to allow her needs to be met.

Exercises

We've been asked many times where in our model we make room for sex therapy exercises. While some who integrate couples and sex therapy do not seem to place a high value on exercises (Schnarch, 2009), others consider them to be one of the hallmarks of their treatment (McCarthy & McCarthy, 2013). In MCT, we apply exercises judiciously. We generally find that understanding one's conflict and learning to manage it will alleviate sexual symptoms, but we are certainly not beyond using exercises in conjunction with treatment. Sensate Focus I and II (Masters & Johnson, 1966) continue to prove useful in treating anxiety and performance demand by encouraging couples to stay in the present (Weiner & Avery-Clark, 2014). Stop-start exercises (Kaplan, 1989; Semans, 1956) are still used by many to treat PE in couples work (Betchen, 2015), and the use of dilators for GPPPD, or what was once referred to as vaginismus (Masters & Johnson, 1970), remains an important means of intervention (Meana, Maykut, & Fertel, 2015).

Exercises are featured more prominently in *Stage 3. Examining the options on a behavioral level*. But they may be assigned throughout the five stages of treatment and as early as the end of the first session. This will depend on the therapist's determination of the following: (1) the couple's presenting problem. For example, we do not assign exercises for couples with low desire. We prefer to rely most often on the uncovering of the couple's master conflict that we feel is responsible. But we almost always prescribe dilator use in conjunction with insight therapy for GPPPD; (2) the pressure the therapist is under to prescribe exercises. The therapist may be under fire at times to assign exercises even when the assessment reveals that the relationship dynamics and underlying master conflict will render the exercises useless. To avoid prematurely losing the couple, Kaplan (personal communication, October 7, 1987) recommended assigning Sensate Focus exercises. She believed that most exercise failure could increase hopelessness and anxiety. But the relatively benign Sensate Focus exercises would do little harm if a couple were unable to use them effectively. We warn a couple when we think that exercises are inappropriate or if the timing will render them unsuccessful, but if they proceed and fail, we have found that they often will then turn themselves over to a deeper treatment; (3) the couple's ability to tolerate exercises. Some couples have refused exercises. While some claimed a fear of failure, many found this type of treatment "mechanical." Some partners could not agree on whether to engage in exercises. Oftentimes this dynamic reflected an ongoing control struggle in the couple's general relational process that needed to be addressed before exercises were to be assigned; and (4) the volatility of the couple's process. If a couple are consistently at odds, we try and de-escalate their process before assigning any exercises. Under these conditions, we find that exercises will only be used by the couple to further their complaints against one another. It is not unusual for one or both partners to sabotage exercises by avoiding participation, failing to initiate exercises when previously agreed, or by changing the assignment to their liking. To us, this represents resistance generated by the power and intensity of a couple's underlying master conflict.

Detailed ways in which we incorporate sex therapy exercises into the MCT model are offered in subsequent chapters. But the following brief example of Bonnie and Peter specifically demonstrates how we utilize them in our 5-stage approach. Bonnie presented with what she referred to as vaginismus (now GPPPD). She was investigating her symptoms online and decided that this was her issue. Bonnie was an unhappy 35-year-old virgin in an unconsummated marriage. Her husband, Peter, 39, claimed that he longed for sex and wanted children. He was threatening to file for divorce if Bonnie could not fulfill his wishes. The couple were married for five years and dated for three. They did have other forms of sex, including oral and manual, but Bonnie was not able to experience penetration via a penis. She was, however, able to insert tampons and could complete a gynecological exam. Follow this couple's *giving vs. withholding* conflict:

Stage 1: Exposing Contradictions and Conflict on the Interactional Level

When one or both partners claim to want otherwise, but demonstrate an unusually high degree of tolerance for pain or deprivation—in this case, absence of intercourse—the MCT practitioner starts with the assumption that there is a part of each partner that is unconsciously rejecting a change that would help to achieve their stated objectives. This can confuse the therapist who chooses to take clients at face value rather than considering that they might be in conflict.

Bonnie: We had a big fight on the way over here. Peter doesn't want counseling.

Therapist: That's interesting, Peter. You've been complaining about the lack of intercourse for many years. You're even threatening divorce. Now that you're finally about to do something about it, you're against it. You're threatening to withhold the pleasure of sex and the possibility of having children. I thought you wanted sex ... and children.

Peter: We can handle it ourselves.

Therapist: But you haven't been able to so far. Again, a man who is threatening divorce doesn't sound as if he has a lot of time left to kill.

Peter: It's not just me. Bonnie wouldn't be here if I wasn't threatening to leave.

Therapist: Is that true, Bonnie?

Bonnie: Yes, I admit that I've procrastinated. My OB-GYN has cleared me of any medical issues and recommended sex therapy several times. I don't know why I haven't followed up, but I really want to have sex. I've been trying my whole life and I haven't been able to do it.

Therapist: You both say you want sex, but you've done so little to achieve it. Bonnie, you've avoided treatment to this point. And Peter, now that you both are here, you're about to sabotage the process. It seems to me that you both are in conflict giving or withholding sex and children.

Bonnie: Well, I want to stay in treatment. I'm sick of being a virgin and I don't want a divorce.

Stage 2: Examining the Origin of the Conflict on a Psychodynamic Level

It turns out that Peter had a good reason to avoid getting what he claimed to desperately want from Bonnie. Unfortunately, the reason was buried deep in his unconscious, and he wasn't very interested in making any connections at that level. Peter was not a fan of marital therapy and he made it clear he didn't believe there was any relationship between his family of origin, his unbalanced internalized master conflict, and his wife's GPPPD. Notice how the therapist uses other contexts, such as employment, to broaden the process. Again, this technique serves to reduce self and other blame and to show the pervasiveness of a master conflict.

Therapist: Peter, you've been waiting a long time for intercourse with Bonnie. Is there anything else in your life that you've had to

	wait for? Is there anything else that you feel someone has withheld from you?
Peter:	What are you talking about?
Therapist:	Have you waited for a job or a promotion at work, or for a girlfriend to take a liking to you when you were in high school or college?
Peter:	No, not really.
Bonnie:	Come on, Peter, you've been waiting for a promotion for years. His company always passes him over. He works hard and always does his job. I feel sorry for him.
Peter:	What does this have to do with Bonnie's sexual problems?
Therapist:	I don't know yet. But didn't you tell me that your mother never paid attention to you as a kid? Didn't you also say that she has never wished you a Happy Birthday? And doesn't she still ignore you?
Bonnie:	Peter is the good son. He's a giver. No matter how neglectful his mother is—and she is awful—he keeps trying to change her.
Therapist:	Didn't your father leave her?
Bonnie:	And his older brother and sister don't even talk to her. Everybody's given up on her but Peter.
Peter:	Okay, she's difficult. But we came here for sexual issues and we're spending valuable time talking about my mother.
Therapist:	Well, there may be a link between your failure to persuade your mother to give you the love and approval you've longed for, your inability to get a promotion at work, and your unsatisfactory sex life.
Peter:	I don't think any of them are related.
Bonnie:	I do.
Peter:	What about Bonnie? Why is she holding back sex?
Therapist:	Any ideas, Bonnie?
Bonnie:	I've been thinking about this. My parents gave all their love to my brother and sister. Maybe I'm not so different than Peter in that way. Maybe I'm testing Peter to see if he'll love me unconditionally.
Therapist:	That makes sense. You might also like someone pursuing you, but at the same time dislike the pressure of the pursuit. You claimed that you were always under pressure to look after your younger siblings, and one is autistic.

Stage 3. Examining the Options on a Behavioral Level

Peter settled into treatment but still wasn't buying the psychodynamic influences at work. Bonnie was less anxious and had read about dilator treatment. Her OB-GYN was more than happy to approve the treatment process and helped Bonnie to obtain a set of dilators.

Therapist: Well, are you both ready to give yourselves behavioral exercises?
Bonnie: I'm nervous but I've read about them and I'm ready to give them a try.
Peter: Is there any other option?
Therapist: Well, Bonnie could try medication to reduce her anxiety, but she doesn't want to go that route. And it is probable that a combination of the psychotherapy and dilator treatment will get you both where you say you want to go faster. How would you like to start, Bonnie?
Bonnie: I'd prefer if Peter helped me. Is it okay if he inserted the dilators?
Peter: Really?
Therapist: Is there a problem? You've inserted your finger for other reasons without a problem.
Peter: I guess not. Do I have to use a lubricant?
Bonnie: I have some.
Therapist: Okay, start with the smallest. Lubricate the dilator, insert gently, and twist as you insert. Bonnie, you may want to breathe in when Peter is inserting and out when he's done. Don't move onto the next one until we talk again.

Stage 4: Examining the Options on a Psychodynamic Level

Bonnie seemed to gain a significant amount of insight during the treatment process. She also demonstrated a healthy desire to alleviate her GPPPD with or without Peter. Peter struggled with treatment. He was especially skeptical of the psychodynamic interventions, but Bonnie's perseverance and tenacity challenged him to hang in there. Despite withholding sex, Bonnie had an empathic, parenting style that she often used to give Peter a boost when he needed it.

Bonnie: I was doing great, and now that I'm ready for the fourth dilator, Peter is threatening to stop therapy and divorce. He won't help me with the last dilator. I don't get it. We're so close.
Peter: This is taking too long.
Therapist: I agree. I believe that you both have waited long enough. But I fear you might want to wait even longer.
Peter: What does that mean?
Bonnie: He means if you quit now it won't happen for us.
Therapist: You can stop, that is an option. But if you truly want to finally give yourselves what you say you want, you will have to sacrifice.
Peter: I've sacrificed.
Therapist: I mean that you will have to stop trying to get something that may be impossible to get and take what you can and do deserve. It means you will have to rethink your dynamic with your mother. You may even have to consider a different company to work for.

Bonnie: I'm ready to give up being pursued. My parents worried more about my brother and sister, and it's too late to change that.
Peter: (Suddenly tearful). Am I asking for too much?
Bonnie: (Surprised and sad). No, you're not. You should have given up on your mom years ago. Maybe you should have given up on me. But we're close now. We must finish, or we'll never even have kids.

Stage 5: Moving Toward the Resolution of the Underlying Conflict and Increased Differentiation

Bonnie continued to do well and got through the fourth dilator without Peter. She grew stronger as Peter began to see intercourse as a not-too-distant reality. Challenged by his wife and the therapist, Peter re-engaged in treatment, and the couple achieved intercourse.

Bonnie: (Smiling). I am officially no longer a virgin.
Therapist: Great! How did it feel? Did you experience any pain?
Bonnie: I was a little tight at first, but no pain. We used a lubricant. I even used the fourth dilator first to prime me for intercourse.
Therapist: Sound wisdom. How about you, Peter?
Peter: (Smiling). It was good. It felt a little weird after all these years, and I had to hold back from feeling angry with Bonnie for her withholding. But on the other hand, if it weren't for her pushing us both, we wouldn't be having sex now.
Bonnie: I see the connection between my family and my sexual issues. I'm not sure Peter still buys into it all.
Peter: Well, whatever happened worked. I at least get the fact that I've overworked for very little, and I need to keep looking at that.

The therapist held a "booster" session (Wachtel, 2017, p. 240) approximately six months following termination. At that time, Bonnie and Peter reported that they were averaging satisfactory intercourse twice per week. Bonnie reported continued minor tightness courtesy of her vaginal muscles. But she rejected an offer to send her for an evaluation for medication, which the therapist thought would relax her and help to increase her pleasure. In sum, the couple's *giving vs. withholding* conflict appeared to be under control, as was their associated GPPPD symptom.

Neutrality, Balance, and Boundaries

Weeks and Fife (2014) referred to balance as a "central systemic concept" (p. 67). The art of balancing is the key to successful couples therapy. As demonstrated in *Chapter 4. Assessment*, the therapist begins to balance the couple at first contact and continues to do so throughout the 5-stage treatment process. To accomplish this, the therapist must maintain a neutral stance.

It is not unusual for the therapist to favor one partner over the other (Wachtel, 2017). Time and again, we have heard colleagues and students say something like: "He's a real jerk. What is she doing with him?" While this reaction may be unavoidable at times, prejudice should be controlled in the treatment setting. It is dangerous for all parties involved for the couples therapist to take sides. This can not only destroy the opportunity for a relationship to survive but end in one or both partners accusing the therapist of ruining their relationship. If the therapist finds that a "pattern" of prejudice exists, such as chronically siding with the opposite-sex partner, or holding a negative attitude towards gay couples, we believe supervision, a referral, or personal therapy for the therapist may be warranted (Weeks & Fife, 2014).

In MCT, we guard against imbalance by pointing out that people choose one another for a good reason—they share a master conflict that is anchored in their families of origin and protecting them from making some potentially painful changes. And while their styles or roles in their relationship may differ, on a deeper level, they are very similar. If the therapist loses balance and leans towards one partner over the other, he or she is losing sight of the couple as a system and practicing from a linear perspective. We find that while the therapist may be turned off by a partner, it may indicate that the partner is doing an excellent job helping the couple to maintain their master conflict. This, in turn, means that both partners are getting their needs met. The therapist may not approve of the way one partner is going about achieving this objective, but chances are great that the couple are colluding in its continuance. One balancing technique that we have found useful is for the therapist to visualize what it would be like to be married to or live with each partner. We picture this, regardless of racial or gender differences. This exercise helps us to better understand what each partner must tolerate.

Throughout the course of treatment (i.e., through all five stages), the therapist is to continue to balance the therapeutic process by challenging each partner, challenging them relatively equally, and treating each with the same level of importance and respect in the therapeutic process. On occasion, one partner will accuse the therapist of being unfair or prejudiced. Others may make comments such as, "You two (meaning the therapist and other partner) aren't listening to me." The couple's therapist should examine these accusations and make a correction if they ring true. However, some clients use accusations and sensitivity to block the therapist from giving them equal responsibility for their contribution to the relationship problems. The therapist should consider a gentler approach and confirm a commitment to neutrality but not back away from intervening when appropriate. We recommend attempting to connect the alleged victimized partner's sensitivity to his or her family of origin and the way in which it is being used to maintain the couple's master conflict.

Not all balancing is expressed verbally. The therapist, for example, can utilize empathic facial expressions and body language judiciously. But these can be destructive to the balancing process as well. For example, if the therapist laughs or snickers at something hurtful that one partner said to the other, the neutrality is lost and could do irreparable damage to the treatment process. As a balancing technique, we recommend that the therapist maintain direct eye contact with whichever partner is speaking and intermittently glance at the non-speaking partner. This will take quite a bit of eye shifting, but it serves to pull the couple together and give them the message that both partners are—at all times—considered vital to a successful therapeutic process.

On occasion, one or both partners will attempt to blur therapeutic boundaries. If the therapist fears hurting a partner's (or the couple's) feelings or losing the case, he or she may be exchanging a relatively minor problem for a potential future catastrophe. We recommend that the therapist warn the couple from the outset that couples therapy is hard and that MCT is a confrontive model, and some sacrifice will be required for change to occur. Consider the following example: A troubled post-graduate student mentioned in supervision that the anxious wife of a couple she was treating routinely contacted her via email between sessions. The woman unabashedly used this extra time with the student to complain about her husband's behavior. The student believed that the woman was hoping the therapist would join with her against her husband and allow her more control in the therapeutic process. The student was directed to re-set the therapeutic boundaries and re-balance the couple. To do so, she was to explain to the wife that contact between sessions might make her husband feel ganged up on and lead to premature termination. To be fair, and to preserve the therapeutic process, contact of this nature was limited to emergencies only. While the student eventually did her job, she admitted that it was challenging. The wife in this case was holding the couple in therapy, and the student feared that if she set limits, she would lose the case entirely. It was explained to the student that if she failed to re-gain control of her case, the therapy might last a bit longer, but the diffuse boundaries would incentivize the wife to continue blaming the husband for the all the relationship difficulties and de-incentivize her to change. The relationship might then destruct, and the student's reputation as a couples therapist might suffer.

In the MCT approach, each partner will, separately and together as a couple, attempt to use the therapist to help maintain the imbalance of their master conflict—this motivation is wholly unconscious. It is the job of the therapist to recognize this objective and to avoid colluding in it. The couple and therapist do not need to share the same conflict to provoke this process, but if the conflicts happen to be the same, the opportunity is greater for the collusion to occur—a logical conclusion given that the therapist and couple must have experienced the same type of master conflict in their respective families of origin. Under these conditions, a positive transference may be more likely, in part because the therapist will be better able to join with and engage the couple. The couple will experience a natural attraction, just as there is between the two partners; they will most likely feel as if the therapist "understands them" or can relate to them. The therapist may or may not necessarily reveal anything personal for this connection to occur. But he or she may unconsciously use a certain word like "unfair" several times, which might indicate that the therapist may share a *justice vs. injustice* conflict with the couple.

The way in which the therapist expresses empathy might also help to reveal a master conflict. For example, if the therapist responds to a couple's feelings of inadequacy by admitting similar feelings, the couple might sense that the therapist shares an *adequacy vs. inadequacy* conflict. I am not suggesting that the couple will be able to identify or label their own or the therapist's master conflict without the therapist's help, but they will sense that all parties have something important in common.

While sharing the same conflict as a couple might help promote a positive transference, it is no guarantee of therapeutic success. Solomon (1997) contended: "The therapist's reception of one or both partners' unwanted affectivity can become the basis for pathological collusion" (p. 27). If the therapist is aware of his or her master conflict, it will be easier to maintain balance and an appropriate level of differentiation to help the couple. If not, the therapist may enable the couple's problems. For example, if a couple have a *success vs. sabotage (big vs. small)* master conflict, they might allow the therapist to experience a certain amount of success in treatment but will ensure a modicum of failure as well. If their conflict is unbalanced towards failure or sabotage, so too might the treatment. This could prove frustrating to the therapist. Pointing out the connection between the couple's conflict and its impact on the therapist and the therapeutic process will help to reduce resistance and balance a couple's conflict. Here's an example of a couple in their early 40s, Alex and Jason, who have an unbalanced *adequacy vs. inadequacy* master conflict. The chief complaint was the wife's low sex drive.

Jason: I don't think I'm asking for much. I'd like to have sex at least twice a week. Is that so bad?
Therapist: How often are you having it now?
Jason: About twice a month. But I always initiate it, and Alex doesn't seem happy when I do. Everything is on her terms.
Therapist: So, Alex is in control of your sex life?
Jason: I didn't say that. It's just on her terms.
Therapist: You don't see "control" and "on her terms" as the same?
Jason: Not really.

Therapist:	Okay, what's the difference?
Jason:	I don't know.
Therapist:	I don't think there is a difference. But I do think you've just tried to do the same thing to me that you do to Alex.
Jason:	What?
Therapist:	Do you know what I'm talking about?
Jason:	No.
Therapist:	Well, I offered you an intervention, and you dismissed it. Perhaps this was your way to unconsciously render me inadequate. When Alex does have sex with you, my understanding is that you fail to offer any positive reinforcement. In fact, as soon as you have finished, you cajole her to have it again that same day or the early morning after. Can you comment on this, Alex?
Alex:	Not really.
Therapist:	What do you think about what I just said to Jason?
Alex:	I think I'll never satisfy him. That's why I barely try anymore.
Therapist:	Alex, do you think you would have sex more often if Jason complimented you more?
Jason:	I tell her she's beautiful all the time, but I get no response.
Alex:	I'm not good at taking compliments. And I don't see myself as beautiful.
Therapist:	So, you dismiss Jason's compliments. Perhaps this is your way to render him impotent. I also notice that you rarely react to any of my interventions. I had to pull a reaction out of you a minute ago even though it turned out that you agreed with me.
Alex:	Sometimes I have nothing to say.
Therapist:	But this time you did have something to say. You rarely react unless pushed. It's hard to tell whether you think what I say is resonating with you.
Alex:	I'm just shy.
Therapist:	Maybe, or you might be trying to make me inadequate, unconsciously, of course.
Jason:	Why would we want to make each other inadequate? That doesn't make any sense. That won't help us.
Therapist:	Both of you had very intrusive, controlling parents that neither of you could control. Even today, you both seem powerless to set limits with them. Maybe this is where your shared conflict originates from, and you both are unconsciously transferring a wish for them to be less powerful onto me and the therapeutic process.

If all parties share the same conflict, the therapist may experience a positive transference and truly like the couple. He or she may develop a sincere appreciation and respect for them; they do, after all, share the same or similar struggles. But the therapist must be careful to avoid turning the positive into a potentially harmful experience. This may occur if the therapist's master conflict is unbalanced. This can be reflective of the therapist: (1) unbalancing the couple—this can take the form of the therapist siding with one partner who the therapist views as more in line with his or her fantasies. For example, if the therapist longed to be rescued from the wrath of a controlling, dominant parent by his or her passive parent, the therapist may side with the stronger of the two partners in treatment; (2) overworking rather than encouraging the couple to do the work—to please the couple, the therapist may take on the bulk of the clinical work, thereby increasing their dependence on the therapist; (3) failing to set limits—allowing the couple to act out or get away with inappropriate behaviors such as building too large an account or routinely coming late to sessions and expecting the therapist to make up the time; (4) neglecting to maintain boundaries—allowing the couple to get too close in inappropriate ways, such as developing a friendship or dual relationship; and (5) failing to confront the couple when appropriate—out of fear of upsetting the couple or a need to join with them, the therapist aims to remain in the couple's favor by failing to challenge them. The therapist remains passive, and the couple fail to grow.

If the therapist experiences anxiety related to the need to help the couple, the therapist's master conflict is most likely out of control. Eventually, the failure to help the couple may produce in the therapist a wide array of feelings, such as guilt, shame, sadness, and a sense of helplessness or hopelessness—the therapist may even come to view his or her conflict as impossible to manage. The therapist may also blame the couple for their treatment failure and in turn experience anger and frustration.

While they may not be as exaggerated, many of these signs also apply when the therapist and couple have different master conflicts. Consider the following example of Craig and Denise. A married couple in their mid-40s, Craig and Denise hadn't had sex in two years primarily because Craig claimed that he had no desire to sleep with his wife. A successful attorney, Denise seemed to be particularly insecure about her looks. Growing up, her mother proved jealous of her intellect and chose to pick on her looks as a way of reducing her. Craig was a strikingly handsome man, but he struggled to keep his clothing store solvent. He said that his father, a terrible businessman, was his role model. Denise admitted that she thought Craig's business acumen was less than adequate. The couple was struggling with an *adequacy vs. inadequacy* conflict. Denise was more than adequate in her career but suffered from insecurity. By all standards, Craig was a very handsome man but suffered in business. The therapist's master conflict was that of *justice vs. injustice*. The therapist believed that Craig was evading personal responsibility and unjustly blaming the therapist for his marital issues. But because the therapist's master conflict was under control, the therapist remained calm and stayed the course in treatment.

Craig: (To the therapist). You're making my wife angry at me. Look at her.
Therapist: My understanding is that your wife is upset with you for not having had sex with her for several years. If I said something to make things worse, I'm sorry, but that wasn't my intention. I'm under the impression that you are angry with her as well.
Craig: I'm not angry with her.
Therapist: You seemed angry when you were complaining about her spending habits. I simply offered that there might be a link between your anger and your lack of sexual interest in her.
Craig: Well, I don't think there is a connection between the two.
Denise: I don't think there's a connection either. I think he's gay.
Craig: That's crazy.

The therapist was sure the hypothesis he offered Craig was on target, but he remained in control. However, when he began to search for the underlying cause of Denise's prodigious spending habits, she immediately terminated the therapy. Craig did not fight to save the treatment. Although he was not the dominant personality in the couple, the therapist believed that he enabled the premature termination of treatment so that he, too, could hold onto his inadequacies.

Siegel (1997) contended that the couples therapist must be able to deal with a wide array of issues, including how each partner expresses anger and sexuality. We agree that it would be difficult for a therapist who has not come to terms with his or her own discomfort concerning these subjects—especially those related to sexuality—to effectively treat couples with sexual symptoms. Because MCT has been developed to treat couples with sexual issues, it is especially important for the practitioner of this approach to maintain appropriate boundaries. As Meana (2010) pointed out, there is a tendency for the couple to idealize the couples therapist. She added that when couples present with a sexual problem, any idealization of the therapist may be eroticized. Because it is more likely that only one partner participates in this fantasy, there exists a danger that the therapist may abandon the neutral stance and lose balance. This may in turn stir up feelings in the other partner such as anger, jealousy, sadness, and feelings of inadequacy, to name a few. Even worse, the therapist may experience an erotic countertransference (Rosiello, 2000) and become overly involved emotionally and or physically with the partner. The therapist must be in touch with his or her own sexual feelings and refrain from buying into the partner's fantasy that "he or she is the one." It is normal to find someone attractive in the therapeutic setting. And if therapist and partner share the same master conflict, this attraction will no doubt be a strong one, in part because common master conflicts attract.

If the therapist's master conflict is unbalanced, he or she will be more likely to collude in unbalancing the couple's master conflict. The mutual attraction does not indicate that the therapist and partner are a good match. More than likely, both are unconsciously fighting to maintain the imbalance of their respective master conflicts—nothing more. A therapist with a *success vs. sabotage (big vs. small)* conflict might be aiming to sabotage his or her career. A partner with a *justice vs. injustice* conflict may be setting up an injustice that he or she can one day protest. A supervisee once admitted that she had fallen in love and was on the verge of having an affair with the husband of a couple she was treating. The couple had presented for treatment because of the husband's inability to commit to his marriage, as evidenced in part by his serial infidelities. Not ironic to MCT, both supervisee and client had unbalanced *commitment vs. freedom* master conflicts. The possibilities are truly endless in the sexual context, but rarely are they healthy.

Broadening the Process

Earlier, we distinguished content from process. A couple's sexual symptom is considered content; the dynamic that depicts their master conflict is the process. In this section, we discuss perhaps our most effective therapeutic technique: "broadening the process" (Betchen, 2005). We did demonstrate this technique briefly in our 5-stage process but we will now address it at some length. Broadening the process is utilized to better show each partner that their dynamic is not new to their current relationship; that, in fact, they have most likely used it before in prior relationships or situations. Two ways to broaden a couple's process appear to us to be most effective: (1) Use information about each partner's prior experiences in a similar context and link it to real time; in this case, sexual issues in prior relationships; and (2) Broaden the process even further by showing each partner how they have utilized the same process in "other" contexts or content areas of a nonsexual nature, such as at work or with friends. If the therapist can employ both, so much the better.

Couples tend to present with one or two symptoms and want the attention focused on these problem areas as if the symptoms have no roots or as if they exist in a vacuum. This is particularly common when the chief complaint carries the responsibility of a couple's sex life. The therapist can broaden the couple's process containing the same content but with others from each partner's pasts. If during the assessment phase the therapist can determine that each partner has replicated their process with the same content in relationships prior to their current relationship, he or she can use this information to join the couple, reduce mutual blame, foster empathy, encourage individual responsibility, and increase insight. For example, if a man attributed his low desire to his wife, or the wife blamed her husband for failing to meet her sexual needs, the therapist could use their pasts to make the case that the problem of withholding existed in each partner long before they met one another—the husband withheld sex from other women, and the wife consistently chose men who failed to meet her needs. If the couple grappled with low sexual desire or withholding behavior during their dating process, the therapist could point out that each partner played a hand in the replication process by choosing one another despite their obvious sexual symptoms.

Broadening the process using other content can be an even more powerful technique, in part because it shows each partner how pervasive their process is in their lives. For example, a couple reported with Delayed Ejaculation. It was soon discovered that the man, who was in middle management, was having a great deal of difficulty asserting himself with his employees. He often withheld information from them and took on much of their work. His communication skills reflected his inability to "let go" and express himself. The man's wife also reported that her husband was financially frugal to the point of being cheap. She said that, as a result, their house was falling apart because he refused to spend any money on its upkeep.

A second example concerns a married woman's inability to achieve orgasm with her husband. She could do so with a vibrator but never with a man. The woman claimed that she was very attracted to her husband, but as soon as she came close to orgasm with him, she would "shut down." It was eventually revealed that the woman had a series of control struggles with many people in her lives, including family and friends. When she became upset with someone, there was no negotiation. Her husband even claimed that their house was immaculate and that she could not tolerate anything out of order. Her inhibited orgasm represented another attempt to maintain control. She gave to others, but in a calculated and incremental way. The following vignette is that of Jay, a 48-year-old physician with Delayed Ejaculation. He could ejaculate via oral and manual sex but not inside Carol, a dental hygienist and his fiancée. This was his first experience with this problem. Notice, the therapist pointed out that the man's issue was ever-present in his life and was causing him difficulty in and out of relationships.

Carol: (Teary eyed). Jay is so critical of me. He never gives me any credit for all I do for him. He's always putting me down. Even if he can ejaculate inside me, I'm not sure we should marry.
Jay: You're too sensitive. I'm just teasing.
Therapist: Apparently, she's taking your comments seriously. What kinds of things does Jay say to you?
Carol: He tells me I'm stupid. He's the big, smart cardiologist, and I didn't go to college, so he thinks I'm an idiot.
Jay: I want to talk about ejaculation.
Therapist: I think we are.
Jay: What do you mean?
Therapist: Didn't your ex-wife leave you because you always put her down and because you refused to have sex with her as frequently as she wanted it? Wasn't that behavior partly responsible for her affairs?

Jay: So, what does that have to do with ejaculation?
Therapist: Well, ejaculation is a form of withholding. Maybe you withhold affection, sex, or even positive things the same way you withhold your ejaculate.
Jay: But I can ejaculate other ways.
Therapist: But not inside Carol. This act must serve some special purpose—perhaps a special form of withholding.
Carol: Maybe he doesn't want to marry somebody he thinks is so stupid.
Jay: But I do want to marry you. I've told you a thousand times that I love you.
Carol: Then you call me an idiot the next day.
Therapist: You did give Carol an engagement ring, but you might be withholding a marriage. You also come to therapy regularly but often criticize my interventions.
Carol: He treats everybody this way. Even his partners couldn't stand him. That's why he's on his own now.
Therapist: Are you a solo practitioner?
Jay: Yeah, but I like it better this way.
Therapist: Are you sure? It sounds as if this is causing you a lot of loss. And it doesn't sound as if you want to lose Carol, too.

Broadening the process can be a most powerful technique if the therapist does the investigative work in the assessment phase and beyond to explore each partner's respective families of origin and their past relationship experiences. It is primarily for this reason that we urge the therapist to complete an extensive sexual and nonsexual history, including a history of each partner's relationships dating back to high school years. Armed with the evidence to prove the pervasiveness of each partner's process will make it far easier to attack the defenses that surround their troublesome master conflict.

Treatment: Success and Failure

When we lecture at colleges and universities, there is usually at least one student—a research-minded one—that asks us: "What is your success rate?" Sometimes the question is put differently: "How many relationships do you save on average?" We respond to these questions with a question of our own: "What constitutes successful couples therapy?" We explain that successful treatment is not always predicated on "saving" a relationship. The reality is that some couples are better off apart. And if they have recently discovered this or have always known it and finally acted with our help, we consider the treatment a success. MCT is, after all, about decision-making and the avoidance of painful paralysis. Save for an impulsive or fantasy-driven decision—these we question—we respect and admire the couple that makes tough decisions. Couples who have separated have thanked us. Many of them have claimed to have gotten enough from therapy to help make a long-suffering choice. We have, on occasion, received referrals from former couples who have divorced and found happiness with and without others.

Treatment tolerance, on the other hand, varies and can be a barometer for therapeutic success or failure. For example, some couples do not wish to uncover their conflicts: they find the process too expensive and time-consuming. We may remind these couples of the expense of a separation or divorce and the odds of replicating their conflict with future partners. Other couples find the discovery process too anxiety-provoking. To these couples, we assert that there is almost always a price for change, but only they can decide whether it is worth it. In some cases, one partner wants to pursue change, and the other is against it—this is surely a recipe for failure. We have mentioned previously that some of these cases are over before they begin because one partner has made up his or her mind to end the relationship, but these still merit some investigation to see if there is a chance for survival. And then there are some who learn of their conflicts but admit that they are unwilling to make the difficult choice that it would take to re-balance them (Betchen, 2010). Perhaps a 38-year-old wife put it best when she said: "I understand my conflict—I see it. But I just don't feel like taking it on at this point in my life. I will continue to live with it and do the best I can." The woman was referring to her difficulty achieving orgasm—a symptom tied to her enmeshed loyalty to her father and a *self vs. loyalty (others)* conflict.

It makes sense to consider treatment a success if the couple's sexual problem has been alleviated. That is what the couple usually comes to us for. Couples and sex therapy models of a cognitive-behavioral bent consider this the main objective of their treatment (McCarthy, 2015). While there are several studies reporting the efficacy of couples therapy (Halford, Pepping, & Petch, 2016; Lebow, Chambers, Christensen, & Johnson, 2012; Snyder & Halford, 2012), it is surprising given the behavioral nature of sex therapy that there are so few evidence-based studies on the treatment of sexual disorders (Binik & Hall, 2014; Meana, Hall, & Binik, 2014). Some sex therapy cases merit more education than intervention, while others require little psychological depth. However, in our experience, many require the uncovering of a master conflict to achieve long-lasting symptom relief. As we have mentioned earlier, if an unbalanced master conflict is out of control, even the most benign sex therapy exercise, such as Sensate Focus I, will prove ineffective. Under these circumstances, we also worry that symptoms will reoccur.

We know how difficult it is to change. And if one or both partners cannot or will not make the sacrifices that change demands, so be it—they do not need to be made to feel bad about this. On the contrary, while we may express sadness, we also offer our admiration for the attempt to take on such a challenging task. We take this stance even if the couple leaves because they simply don't like us or our model. It is the couple's journey, and we wish them well. We do not view ourselves as saviors. We prefer to think of ourselves as guides, taking the couple on a journey of individual/personal and interactional discovery. What the couple does with what they discover is up to them. If in the process the couple learns to manage their conflict and alleviate their sexual symptoms, so much the better. This would be an optimal outcome—an unequivocal success. In sum, MCT has a very narrow view of treatment failure, in part because of its deterministic bent and the value of getting unstuck.

Termination and Relapse

In MCT, the timing of termination is usually agreed upon by both the couple and the therapist. Optimally, this would mean that the couple's underlying master conflict has been revealed and balanced, and their sexual symptom has been alleviated. If the couple feels confident enough to identify their master conflict in other contexts (e.g., nonsexual relationship symptoms), so much the better. This will reduce the recidivism rate.

It is imperative that the couple terminate with the understanding that there is no such thing as a complete cure. The symptom should dissipate, but the underlying master conflict will live on. The therapist should therefore warn the couple that their master conflict: (1) will not disappear; (2) will remain an integral part of them whether they are together or apart; (3) may require constant vigilance and therefore should be kept at the forefront of their minds; and, (4) should be the first thing they consult when a problem arises. If all went well in treatment, the couple should experience a reduction or complete amelioration of their sexual symptoms.

Premature termination is part of the business of psychotherapy. In couples therapy, this could mean that one partner wants out of treatment before the other, or that the couple have reached an agreement to stop treatment. When one partner elects to terminate against the other's wishes, a control struggle might be the culprit. The objective, in this case, albeit unconscious, would be to avoid making a difficult choice and preserve the couple's unbalanced conflict—the very same conflict that has plagued the couple's relationship for some time. We recommend that the therapist point this out as quickly as possible and link it to the couple's master conflict.

In our experience, the couple's dynamic will give an indication of how the relationship or treatment might end. For example, if a couple were volatile during their relationship and in therapy, their dissolution would most likely reflect this strife. If the couple struggled for control or power, their divorce might reflect a similar end, with each partner fighting over needless issues. If the couple were relatively passive in their relationship, their end might come calmly and quietly. And if the couple were inconsistent in their relationship, or there was a pattern of coming together and separating, they may demonstrate an inability to stick with the treatment or sustain it on a consistent basis. Understanding this concept should arm the therapist with the ability to predict premature termination or the tone of the termination. We always warn a couple not to take their dynamic into the legal system. Doing so can result in an expensive and emotionally draining process that may seem endless.

When both partners agree to terminate, they sometimes do so because they erroneously feel well enough. This may mean that they believe they have balanced their conflict. But many of these couples have only done so on an intellectual, not an emotional, level. Under such circumstances, we find that the couple's symptoms will soon return. For example, Larry's second wife had an affair with his good friend, and Larry was outraged. But Larry did not want a divorce because he was already paying alimony to his first wife and did not want to put the children he recently had with his second wife through the divorce process. Larry's wife begged for forgiveness and turned to therapy to help her through this situation; she did appear sincere when she expressed a desire to save her marriage. But despite Larry claiming that he had a handle on his *justice vs. injustice* conflict, he could not control his rage and would intermittently blow up in the couple's sessions. Larry finally gave in and admitted to himself that he could no longer stay married to his wife. Intellectually, he decided that he wanted his marriage, but he could not reconcile this emotionally. To control a master conflict, each partner must decide both intellectually and emotionally to do so.

Most couples who terminate prematurely are viewed in MCT as unconsciously colluding to maintain their unbalanced conflict and sexual symptom—a dynamic that the therapist needs to address. The couple should be sufficiently warned that if they stop treatment at this juncture, they might continue to have symptoms or that their symptoms might soon reappear (Greenan, 2010). There are, however, circumstances in which the couple cannot tolerate the anxiety that often accompanies deep psychotherapy (Siegel, 2010). And not every therapist and couple make a good match. While both conditions may be a form of resistance, if a couple conveys this, the therapist should maintain an air of professionalism and make an appropriate referral. Other couples can no longer financially afford the treatment. Here we recommend that the therapist aid the couple in finding a therapist or clinic that charges on a sliding scale. After experiencing a premature termination, the therapist should examine how the treatment was handled or mishandled and make appropriate adjustments to prevent this from happening in the future.

In some instances, a couple will decide to separate during treatment and one partner wishes to continue with the couples therapist. Wachtel (2017) is reluctant to see one partner following couples therapy. It is safer to consider yourself the couple's therapist only, and to terminate when the couple does. But because most couples therapists we know will continue to see one partner in treatment, we suggest that it is done so with the terminating partner's permission, and only with the partner who is being abandoned. This way, the therapist is less likely to be accused of turning the terminating partner against the absent one.

In MCT, we prefer that a couple terminate gradually. We usually see a couple on a weekly basis, but when they are in the termination process, we will first recommend bi-weekly sessions, slowly moving to monthly. This will give the couple a chance to test their skills and to see if the sexual symptom remains under control. It will also give the therapist time to discuss the positive gains that the couple has made over the course of their treatment (Morrill & Córdova, 2010).

McCarthy (2001) has placed a high value on relapse strategies with couples who suffer from sexual disorders. In MCT, we reiterate the power of their conflict and how it may appear in different contexts. We recommend that when they have difficulty in any context, they pause and "think conflict." We predict that the conflict will show itself, and we warn the couple to expect this. But we add that they now have the skills to cope with such a moment. To reduce shame or embarrassment in the couple, we normalize the need for a couple to come back for a "tune up" if their master conflict begins to be a problem. Daniel and Terry, a married couple in their early 40s, were successful in alleviating Terry's low sexual desire with MCT, but approximately two years later, Daniel dropped in for a few sessions—with Terry's encouragement—because he was provoking his boss at work and in turn being reprimanded and passed over for promotions. Initially, Daniel was having difficulty "thinking conflict," but he was quick to see that his *success vs. sabotage (big vs. small)* conflict was acting up again. He was happy to recognize his old nemesis and to regain control over it.

Summary

In this chapter, we have attempted to demonstrate how we utilize MCT in the context of a sexual symptom. This will also be illustrated with a wide variety of sexual issues in the chapters to follow. But here we presented our 5-stage process, which colleagues and students have told us they have found particularly helpful in understanding the MCT treatment process. They are as follows: *Stage 1. Exposing contradictions and conflict on the interactional level.* In this stage, the couple's therapist observes the couple's interactional style or dynamic and points out contradictions and any other evidence that may lead to the discovery of the couple's master conflict; *Stage 2. Examining the origin of the conflict on a psychodynamic level.* In this stage, the therapist helps the couple to determine how the influences from their families of origin have helped to develop their shared master conflict; *Stage 3. Examining the options on a behavioral level.* Here the therapist and couple examine the behaviors the couple might employ to control their conflict; *Stage 4. Examining the options on a psychodynamic level.* In this all-important emotional stage, the therapist helps the couple to gain insight into what they would have to give up or *sacrifice* to rebalance their conflict; and *Stage 5. Moving towards the resolution of the underlying conflict and increased differentiation.* In this stage, the therapist helps the couple to rebalance their conflict and alleviate their symptoms. Other sections of this chapter addressed setting boundaries, balancing the couple, the powerful technique of broadening the therapeutic process to show the pervasiveness of a couple's master conflict, treatment success and failure, termination, and treatment relapse prevention.

References

Betchen, S. (2005). *Intrusive partners, elusive mates: The pursuer-distancer dynamic in couples.* New York, NY: Routledge.
Betchen, S. (2010). *Magnetic partners: Discover how the hidden conflict that once attracted you to each other is now driving you apart.* New York, NY: Free Press.
Betchen, S. (2015). Premature ejaculation: An integrative, intersystem approach for couples. In K. Hertlein, G.R. Weeks, & N. Gambescia (Eds.), *Systemic sex therapy* (2nd ed., pp. 90–106). New York, NY: Routledge.
Binik, Y., & Hall, K. (2014). (Eds.). *Principles and practice of sex therapy* (5th ed., pp. 551–558). New York, NY: Guilford.
Grennan, D. (2010). Therapy with a gay male couple: An unlikely multisystemic integration. In Gurman (Ed.), *Clinical casebook of couple therapy* (5th ed., pp. 90–111). New York, NY: Guilford Press.
Greenberg, L., & Johnson, S. (2010). *Emotionally focused couples.* New York, NY: Guilford Press.
Halford, W.K., Pepping, C., & Petch, J. (2016). The gap between couple therapy research efficacy and private practice effectiveness. *Journal of Marital and Family Therapy, 42,* 32–44. doi:10.1111/jmft.12120
Kaplan, H.S. (1989). *PE: How to overcome premature ejaculation.* New York, NY: Brunner/Mazel.
Lebow, J., Chambers, A., Christensen, A., & Johnson, S. (2012). Research on the treatment of couple distress. *Journal of Marital and Family Therapy, 38,* 145–168. doi:10.1111/j.1725-0606.2011.00249.x
Masters, W., & Johnson, V. (1966). *Human sexual response.* Boston: Little, Brown & Company.
Masters, W., & Johnson, V. (1970). *Human sexual inadequacy.* Boston: Little, Brown & Company.
McCarthy, B. (2001). Relapse prevention strategies and techniques with erectile dysfunction. *Journal of Sex & Marital Therapy, 27,* 1–8.
McCarthy, B., & McCarthy, E. (2013). *Rekindling desire* (2nd ed.). New York, NY: Routledge.
McCarthy, B. (2015). *Sex made simple: Clinical strategies for sexual issues in therapy.* Eau Claire, WI: PESI Publishing & Media.
Meana, M. (2010). When love and sex go wrong: Helping couples in distress. In S. Levine., C. Risen, & S. Althof (Eds.), *Handbook of clinical sexuality for mental health professionals* (2nd ed., pp. 103–120), New York, NY: Routledge.

Meana, M., Hall, K., & Binik, Y. (2014). Sex therapy in transition. In Y. Binik & K. Hall (Eds.), *Principles and practices of sex therapy* (5th ed., pp. 551–558). New York, NY: Guilford.

Meana, M., Maykut, C., & Fertel, E. (2015). Painful intercourse: Genito-pelvic pain/penetration disorder. In K. Hertlein, G.R. Weeks, & N. Gambescia (Eds.), *Systemic sex therapy* (2nd ed., pp. 191–209). New York, NY: Routledge.

Morrill, M., & Córdova, J. (2010). Building intimacy bridges: From the marriage checkup to integrative behavioral couple therapy. In A. Gurman (Ed.), *Clinical casebook of couple therapy* (pp. 331–354). New York, NY: Guilford.

Rosiello, F. (2000). *Deepening intimacy in psychotherapy: Using the erotic transference and countertransference.* New York, NY: Aronson.

Schnarch, D. (2009). *Passionate marriage: Keeping love & intimacy alive in committed relationships.* New York, NY: W.W. Norton.

Semans, J. (1956). Premature ejaculation: A new approach. *Southern Medical Journal, 49,* 198–200.

Siegel, J. (1997). Applying countertransference theory to couples treatment. In M. Solomon & J. Siegel (Eds.), *Countertransference in couples therapy* (pp. 3–22). New York, NY: Norton.

Siegel, J. (2010). A good-enough therapy: An object relations approach. In A. Gurman (Ed.), *Clinical casebook of couple therapy* (pp. 134–152). New York, NY: Guilford.

Snyder, D., & Halford, W.K. (2012). Evidence-based couple therapy: Current states and future directions. *Journal of Family Therapy, 34,* 229–249. doi:10.1111/j.1467-6427.2012.00599.x

Solomon, M. (1997). Countertransference and empathy in couples therapy. In M. Solomon & J. Siegel (Eds.), *Countertransference in couples therapy.* New York, NY: Norton.

Wachtel, E. (2017). *The heart of couple therapy: Knowing what to do and how to do it.* New York, NY: Guilford.

Weeks, G., & Fife, S. (2014). *Couples in treatment: Techniques and approaches for effective Practice* (3rd ed.). New York, NY: Routledge.

Weiner, L., & Avery-Clark, C. (2014). Sensate focus: Clarifying the Masters and Johnson's model. *Sexual and Relationship Therapy, 29*(3), 307–319.

Section III

Case Studies

Chapter 6

Female Sexual Disorders

Female Orgasmic Disorder

Female Orgasmic Disorder is defined by the *DSM-5* (American Psychiatric Association, 2013) as: (1) a delay, infrequency, or absence of orgasm, and (2) a significant reduction of the intensity of orgasm. The symptoms must be experienced during sexual activity 75% to 100% of the time and persist for at least six months. Symptoms must also cause the individual distress and not emanate from another mental disorder, relationship distress, other life stressor, the use of medication, or a medical condition. The condition can be lifelong or acquired, generalized or situational (p. 429).

The wide range in prevalence of Female Orgasmic Disorder makes it hard to accurately assess its commonality (Fugl-Meyer & Fugl-Meyer, 2006). Studies have shown it to be 3% to 34% (Graham 2010). Apparently, only half of the women who cannot achieve orgasm report distress—one of the diagnostic criteria for the disorder (Oberg, Fugl-Meyer & Fugl-Meyer, 2004; King, Holt, & Nazareth, 2007; Shiffren, 2008). Female Orgasmic Disorder is oftentimes comorbid with other sexual dysfunctions, including lack of interest or arousal (Weeks, Gambescia, & Hertlein, 2016).

Medical conditions such as diabetes, multiple sclerosis, or conditions that result in sexual pain can impact a woman's ability to achieve orgasm. Changes related to childbirth or menopause, as well as the use of certain medications, such as antidepressants—especially selective serotonin reuptake inhibitors (SSRIs) and selective noradrenergic serotonin reuptake inhibitors (SNRIs)—may also play a role (Donahey, 2010; Graham, 2014; McCabe, 2015; Weeks, Gambescia, & Hertlein, 2016).

Nonmedical causes of Female Orgasmic Disorder may include: communication difficulties with a partner (Kelly, Strassberg, & Turner, 2004; McCabe & Giles, 2012), fear, guilt, shame, lack of attraction, and a lack of education (Birnbaum, 2003; Ramage, 2004). Cultural or religious beliefs, a history of sexual trauma (Donahey, 2010), daily life stressors (Morokoff & Gilliland, 1993), performance anxiety, and a lack of sexual experience (McCabe, 2015) may also contribute.

Evidence-based treatment techniques for the disorder include cognitive behavioral strategies such as: identifying obstacles to orgasm, providing appropriate psychoeducation, masturbation exercises, increasing fantasy, developing more effective communication skills training, Sensate Focus exercises, and using mindfulness techniques (Graham, 2014; Weeks, Gambescia, & Hertlein, 2016).

Rodrigo and Angela: Closeness vs. Distance

Rodrigo and Angela (see Figure 6.1) were an engaged couple in their early 30s who had been living together for approximately three years. They sought treatment for two reasons: (1) Rodrigo reported anxiety, or in his words, "cold feet," regarding his upcoming marriage to Angela; and (2) Angela reported increasing difficulty achieving orgasms with Rodrigo. When she did have an orgasm, it was clitoral; she had never achieved a vaginal orgasm with anyone. Angela did experience orgasms with past lovers via manual

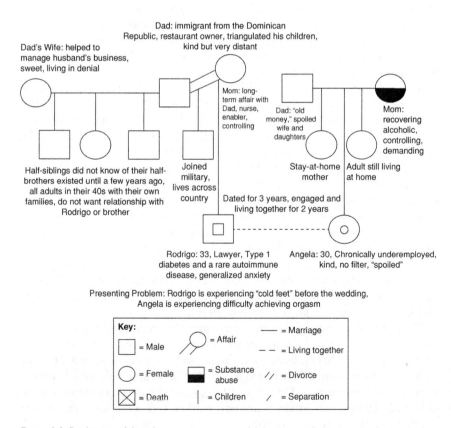

Figure 6.1 Rodrigo and Angela.

masturbation, and with the aid of a vibrator. However, at the time she presented for treatment, she had abstained from self-pleasuring.

The couple estimated that in recent months, their sexual problem had escalated. Angela's ability to achieve orgasm decreased from 90% of the time to 25% of the time. She was not taking any medications that would impact orgasm, and there were no medical changes. Upon assessment, the therapist determined the couple suffered from an unbalanced *closeness vs. distance* master conflict.

Rodrigo, a lawyer, had just recently passed the bar exam. He discussed his family history with some embarrassment; a behavior which hinted at an unbalanced master conflict. Rodrigo claimed that his father was a Dominican who had immigrated to the United States with his family approximately 40 years ago. He proceeded to work hard as a restaurateur and to achieve enough financial success to comfortably support his family.

Rodrigo resented his father and rarely saw him because of his work schedule and because he had another wife and family. Rodrigo discovered this family when he was 8 years old. He knew that he had three half-siblings since childhood, but they did not know that he existed until a few years ago. Rodrigo reported that his half-siblings had rejected his attempts to contact them.

Born with Type 1 diabetes, Rodrigo also suffered from a rare autoimmune disease which resulted in frequent hospitalizations during his childhood. Both diseases were difficult to manage and nearly cost him his life. He attributed these experiences to his apparent anxiety. Both he and his father shared a fear of hospitals. His father rarely visited him in the hospital, and when he did, he was highly anxious. Rodrigo recalled his first panic attack in the hospital as a small child.

Rodrigo's mother was a white, working-class woman. She was initially employed as a secretary but eventually returned to school to study nursing. Rodrigo said that his mother always seemed to be waiting for his father to join their family. During this time, she would experience periods of anger and depression, which she displaced onto him and his brother. She treated the boys as her surrogate husbands. His older brother left home at 18 and joined the military. Heartbroken by her elder son's absence, Rodrigo's mother hid Rodrigo's acceptance letters from colleges that she deemed too far away. Once at college, Rodrigo struggled with anxiety. Although he took a semester off to ease the pressure, he finished and went to law school at a nearby university. He explained that after his brother left home, he felt obligated to stay and care for his mother. He lived with her up until moving in with Angela at age 30. Rodrigo described his sexual development as "stunted" because of health problems. He had no sexual experiences until he completed college and began to date online.

Angela came from a very wealthy Italian-American family in which she and her two sisters were spoiled. Her father worked in commercial real estate and was gone much of the time. Her mother was a housewife who Angela described as a "helicopter parent": a very controlling individual. Her mother also struggled on and off with alcohol abuse during Angela's childhood. She found sobriety only when Angela's father threatened to leave her.

Angela presented as sweet but naïve and somewhat immature. Despite having a master's degree in accounting, she was historically "underemployed." Both parents wanted their daughters to "live at home with them forever," and encouraged them to quit any job if it became too challenging. Angela described a relatively uneventful childhood and denied any trauma. Angela did struggle with separation issues, especially with her mother, who was both over-involved and extremely critical.

A self-admitted "serial dater" since high school, Angela found it difficult to stay in any one relationship for long. Her relationship with Rodrigo had been by far the longest.

Angela claimed that her family openly disapproved of Rodrigo because of his race and socioeconomic status. Angela's father had individually offered them several thousands of dollars to call off the engagement. Despite these attempts at breaking up the relationship, Angela's parents simultaneously were involved in every wedding detail. They also demanded a say in the couple's future, including where they should live and when they should start a family. Several months before the start of therapy, Rodrigo began to experience "cold feet" about marrying Angela.

Rodrigo began to distance himself. He stayed late at work and offered to teach a law course at his alma mater. He also busied himself with projects at his mother's house. Angela began to question whether Rodrigo was having an affair. She would often call frantically, demanding that he come home, but then scream at him to "leave [the relationship] already." In treatment, the couple discovered that Angela's own desire for distance was related to her unconsciously withholding orgasm. The couple realized that part of each of them wanted to be close, but another part of them needed distance and actively created it.

For the couple to better manage their *closeness vs. distance* master conflict, they had to better differentiate from their respective families of origin. For each of them, closeness meant to be nurtured, but it also meant being smothered and controlled. Once the couple began to realize how each colluded with their families of origin to remain dependent, they began to see the negative impact it had on their relationship. This also enabled them to unite in the mutual goal of differentiation. As a result, the couple began to set firmer boundaries with each of their families of origin. As the couple rebalanced their *closeness vs. distance* master conflict through differentiation, Rodrigo made himself more available to the relationship, and Angela's orgasmic issue improved. With the added help of erotic literature, fantasy, and solo pleasuring, Angela found herself better able to let go and be more present or close during sex with Rodrigo. She claimed that it was the jumpstart she needed to get back to her old self. She reported that she could achieve orgasm approximately 60%–75% of the time. In the following brief vignette, the therapist shows each partner how they are enabling their unbalanced *closeness vs. distance* conflict:

Therapist: You both say that you would like to be more independent from your families, but it is impossible to achieve.
Angela: I don't think my parents will ever butt out of the wedding, let alone our lives.
Rodrigo: [Laughs] Yeah, that will never happen.
Therapist: Neither of you can control their behavior, but you may be able to control your own. I do wonder, however, in what ways you enable their behavior.
Angela: What do you mean?
Therapist: For example, when you got engaged, your parents offered to pay for the wedding, and you both agreed. You both could have said no and taken more control over the process. Perhaps you might have been able to join and limit their contributions to certain aspects of the wedding. Instead, you both opted to take the big bucks.
Rodrigo: And now they're making our lives miserable! Honestly, it's not even going to be the type of wedding I want. They've taken over the entire event.
Therapist: That may be the cost of accepting their money.
Angela: I see your point. But I think a wedding is a special exception. Lots of people let their parents pay for their weddings.
Rodrigo: But $80,000! You have no idea what the average person lives on [shaking his head].
Therapist: Rodrigo, you seem frustrated.
Rodrigo: I grew up poor. Angela has no idea what most people live like. And I feel like she's never going to stop taking money from her parents. I want us to make it on our own.
Angela: He thinks I'm spoiled.
Rodrigo: Angela, your parents still pay your credit card balances.
Therapist: Let's focus for a minute on another type of cost. Angela, I want you to look at the costs of being close vs. distant from your family. First, what is the benefit of being so close to them?
Angela: Well, if I'm literally close to them, they pay my bills. And I can quit jobs that are not a good fit. My life is less stressful with their help.
Therapist: Those are some nice perks. So, what will this cost you?
Rodrigo: That you never grow up.
Angela: I guess Rodrigo is right. I haven't been challenged in the same way he has.
Therapist: So that's the cost. What would happen if you were to establish some healthy distance from your parents?
Angela: If I were to refuse their financial help? Drama! And I guess I would have to find a way to make it on my own.

Rodrigo: For "us" to make it on our own.
Therapist: That is a good point, Rodrigo, and an interesting one. You say you want the two of you to make it on your own, but you are distancing from Angela by over-committing to work and to your mother. Your family may not be able to give you financial perks by being close, but you are certainly getting something out of it.
Rodrigo: Well, I do have an obligation to my mother.
Therapist: I understand that, but putting her ahead of your family's needs may also demonstrate an issue with growing up.
Rodrigo: How so?
Therapist: Your closeness to your mother might be a way to create distance between you and Angela, and to avoid to your responsibilities at home. You only just recently purchased a house together, but you seem to spend more time with your mother than you do in your new home.

Genito-Pelvic Pain/Penetration Disorder

The *DSM-5* (American Psychiatric Association, 2013) merged the previous diagnoses of vaginismus and dyspareunia into a singular diagnosis: Genito-Pelvic Pain/Penetration Disorder (GPPPD). The recent *DSM-5* changes reflect the latest research, which indicates the overlap in symptoms and presentation of dyspareunia and vaginismus, as well as research indicating that the idea of vaginal spasm is not adequate in the diagnosis of vaginismus (Cherner & Reissing, 2013). To be diagnosed with GPPPD, a client must experience one or more of the following: (1) difficulty with vaginal penetration during intercourse; (2) vaginal pain during intercourse; (3) fear or anxiety related to vaginal penetration or pain during penetration; or (4) tightening of the pelvic floor muscles prior to or during intercourse. The symptoms must have occurred for at least six months and must cause significant stress to the individual. The symptoms cannot be attributed to another mental disorder, relationship distress, other life stressors, medication, or a medical condition. The subtypes for GPPPD include lifelong (i.e., women who have never been able to experience penetration since becoming sexually active) and acquired (i.e., penetration difficulties began after a period of normalcy) (*DSM-5*; APA, 2013, p. 437).

Pelvic and genital pain can be caused by vulvodynia, endometriosis, interstitial cystitis, various skin conditions, and changes related to childbirth and menopause. The estimates of genital pain range from 6.5% to 45% in older women and 14% to 34% in younger women (van Lankveld *et al.*, 2010). It is common for women to report symptoms for many years, but the actual cause of the pain may fail to be diagnosed (Reissing *et al.*, 2014). Without the appropriate medical treatment, symptoms may worsen, self-esteem may deteriorate, and sexual and relationship distress may increase.

There is some debate as to whether lifelong vaginismus fits the diagnostic criteria for GPPPD or should be considered a specific phobia (Kumar Sahoo, Biswas, Singh, & Kumar Padhy, 2014; Reissing *et al.*, 2014). Women with lifelong vaginismus differed in their manifestation of anxiety and fear during pelvic examinations compared to women with dyspareunia. Many women were too anxious to submit to or complete a pelvic examination (ter Kuile *et al.*, 2009). Fear often leads to the avoidance of any experiences that could result in vaginal penetration, and in turn eliminates opportunities that could challenge the cognitive distortions that maintain the fear and avoidance (Meana, Maykut, & Fertel, 2015; Reissing *et al.*, 2014; ter Kuile *et al.*, 2009). This avoidance negatively reinforces the fear-avoidance cycle of vaginismus, which is often what happens with a specific phobia (Cherner & Reissing, 2013). According to ter Kuile and Reissing (2014), the Fear-Avoidance model of vaginismus developed by Vlaeyen and Linton (2000) explains how vaginal penetration problems are exacerbated in women who already have anxiety and/or pain when attempting intercourse and the cyclical pattern of pain and avoidance that may follow.

When examining the cognitions of women with lifelong vaginismus compared to those with dyspareunia, several differences emerged. The fear of pain was the primary reason women with vaginismus reported an avoidance of intercourse (Lahaie, Boyer, Amsel, Khalifè, & Binik, 2010). Reissing *et al.* (2014) wrote: "Women with lifelong vaginismus report significantly more negative cognitions related to vaginal penetration and have higher pain catastrophizing cognitions when compared to women without sexual pain and women with dyspareunia" (p. 1211). These same women also reported "significantly more causal attributions related to fears of pain, injury, intimacy, and loss of control, and negative images of the body and their own genitals and penis, disgust about intercourse" (Cherner & Reissing, 2013, p. 1606).

The preponderance of evidence has supported the need for a multimodal and holistic approach in the treatment of GPPPD and lifelong vaginismus (Meana, 2009; Reissing, Binik, Khalifè, Cohen, & Amsel, 2003). In addition, using multiple interventions simultaneously may yield better outcomes, as the numerous influencing factors can be addressed. Cognitive behavioral therapy, couples therapy, mindfulness techniques, and exposure therapy with dilators have been effective in the treatment of sexual and pelvic pain (Bergeron, Rosen, & Pukall, 2014; Betchen, 2005; Weeks, Gambescia, & Hertlein, 2016).

Frank and Merjan: Giving vs. Withholding

Frank and Merjan (see Figure 6.2) were a young couple in their early 30s who were referred by Merjan's OB-GYN. The couple explained during their initial session that their marriage was unconsummated and that Merjan had recently been diagnosed with "lifelong vaginismus" or GPPPD. Although

142   Case Studies

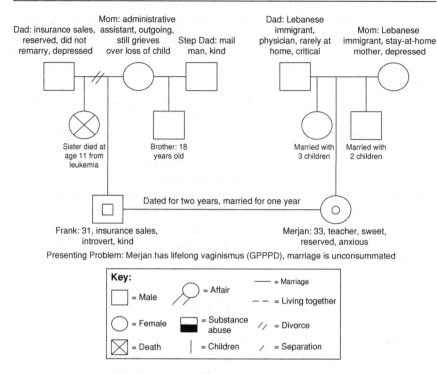

Figure 6.2 Frank and Merjan.

the couple struggled with attempts at penetrative sex for a year since their marriage, Merjan's discovery of an emotional affair that Frank was having with a coworker was a "wake-up call." Merjan had avoided getting treatment for vaginismus, but she was now in a crisis. During the first few sessions it became evident that the couple was struggling with a *giving vs. withholding* master conflict.

Merjan was raised in a conservative, Christian family. Her father and mother immigrated to the United States from Lebanon shortly after marrying. In her youth, many friends and relatives stayed with Merjan and her family in the United States—most escaped the 1982 Lebanon War and needed a place to stay while they transitioned to life in the United States. Although her father had a stable income as a physician, he spent most of his money helping his people make this transition. There was so little money left over that Merjan and her siblings were not able to participate in extracurricular activities. They also had to use hand-me-down clothes and the local food bank.

Merjan's mother was a housewife. Merjan recalled her mother as emotionally distant, busy with relatives, and preoccupied with the news from Lebanon. When Merjan was a teenager, one of her mother's sisters died in the war. This left her mother extremely depressed and even more distant.

Merjan was a compliant but independent child. She held several jobs to support herself. Merjan also excelled in school but felt as if she did not fit in with her peers. She rarely dated, and even when she did, boyfriends meant little to her. She abstained from sex because of her religious beliefs but also feared that sex would be painful. She denied any sexual trauma and reported having little to no education about sex. Her brother and sister married in their 20s to other Lebanese Americans and started families.

Merjan's parents began to worry that their daughter, still single at 25, would never marry, so they arranged for her to meet eligible men in the family's religious community. But Merjan resented and rejected these attempts. She also upset her parents by moving out of the family home and securing her own apartment. Merjan met Frank through mutual friends, and the two soon began to date. They claimed to have experienced an immediate physical attraction and shared many interests. While Merjan's parents were less than thrilled that Frank was not Lebanese, they were pleased that she was getting married, and to a Christian.

Frank was raised in a Catholic, Italian-American family. Frank's childhood was disrupted by his older sister's six-year battle with childhood leukemia; she was 11 when she passed. Frank explained that shortly after her death, his parents divorced. He blamed their unbearable grief for the separation. Following the divorce, Frank's father lived nearby, but Frank rarely saw him. He did, however, contribute to the financial cost of raising Frank. Frank's mother remarried a man who Frank described as kind and emotionally involved, but of little means.

Frank was not a confident teenager, and like Merjan, he rarely dated. He did, however, have many friends, and he excelled in academics. In college he did manage to have a two-year relationship in which he lost his virginity. He had one other long-term girlfriend before meeting Merjan. Although Frank had previously had sex, he said he was willing to wait until Merjan was ready. He admitted that he missed having intercourse but claimed to be generally happy with his relationship. The couple did attempt intercourse during their engagement period, but it was unsuccessful.

Like Merjan, Frank thought his wife's issues would resolve once they were married. But attempts at intercourse on their honeymoon failed and left the couple frustrated. Frank urged Merjan to consult with a physician, but she refused. It was only when she discovered a series of inappropriate texts and photos between Frank and one of his coworkers that she agreed to see an OB-GYN.

With a mixture of individual and couples sessions, Merjan eventually discovered that her anxiety about penetrative sex represented a conflict about giving all of herself to her husband. She took care of him in many ways, as her parents did of her, but just as her parents fell short, so did she. Once she began to understand how her parents' withholding affected her, she was better able to empathize with what Frank was missing in their relationship.

With the cooperation of Merjan's OB-GYN, the therapist employed MCT, anti-anxiety medication, and dilator use to help Merjan and Frank. Merjan was progressing until she reached the fourth and final dilator. She then began to obsess about Frank's transgressions. In the following vignette, the therapist will address the therapeutic backslide and connect it to the couple's shared master conflict. Frank's contribution to the conflict was also exposed:

Frank: I swear on my mother's life I did not have any physical contact with Rachel [Frank's coworker/affair partner].
Merjan: I find that hard to believe after seeing those texts and photos.
Therapist: I know we have talked a bit about your *giving vs. withholding* master conflict, Merjan. And while I cannot say for certain that Frank had physical contact with his affair partner, it would certainly fit your shared master conflict if he gave to her emotionally but withheld sex.
Merjan: I guess so. But it is still hard for me to believe.
Therapist: Initially you sought treatment immediately and seemed to forgive Frank. Now you're on the last dilator and are very close to being able to have sex. And suddenly you're revisiting the affair. I do wonder how this relates to your conflict.
Merjan: Well, one side of me wants to give to Frank. After all, I am here. And I do give to Frank in many other ways. But another part of me wants to withhold, which I did for a long time.
Therapist: I wonder what you get out of withholding.
Merjan: I think it's some sort of unconscious insurance.
Therapist: Can you explain that a little more?
Merjan: I saw both of my parents give to the point that they had nothing left. Not even for each other; certainly not for me and my siblings. A part of me is afraid of that happening again. Maybe I'm afraid of losing myself in giving.
Therapist: I would like both of you to keep in mind that once you start having penetrative sex and essentially begin to "give" to each other, you will both probably withhold in some other way. You need to be mindful of this to keep your master conflict balanced. Remember, this conflict will always be there, and you must manage it.
Frank: That's an interesting point. If that's true, then we can both choose what to give and what to withhold.
Therapist: Yes. And awareness of this can help you to make less destructive choices.
Merjan: (Rolling her eyes at Frank) Yes, like not having an affair.
Frank: Okay, okay. I already said I am sorry several times. I promise you I will never let that happen again.

Therapist: But you will have issues with giving and withholding again. How can you guarantee that it won't lead to another affair?
Frank: I think I need to work on communicating my displeasure with Merjan rather than withholding this information and punishing her. I know I am responsible for my own actions, but the truth is, I was feeling lonely. I think loneliness drove me to the affair. Although again, it was not physical.
Therapist: Why do you think loneliness is the prime emotion that is evoked when Merjan withholds?
Frank: My entire childhood was lonely. That is always the first emotion I feel. When my sister was alive, my parents were totally preoccupied with her illness. No one ever read to me at bedtime or came to my baseball games. Yes, I went to the best private schools and summer camps. But I think I participated in whatever activity I could to keep from feeling pain.
Therapist: How do you think you will feel once Merjan is able to have intercourse with you? When she will "give" to you in this way?
Frank: [Tears up] I don't want to feel Merjan is giving me sex out of obligation. I feel like my parents only gave to me out of obligation, too. They provided the basics.

Female Sexual Interest/Arousal Disorder

The *DSM-5* (American Psychiatric Association, 2013) created the diagnosis of Female Sexual Interest/Arousal Disorder (SIAD) by merging Hypoactive Sexual Desire Disorder (HSDD) with Female Sexual Arousal Disorder (FSAD). These changes were also made to reflect new research findings that women's sexual desire is receptive or responsive rather than spontaneous, like sexual desire in men (Brotto & Luria, 2014). These changes also demonstrated that a woman's sexual desire can be influenced by a range of factors, including daily life stressors and relationship stress (Hamilton & Julian, 2014). And finally, the changes were driven by findings that a woman's motivation to engage in sexual activity varied (Weeks, Gambescia, & Hertlein, 2016).

The *DSM-5* (American Psychiatric Association, 2013) claimed that to be given the diagnosis of Female Sexual Interest/Arousal Disorder, at least three of the following symptoms must be present for at least six months: (1) absent or reduced interest in engaging sexually; (2) absent or reduced sexual thoughts and/or fantasies; (3) absent or reduced attempts to initiate sexual activity and not be responsive to a partner's attempts to initiate; (4) absent or reduced sexual excitement or pleasure during sexual activity in 75%–100% of sexual encounters; (5) absent or reduced response to internal and external sexual or erotic cues; and (6) absent or reduced genital or nongenital feelings in about 75%–100% of sexual encounters. In addition, the symptoms must cause distress to the individual. The disorder can be either lifelong or acquired, generalized or situational (p. 433).

SIAD is more likely to occur in menopausal and postmenopausal women (Sims & Meana, 2010). The disorder is often found comorbid with mental health conditions such as depression and medical problems that impact the cardiovascular and neurological systems. However, it is believed that how a woman feels towards her partner may be more influential than hormonal and other medical factors (Brotto & Luria, 2014). In addition, sociocultural factors must be considered. A negative view of masturbation, guilt that is driven by religious beliefs, and the reality that women are socialized to be sexually passive in many cultures may contribute to problems with sexual interest and arousal (Boul, Hallam-Jones, & Wylie, 2009; Woo, Brotto, & Gorzalka, 2011; Woo, Morshedian, Brotto, & Gorzalka, 2012).

Because biological, psychological, and relational factors may influence a woman's sexual desire, the treatment of this disorder must be guided by the specific factors impacting the drive. Treatment strategies and interventions sometimes include: providing appropriate psychoeducational materials; addressing nonsexual relationship issues or dynamics that influence desire; reducing anticipatory anxiety; creating positive anticipation; cultivating sexual fantasies; and developing more effective communication strategies to use with a partner. Other strategies include helping a woman to develop a positive body image and a positive view of her sexuality (Weeks, Gambescia, & Hertlein, 2016). A thorough assessment is imperative to determine an effective treatment plan tailored to the couple's specific needs. MCT can be useful in helping to determine the role a couple's shared underlying conflict is contributing to this symptom formation. This is illustrated in the following case:

Adam and Rebecca: Self vs. Loyalty (Others)

Adam and Rebecca (see Figure 6.3) were a married couple in their early 30s. Rebecca was referred to therapy by her OB-GYN because she had been suffering from low sexual desire since the couple married approximately one year earlier. Rebecca's blood work tested as normal, and there had been no changes in her health. She was not taking any medication.

Adam and Rebecca claimed that during their three-year dating period prior to marriage, their sex life was satisfying; the couple averaged sex once per month. However, once married, Rebecca's drive significantly decreased, and the couple neglected to have sexual contact for several months. Both Adam and Rebecca had little insight regarding the cause of their problem. During the assessment, the therapist was convinced that the couple suffered from an unbalanced *self vs. loyalty (others)* master conflict.

Adam worked in IT for a major company. Adam's parents divorced shortly after his birth, and he was raised by his mother and maternal grandparents in a middle-class suburban neighborhood. Adam said both his

Female Sexual Disorders 147

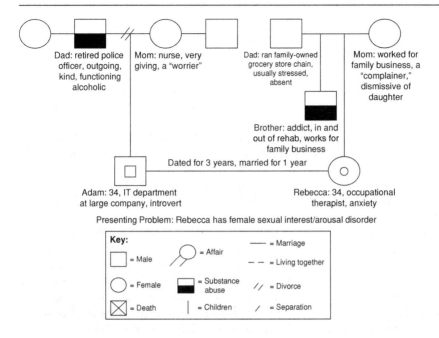

Figure 6.3 Adam and Rebecca.

parents remarried but maintained a friendship with one another; they shared his birthdays and various other holidays.

Adam described himself as an introvert. He said that he excelled in school but had few friends. He believed that he suffered from social anxiety acquired from his anxious and controlling mother. He said that this anxiety hindered him from spending more time with his father and from making friends. While in high school, Adam wanted to go out with others, but his mother wanted him at home. When he would venture out, he would return to find his mother in an "extremely anxious state." He eventually decided that having a social life was not worth the pain he was causing his mother.

Upon his mother's request, Adam attended a local college. Luckily, his father sanctioned that Adam move out of his mother's home and into a college dorm. Adam enjoyed college and did well academically. After completing his undergraduate degree, he went on to obtain a master's degree in computer science, but again he commuted. Adam's father was disappointed by his son's decision to reject a prestigious program in California that was interested in him. Adam later agreed with his father and regretted his decision. He admitted that most of his life decisions were attempts to appease his anxious mother.

Adam had one other relationship prior to Rebecca. It ended, however, because he was unwilling to relocate with this woman after her employer transferred her to a major metropolitan city. Adam claimed there were "other issues" that prevented him from moving, such as poor communication. A mutual friend of Adam and Rebecca's served as a matchmaker, and the couple quickly began to form a relationship.

Rebecca, 34, was employed as an occupational therapist for children with special needs. She grew up in the suburbs of a major city in the Mid-Atlantic region. Her father had taken over his father's chain of grocery stores and did quite well, but they required a lot of time and effort. Rebecca claimed that her father was "rarely around," and when he was, he was overwhelmed by stress. Rebecca's mother helped to manage the stores and was also rarely available to her daughter. Rebecca described her mother as a "chronic complainer" who was unhappy and overworked. Given the little parenting time they put into Rebecca, she questioned why her parents even had children; she added that they did not seem to enjoy the role of being parents.

Rebecca said that her childhood was both lonely and distressing. She described her older brother as having sociopathic tendencies. Rebecca recalled that she was frightened of him as a child. She had vivid memories of her brother physically torturing her: hitting and biting her, purposefully slamming her fingers between doors, and pulling out some of her hair. He also abused the family pet. She recalled that as a teenager he tried to touch her inappropriately, but she resisted. He did, however, flash her several times when he had an erection. Rebecca reported her brother's behavior to her parents but was dismissed. Both parents accused her of being "crazy" and "dramatic." By age 10, Rebecca gave up on her parents and spent as much time outside the family home as possible.

Rebecca claimed that her brother often stole money from her parents to purchase drugs to feed his heroin habit. She said that her parents were so overwhelmed with her brother's behavior that they neglected her in the process. They were late for her high school graduation because of an incident with her brother, and they proceeded to be miserable the entire time. When Rebecca challenged her parents about this, her mother said: "You can only be as happy as your saddest child." Rebecca felt that this very attitude prevented her parents from celebrating her life events.

To make matters worse, Rebecca's parents spent a small fortune paying for several expensive rehabilitation centers for their son, none of which helped. During his most recent stint in treatment, Rebecca's brother admitted to a treatment team that he was physically and sexually abusive to Rebecca as a child. Unable to deny this any longer, Rebecca's mother confronted Rebecca via telephone, but Rebecca denied much of it. She thought that it would kill her mother to know the truth about her brother.

Rebecca was an excellent student and found school to be her safe haven, so to speak. She had plenty of friends and participated in several student activities. Rebecca left home for college and studied abroad in Europe. Unfortunately, her brother ruined that experience with a nearly fatal overdose that required her to return home sooner than expected. After graduating from college, Rebecca pursued her master's degree in occupational therapy and purposefully chose to remain several states away from her family. She said that she has not seen her brother in several years and did not plan to do so despite her parents' urging.

Rebecca had several boyfriends in college and adulthood. She reported having generally positive sexual experiences that were consensual save for one: a college boyfriend cheated on her and passed on herpes. She said that this experience, coupled with her brother's abuse and her father's inability to protect her, changed her views about men for the worse, a perspective that only began to improve once she met Adam.

Rebecca said that her relationship with Adam was serious from the beginning. When the couple became engaged, however, her parents once again focused the spotlight on their son by demanding that Rebecca form a truce with him and involve him in the wedding. Succumbing to the pressure, Rebecca agreed but opted for a courthouse wedding and a small garden party for a reception—decisions that upset her parents.

During the assessment phase, it became clear that the stressors outside of Rebecca's relationship were significantly impacting her sexual desire. Rebecca's parents were extremely angry with her for not having a formal wedding and for her continued resistance to a relationship with her brother. Their increased criticism and dismissal of Rebecca's needs served as a trigger to Rebecca. She was also "burned out" from her job. She admitted to spending several nights after work crying about job-related issues. Working with severely handicapped children in an underfunded urban school district had become "unbearable" to her. Her emotions were often triggered by the neglectful behavior of some of the parents. These two factors alone emotionally and physically drained Rebecca. Nevertheless, the timing of her loss of desire seemed to coincide with her marrying—and this did not escape the therapist.

Rebecca made several changes with treatment that eventually led to an increase in sexual desire. She left her job and found a new position in a private hospital system that was well-funded and less triggering. And she set firmer boundaries with her parents, who continued to badger her about engaging her brother. Once Rebecca felt emotionally stable, the couple began Sensate Focus Exercises, which they progressed nicely through over a series of months. Rebecca also worked on creating positive anticipation about sex and increasing fantasy, and the couple worked on setting aside time each week with the intention of connecting sexually.

After approximately eight months of treatment, the couple found themselves having sex on a regular basis (i.e., once a week). At a six-month follow-up appointment, the couple maintained their level of sexual intimacy. To support the therapist's hypothesis, Rebecca reported that whenever her parents placed unbearable pressure on her for any reason, her sexual desire would decline. They knew then that even firmer boundaries had to be set.

This time, Rebecca was smart enough to enlist Adam in this process. The following is a brief vignette depicting the part MCT played in helping Rebecca and her husband:

Therapist: Rebecca, we have discussed some of the factors contributing to your loss of sexual desire. But I wonder what you both think of the timing of it.
Rebecca: I think it's the result of a buildup of all the stress that I've been under.
Therapist: But these stressors have existed throughout your entire relationship. Why is the desire suddenly disappearing?
Adam: I think it's because we became "family."
Therapist: Can you say more about that?
Adam: Well, we apparently both have this *self vs. loyalty (others)* conflict you've mentioned. And I think for Rebecca, it is much more intense than mine. Not to say that mine isn't there—because it is. But my childhood was less traumatic.
Rebecca: That's fair.
Adam: I feel like when I became family to you, maybe you felt I would hurt you like your family has? Or maybe that you had to choose?
Rebecca: I think that is partly true, but I think it's something more.
Therapist: Rebecca, we've talked about how you were sacrificed for your brother's needs as a kid ... and still are. That you haven't been able to safely express your needs to your parents to attempt to get your needs met. "Family" to you might mean having to give up your needs for someone else. Perhaps it is as if there is a constant tug-of-war going on between pleasuring yourself versus others. That's got to be exhausting [Rebecca tearing up]. Perhaps this is what is going on between you and Adam now that he has become family.
Rebecca: That's hitting me. And on top of those other stressors, it's just too much. I don't even think there is room for my sexual desire.

Summary

The purpose of this chapter was to demonstrate how MCT could be used with a range of female sexual disorders. While it was not possible to address every female sexual dysfunction, we believe female sexual disorders can be treated effectively with MCT. The cases selected for this chapter highlighted the most common female sexual dysfunctions we see in our clinical practices: Female Orgasmic Disorder, Genito-Pelvic Pain/Penetration Disorder, and Female Sexual Interest/Arousal Disorder. The cases also represented issues specific to working with women, including sexual trauma and the role of sociocultural influences on sexual and nonsexual relationship problems. We acknowledge that we have used the *DSM-5* to define the sexual disorders addressed, but we do feel that the recent changes to this reference have removed relationships as a primary factor. This can be especially difficult when working with women, given that relationship factors seem to be strongly tied to the way women experience their sexuality and their motivations to have sex with a partner.

References

American Psychiatric Association (2013). *Diagnostic and statistical manual of mental disorders* (5th ed.). Arlington, VA; Author.
Bergeron, S., Rosen, N., & Pukall, C. (2014). Genital pain in women and men: It can hurt more than your sex life. In Y. Binik & K. Hall (Eds.), *Principles and practice of sex therapy* (5th ed.). New York, NY: The Guilford Press.
Betchen, S. (2005). *Intrusive partners – elusive mates: The pursuer-distance dynamic in couples.* New York, NY: Routledge.
Birnbaum, G.E. (2003). The meaning of heterosexual intercourse among women with female orgasmic disorder. *Archives of Sexual Behavior, 32,* 61–71. doi:10.1023/A:1021845513448
Boul, L., Hallam-Jones, R., & Wylie, K.R. (2009). Sexual Pleasure and motivation. *Journal of Sex and Marital Therapy, 35*(1), 25–39.
Brotto, L., & Luria, M. (2014). Sexual interest/arousal disorder in women. In Y. Binik & K. Hall (Eds.), *Principles and practices of sex therapy* (5th ed.) (pp. 17–41). New York, NY: Guilford Press.
Cherner, R., & Reissing, E. (2013). A comparative study of sexual function, behavior, and cognitions of women with lifelong vaginismus. *Archives of Sexual Behavior, 42,* 1605–1614. doi:10.1007/s10508-013-0111-3
Donahey, K. (2010). Female orgasmic disorder. In S. Levine, C. Risen, & S. Althof (Eds.), *Handbook of clinical sexuality for mental health professionals* (pp. 181–192). New York, NY: Routledge.
Fugl-Meyer, A.R., & Fugl Meyer, K.S. (2006). Prevalence data in Europe. In I. Goldstein, C.M. Meston, S.R. Davis, & A.M. Traish (Eds.), *Women's sexual function and dysfunction: Study, diagnosis and treatment* (pp. 34–41). Abingdon, Oxon, United Kingdom: Taylor & Francis.
Graham, C.A. (2010). The DSM diagnostic criteria for female orgasmic disorder. *Archives of Sexual Behavior, 39,* 256–270.
Graham, C.A. (2014). Orgasm disorders in women. In Y. Binik & K. Hall (Eds.), *Principles and practice of sex therapy* (pp. 89–111). New York, NY: Guilford Press.
Hamilton, L.D., & Julian, A.M. (2014). The relationship between daily hassles and sexual function in men and women. *Journal of Sex & Marital Therapy, 40*(5), 379–395. doi:10.1080/0092623X.2013.864364
Kelly, M.P., Strassberg, D.S., & Turner, C.M. (2004). Communication and associated relationship issues in female anorgasmia. *Journal of Sex & Marital Therapy, 30,* 263–276. doi:10.1080/00926230490422403

King, M., Holt, V., & Nazareth, I. (2007). Women's views of their sexual difficulties: Agreement and disagreement with clinical diagnoses. *Archives of Sexual Behavior*, 36, 281–288.

Kumar Sahoo, M., Biswas, H., Singh, V., & Kumar Padhy, S. (2014). Primary vaginismus and associated phobia: Successful treatment with behavior therapy. *Journal of Postgraduate Medicine, Education and Research*, 48(3), 151–153.

Lahaie, M., Boyer, S., Amsel, R., Khalifé, S., & Binik, Y. (2010). Vaginismus: A review of the literature on the classification/diagnosis, etiology and treatment. *Women's Health*, 6, 705–719. doi:10.2217/whe.10.46

McCabe, M.P. (2015). Female orgasmic disorder. In K. Hertlein, G.R. Weeks, & N. Gambescia (Eds.), *Systemic sex therapy* (2nd ed., pp. 171–190). New York, NY: Routledge.

McCabe, M.P., & Giles, K. (2012). Differences between sexually functional and dysfunctional women in psychological and relationships domain. *International Journal of Sexual Health*, 24, 181–194. doi:10.1080/19317611.2012.680686

Meana, M. (2009). Painful intercourse: Dyspareunia and vaginismus. In K. Hertlein, G.R. Weeks, & N. Gambescia (Eds.), *Systemic sex therapy* (pp. 237–262). New York, NY: Routledge.

Meana, M., Maykut, C., & Fertel, E. (2015). Painful intercourse: Genito-pelvic pain/penetration disorder. In K. Hertlein, G.R. Weeks, & N. Gambescia (Eds.), *Systemic sex therapy* (2nd ed., pp. 191–209). New York, NY: Routledge.

Morokoff, P.J., & Gilliland, R. (1993). Stress, sexual functioning and sexual satisfaction. *Journal of Sex Research*, 30, 43–53.

Oberg, K., Fugl-Meyer, A.R., & Fugl-Meyer, K.S. (2004). On categorization and quantification of women's sexual dysfunctions: An epidemiological approach. *International Journal of Impotence Research*, 16, 261–269.

Ramage, M. (2004). Female sexual dysfunction. *Women's Health Medicine*, 3(2), 84–88.

Reissing, E., Binik, Y., Khalifé, S., Cohen, D., & Amsel, R. (2003). Etiological correlates of vaginismus: Sexual and physical abuse, sexual knowledge, sexual self-schema, and relationship adjustment. *Journal of Sex & Marital Therapy*, 29, 47–59. doi:10.1080/713847095

Reissing, E., Borg, C., Spoelstra, S., ter Kuile, M, Both, S., de Jong, P., van Lankweld, J., Melles, R., Weijenborg, P., & Weijmar Schultz, W. (2014). Throwing the baby out with the bathwater: the *demise* of vaginismus in favor of genito-pelvic pain/penetration disorder. *Archives of Sexual Behavior*, 43, 1209–1213. doi:10.1007/s10508-014-0322-2

Shifren, J.L., Monz, B.U., Russo, P.A., Segreti, A., & Johannes, C.B. (2008). Sexual problems & distress in United States women. *Obstetrics and Gynecology*, 112, 970–978.

Sims, K., & Meana, M. (2010). Why did passion wane? A qualitative study of married women's attributions for declines in sexual desire. *Journal of Sex and Marital Therapy*, 36(4), 360–380.

ter Kuile, M., & Reissing, E. (2014). Lifelong vaginismus. In Y. Binik & K. Hall (Eds.), *Principles and practice of sex therapy* (5th ed.). New York, NY: The Guilford Press.

ter Kuile, M., Bulté, I., Weijenborg, P., Beekman, A., Melles, R., & Onghena, P. (2009). Therapist-aided exposure for women with lifelong vaginismus:

A replicated single-case design. *Journal of Consulting and Clinical Psychology*, 77, 149–159. doi:10.1037/a0014273

van Lankveld, J.J., Granot, M., Weijmar Schultz, W.C., Binik, Y.M., Wesselmann, U., Pukall, C.F., Bohm-Starke, N., Achtrari, C. (2010). Women's sexual pain disorders. *Journal of Sexual Medicine*, 7, 615–631.

Vlaeyen, J., & Linton, S. (2000). Fear-avoidance and its consequences in chronic musculoskeletal pain: A state of the art. *Pain*, 85, 317–332. doi:10.1016/S0304-3959(99)00242-0

Weeks, G.R., Gambescia, N., & Hertlein, K.M. (2016). *A clinician's guide to systemic sex therapy*. New York, NY: Routledge.

Woo, J.S.T., Brotto, L.A., & Gorzalka, B.B. (2011). The role of sex guilt in the relationship between culture and women's sexual desire. *Archives of Sexual Behavior*, 40(2), 385–394.

Woo, J.S.T., Morshedian, N., Brotto, L.A., & Gorzalka, B.B. (2012). Sex guilt mediates the relationship between religiosity and sexual desire in East Asian and Euro-Canadian college-aged women. *Archives of Sexual Behavior*, 41(6), 1485–1495.

Chapter 7

Male Sexual Disorders

Premature (Early) Ejaculation

Premature Ejaculation (PE) is defined by the *DSM-5* (American Psychiatric Association, 2013) as "a persistent or recurrent pattern of ejaculation occurring during partnered sexual activity within approximately one minute following vaginal penetration and before the individual wishes it" (p. 443). The symptom must be present 75%–100% of the time and must cause the individual significant distress for more than six months. The condition must not be better accounted for by another mental disorder, severe relationship distress, other significant life stressors, the impact of medication, or a medical condition. PE can be lifelong or acquired and generalized or situational (p. 443).

PE is the most common male sexual dysfunction worldwide, impacting one third of men (Althof, 2014; Namavar & Robati, 2011). Several factors contribute to PE, such as: excitement, performance anxiety, and sexual inexperience (Weeks, Gambescia, & Hertlein, 2016). Biological causes may include penile sensitivity (Abdel-Hamid, Abdel-Razek, & Anis, 2013), endocrine disorders (Corona *et al.*, 2011), urological problems, including diseases of the prostate (Liang *et al.*, 2010), Type 2 diabetes mellitus (Hidalgo-Tamola & Chitaley, 2009), and cardiovascular disease, especially if the PE is associated with ED (Palmer & Stuckey, 2008). PE can also develop from the chronic use of or withdrawal from substances such as opiates (Chekuri, Gerber, Brodie, & Krishnadas, 2012) and alcohol (Arackal & Benegal, 2007; Betchen, 2009).

There is no specific medication for the treatment of PE, but some physicians recommend the off-label use of SSRIs such as paroxetine (Paxil) (Betchen, 2015; Waldinger, Zwinderman, Schweitzer, & Olivier, 2004). Psychotherapy techniques focus on increasing ejaculatory control and reducing performance anxiety. This is to be achieved by providing psychoeducation to both the male and his partner and utilizing a series of masturbatory and penetrative sex techniques (Althof, 2014; Weeks, Gambescia, & Hertlein, 2016). Perhaps the most popular of these methods remains Kaplan's (1989) adaption of the stop-start technique (Semans, 1956).

Male Sexual Disorders 155

PE can "result" from dyadic distress emanating from poor communication and power and control struggles (Betchen, 2001) or be the "cause" of general relationship difficulty (Althof, 2013). But although PE, along with most other sexual disorders, occurs within the context of a couple, the *DSM-5* seemingly reduces the significance that relationship issues play in the disorder (Hall, 2015). While we believe that each partner brings his or her own master conflict to the relationship, the relational dynamics that ensue will be behind or exacerbate the PE symptom. We therefore find that MCT can be a very effective tool in alleviating the symptom. The following case will be used to demonstrate this process:

Jack and Carolyn: Success vs. Sabotage (Big vs. Small)

Jack and Carolyn (see Figure 7.1) were a married couple in their middle 50s. Jack, a physician, suffered from Lifelong PE. He first experienced it when he lost his virginity to his high school girlfriend and has had difficulty ever since. Jack reported that he could achieve a full erection and enter Carolyn successfully but that he ejaculated within 10 seconds or approximately two to three thrusts. Jack was clearly distraught when he and his wife first presented for treatment. He said that he was very attracted to Carolyn, a brilliant scientist, and that his PE was "ruining his life."

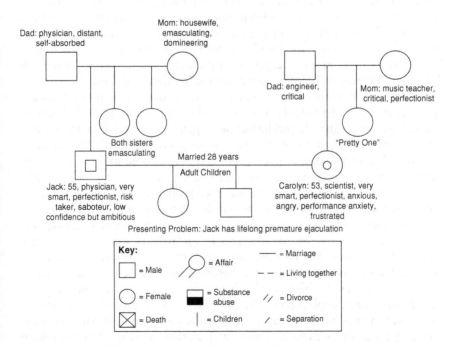

Figure 7.1 Jack and Carolyn.

Unlike many men who avoid challenging their PE out of fear or shame (Betchen, 2015), Jack made numerous attempts to treat his problem, including prior individual therapy. He did, however, reject the idea of taking any medication. Jack and Carolyn decided to seek therapy after Jack's urologist cleared him of any organic issues. Carolyn expressed a moderate amount of anger and frustration because most of her orgasms were experienced through intercourse.

Although the couple's chief complaint was Jack's PE, it was soon revealed that Carolyn was upset about some of Jack's nonsexual behavior as well, which she berated him for. She commented that Jack's private medical practice was floundering, in part because he failed to bill, demand adequate performance from his employees, and see patients in a timely fashion. According to Carolyn, Jack failed to make the kind of money he was capable of earning. She also stated that Jack had participated in some shady business practices that could have jeopardized his license. Jack did not deny any of these accusations. Instead, he showed remorse.

Jack was the oldest brother of two sisters. His father was a physician who practiced general medicine in the town that Jack was raised in. Although his father was well liked, Jack saw him as an average doctor who enjoyed vacations more than his work. Jack had higher aspirations for himself. He worked hard and attended an Ivy League college and medical school. He eventually took over his father's medical practice after his father retired. Despite this connection, Jack was closer to his mother, a housewife, and was considered by her to be exceptionally bright—a budding academic star. Although he believed his father respected and appreciated him enough to allow him to take over his medical practice, Jack claimed that his father worked too much and had too many hobbies to spend any quality time with him.

Jack's sexual history was significant. He reported that he had always thought that he had a "small penis." He said that his sisters would tell him so. Jack also reported that the girl he lost his virginity to in high school was experienced and commented that she also felt his penis was small. The therapist asked Jack if he had a micro-penis. He said that he used to think so, but in fact he was well above average size (i.e., 8 inches). Jack was not only initially wrong about his penis size, but he was a very smart man with a very expensive education. Yet he seemed to fail a little too much for his credentials.

Jack described his mother as domineering and at times emasculating, like his sisters. His father was absent. This compilation of information led the therapist to believe that Jack may have internalized a *success vs. sabotage (big vs. small)* master conflict. Once therapy began to take this route in treatment, he and his wife validated the therapist's suspicion with more sabotaging details. For example, on one occasion Jack and his wife were vacationing in Hawaii, when for little reason, Jack started an argument with the hotel concierge. Carolyn was so distraught at Jack that she refused to speak with him for two days. As usual, Jack would later feel shamed by his behavior and beg Carolyn's forgiveness.

Carolyn came from a demanding, perfectionistic family. While she was a very talented musician and student, her parents could be quite critical, and she never felt good enough. Although she was quite attractive, she admitted that she questioned her looks in part because her parents had told her that her sister was the pretty one and that she was the smart one. Carolyn did not appreciate being thought of as exclusively the smart one, but she did admit that it gave her a certain confidence that her sister did not possess.

Carolyn presented as anxious and performance-oriented. She was a sweet person but somewhat intolerant of failure, as were her parents. From a circular perspective, it was easy to see how Jack and Carolyn made each other big: They both achieved academic and professional success and were clearly proud of one another. It was easy for each to proclaim attraction and love for one another. It was more difficult, however, for both to digest that they were simultaneously rendering themselves and one another small. Carolyn felt that her scolding of Jack was meant to encourage him to end his sabotaging behavior, but it only served to make him feel even smaller and more susceptible to sabotage.

The bulk of the couple's work focused on helping each partner to become more cognizant of the big versus small messages they received from their respective families of origin and to connect them to their interactional dynamic and Jack's PE. For their efforts, Jack organized his office and hired an office manager. He began to set better limits with his existing staff and demand that the billing be mailed in a timely fashion. He was more attuned to his marriage and Carolyn's feelings, and he began to take the treatment of his PE more seriously and consider medication as an option.

With a renewed sense of commitment and energy, Jack went back to his urologist and accepted a prescription for paroxetine (Paxil). The urologist felt that Jack was somewhat depressed and that a selective serotonin reuptake inhibitor (SSRI) drug might simultaneously work off-label to help Jack with his PE (Betchen, 2015; McMahon, 2013). The power of his conflict was evident in that the medication had little positive impact on his PE. He also intermittently ignored the treatment recommendations offered him. The therapist told Jack and Carolyn to limit their foreplay to achieving an adequate erection and to begin intercourse with the quiet vagina (Kaplan, 1989) technique, in which Jack would enter Carolyn but delay thrusting for a couple seconds. The struggle to get Jack to follow suggestions went on for approximately four months, but as he gained control over his conflict, his resistance to success eventually began to dissipate. Jack reported that he was following instructions and he was lasting longer and longer with Carolyn. Eventually, the couple were averaging successful sex twice a week. The couple and therapist discussed trying to stop the medication, but they did not want to risk it. They did, however, at times have satisfactory sex without the quiet vagina method. Horrified that she might be working at cross purposes when attacking Jack, Carolyn became much more empathic and supportive of Jack's gains in all phases of their lives.

The couple claimed that the sex they were having was some of the best since they married over 25 years ago. The following is an example of an intervention used to confront Jack after he admitted that he had sabotaged a sexual encounter with Carolyn:

Carolyn: I pleaded with Jack to follow your instructions, but he was like a man possessed. He extended the foreplay, got hard as a rock, entered me, and started thrusting as quickly as he could. He came within seconds.
Therapist: Really!
Jack: Yeah, I screwed things up. I can't even explain it.
Therapist: Sure you can. Give it a try.
Jack: I guess the conflict got me.
Therapist: Explain.
Jack: We were doing so well, and I guess I had to sabotage us.
Therapist: That would be my guess. Remember, a master conflict will be even more likely to resist when you are attempting to make a choice, and you have decided to choose becoming a success—to be big. You were leaning towards the success side of the conflict, and so there was a drive to move towards the other end, or towards sabotage—smallness. If you sabotage, you accept that you have a small penis and that you are small in general.

Erectile Disorder

Erectile Dysfunction is defined by the *DSM-5* (American Psychiatric Association, 2013) as experiencing one of the three symptoms listed for 75%–100% of the time and for at least six months: (1) a problem in achieving an erection for sex; (2) a problem maintaining an erection for the duration of the sexual activity; and (3) a significant decrease in erectile firmness. The symptoms must be causing significant distress to the individual. And the symptoms are not the result of a nonsexual mental disorder, significant relationship distress, other life stressors, or a substance/medication or medical issue. The condition can be lifelong or acquired and generalized or situational (p. 426).

Approximately 10% of men under the age of 35 and 50% or more of men who are older than 60 suffer from ED. Older men with the disorder seem to be less distressed than younger men with the disorder (Rosen, Miner, & Wincze, 2014). ED can negatively alter a man's self-esteem and self-confidence, leading to an avoidance of sex and partner frustration (Weeks, Gambescia, & Hertlein, 2016). ED impacts men more often as they age (Lewis *et al.*, 2010). The condition is also associated with medical conditions including liver problems and cardiovascular disorders (Shamloul & Ghanem, 2013), diabetes and hypertension (Simopoulos & Trinidad, 2013), and spinal injuries (Awad *et al.*, 2011), among others. Emotional problems such as anxiety and depression (Gambescia & Weeks, 2015) may be culprits. Various medications may also be the cause of ED such as thiazides, beta-blockers, anti-androgens, and SSRIs (Plaut, Graziottin, & Heaton, 2004). Because of the high correlation with other medical conditions, it is important that men experiencing ED be seen by a medical professional to determine the extent of biological factors. It is also important to determine whether the erectile difficulties happen under all situations or only with partnered sex.

In 1997, a treatment breakthrough occurred with the discovery of the PDE5 inhibitor sildenafil citrate (Viagra) (Segraves & Balon, 2003). Other PDE5s followed, such as vardenafil (Levitra) and tadalafil (Cialis). Psychotherapy techniques generally focus on reducing performance anxiety and are often used in conjunction with one's partner. Common techniques include psychoeducation, sensate focus exercises, cognitive-behavioral approaches, and sexual stimulation techniques (Metz & McCarthy, 2004; Rosen, Miner, & Wincze, 2014; Weeks, Gambescia, & Hertlein, 2016). While the *DSM-5* also seems to reduce the significance of relationship distress in ED, several scholars have found a correlation between the two (Althof, 2014; Althof & Rosen, 2010; Betchen, 2005; Gambescia & Weeks, 2015). We propose ED can be the result of an unbalanced master conflict, and we offer the following case as an example:

Gopal and Bernadette: Adequacy vs. Inadequacy

Gopal and Bernadette (see Figure 7.2) were a married couple in their early 40s with two young children. Gopal, an engineer, was a Hindu born in India but educated in the United States. Bernadette, a housewife and part-time private music tutor, was a white American woman. The chief complaint was Gopal's ED. He would achieve an adequate erection with foreplay and lose it within seconds of entering his wife. Gopal claimed that his difficulty began soon after college. He noticed that he would function at the beginning of a relationship but eventually have difficulty. He and Bernadette agreed that ED had been a negative factor for at least the last four years of their 12-year marriage.

Gopal claimed that he tried hard to alleviate his ED. He saw it as shameful and embarrassing. He said that when exercises failed to alleviate the problem, he resorted to more drastic means: PDE5s (Shamloul & Ghanem, 2013), which worked sporadically; vacuum constriction device (Yuan *et al.*, 2010), which he and his wife found "too messy" and not spontaneous enough; and intraurethral medication (Shamloul & Ghanem, 2013), which he said was painful. He refused to get an intracavernosal injection (Belew, Klaassen, & Lewis, 2015) because the concept of sticking a needle in his penis did not sit well. His urologist finally referred him for sex therapy.

160　Case Studies

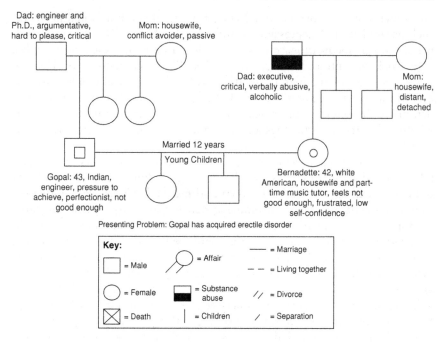

Figure 7.2 Gopal and Bernadette.

Beyond Gopal's ED, it was immediately revealed by the couple's interactional style that they took turns simultaneously praising and picking on one another. Gopal said that he was very physically attracted to Bernadette. He saw her as patient, smart, and a great mother. But he also unmercifully criticized her about a myriad of things, especially about her career and income. Bernadette held a master's degree in music education and tutored private students part-time. Gopal felt a money crunch and wanted her to get a full-time teaching position. He was also critical of her spending habits, but it seemed that Bernadette was relatively frugal.

Bernadette took offense to Gopal's criticisms. While she admitted that he was a good man and a good father, she complained that he was a relentless perfectionist and that neither she nor the children could meet his standards. She also felt that Gopal was undervaluing her role as a housewife and mother. She added that the couple made enough money and that there was no need for her to work more. At times, Bernadette would point to Gopal's sexual deficiencies to even the score with her husband.

Gopal was the oldest of two sisters. He held an M.S. in chemical engineering and worked as an engineer. His genogram assessment revealed that as a youngster, he was under tremendous pressure from his father to achieve professional status. He described his father, a Ph.D.-level engineer, as argumentative and critical. Gopal admitted that his father expressed his admiration of Gopal for coming to the United States on his own and completing a very challenging graduate program. But he was upset when Gopal refused to get his Ph.D. Gopal said his father criticized him frequently and was very difficult to please, but he knew he loved him and was proud of his accomplishments. Gopal reported his mother as a passive, conflict avoider. He said that his father loved his mother and would often say so, but he would also yell at her when he thought she did something wrong. Gopal said his mother kept quiet and took it. Gopal's parents lived in India and valued their cultural traditions, but they encouraged Gopal to seek higher education in the United States. Gopal's parents were not happy with his marrying Bernadette, and they initially made life difficult for the couple. They had hoped that after completing his education, Gopal would return to India and a marriage would be arranged for him. But they also knew that Gopal would have more opportunity if he stayed in the United States.

Bernadette was the oldest of two brothers. She described her father as a critical alcoholic and her mother as distant and detached. She claimed that her father was highly critical of all family members and that they feared him. She said he could be verbally abusive and controlling. He was particularly hard on her about her weight and her seemingly low self-confidence, even though he would not admit that he was a contributing factor in both symptoms. Bernadette was an excellent student, far better than her brothers. Her parents recognized this, and she even heard them brag about her at times to family and friends. Bernadette said that her parents were not happy about her marrying Gopal and only stopped torturing her about this when they became grandparents.

Gopal and Bernadette took turns attacking one another. Neither felt good enough in their own eyes, the eyes of their respective families of origin, or in the eyes of one another. In tune with MCT, it was determined that the couple shared, and continuously reinforced, an *adequacy vs. inadequacy* master conflict. That is, each were both intermittently supportive (i.e., reinforcing adequacy) and critical (i.e., reinforcing inadequacy) of themselves and one another.

The therapist eventually showed Gopal the sophisticated connection between his conflict and his ED: In the beginning of a relationship, his competent sexual functioning lent balance to his *adequacy vs. inadequacy* conflict. But soon, this adequacy was intolerable to both partners, and their need to reduce themselves and one another took precedence. One pathway to reduction in marriage was Gopal's embarrassing erection problems; another was Bernadette's emasculating comments.

When each partner finally saw that they had been using mean and relentless criticisms to feed their conflict and associated sexual symptom, they were then able to stop torturing themselves and one another. But this took time and the horrifying insight that they were treating each other the way they each had been treated in their families of origin and by their fathers. Only then did they begin to develop mutual empathy. To his credit, Gopal tried tadalafil (Cialis) again, only this time with positive results; he was soon able to achieve more consistent erections. Bernadette was more supportive of his ED. She also secured a part-time teaching position and continued to tutor privately. The following is a short exchange depicting how the therapist helped the couple connect Gopal's ED to their master conflict:

Gopal: Why should I have to be the one to earn most of the money? Bernadette is very smart. She likes nice clothes, but she won't work to get them. She can earn a teacher's salary.
Bernadette: We have all the money we need. You are a good provider and father, but you are never satisfied with any of us. Why don't you focus on your own problems? I've been living with your ED for years. I can't go on like this much longer.
Therapist: That sounds threatening. Does Gopal's behavior remind you of anyone?
Bernadette: His father.
Gopal: I'm not my father.
Therapist: Does Bernadette's attitude remind you of anyone, Gopal?
Gopal: She's not like my mother, if that's what you mean.
Therapist: I was thinking that you treat each other the same way your fathers did. They at times praised you both, but neither of you were ever good enough. Similarly, you both are complimentary and critical of one another. It is as if you are supporting adequacy and inadequacy at the same time. Maybe this dynamic can help explain your ED, Gopal. I mean ... your ED came into play in the middle years of your marriage without any known precipitating incident. I wonder if you had too long a period of adequacy. Perhaps you used your ED as a vehicle for some needed inadequacy.
Gopal: If I did that, I didn't mean to.
Therapist: Not consciously.

Delayed Ejaculation

Delayed Ejaculation is conceptualized by the *DSM-5* (American Psychiatric Association, 2013) as the following: (1) significant delay in ejaculation, and (2) pronounced infrequency or absence of ejaculation. The symptoms must have existed for at least six months and cause distress to the individual. The symptoms must be present approximately 75%–100% of the time in partnered sexual activity when the individual does not desire a delay in ejaculation. They also cannot be attributed to another mental disorder, significant relationship distress, other significant stressors, a reaction to medication, or a medical condition. The condition can be lifelong or acquired and either generalized or situational (p. 424).

Delayed ejaculation is the least common and least understood male sexual dysfunction (American Psychiatric Association, 2013; Perelman, 2014; Weeks, Gambescia, & Hertlein, 2016). Prevalence estimates of delayed ejaculation are low: approximately 3% (Laumann, Paik, & Rosen, 1999; Rowland, Keeney, & Slob, 2004). More recently in the *DSM-5*, the disorder was reported to occur in less than 1% of men (American Psychiatric Association, 2013). It is possible that delayed ejaculation has been underreported because it is commonly comorbid with other sexual dysfunctions (Foley & Gambescia, 2015).

Contributing factors to delayed ejaculation include low self-esteem and a negative body image (Metz & McCarthy, 2007), a history of trauma (Lew, 2004), cultural or religious scripts that interfere with adequate sexual functioning, fear of pregnancy, performance anxiety (Wincze & Carey, 2001), and high masturbation frequency or an idiosyncratic masturbation style that does not easily translate to partner sex (Perelman, 2014). Relationship factors may play a role, such as: a conflict about making a commitment (Betchen, 2005), withholding to gain power, predominant focus on a partner's pleasure rather than one's own, inadequate partner stimulation, a lack of attraction to one's partner, and a disparity between a fantasied partner and the real partner (Perelman & Rowland, 2006; Weeks, Gambescia, & Hertlein, 2016). Poor partner communication, such as unexpressed emotions, may also be a factor (Perelman, 2014). Apfelbaum (2000, 2001) believed the disorder could be caused by insufficient levels of arousal during intercourse. He correlated it with low sexual desire in men. Certain medications may contribute to the disorder as well, such as SSRIs, anticholinergics, antiadrenergics, antihypertensives, and antipsychotics (Corona *et al.*, 2011).

A combination of psychotherapeutic treatment techniques often recommended for Delayed Ejaculation are: cognitive behavioral strategies to reduce anxiety; challenge interfering sexual scripts; increase confidence; insight-oriented strategies to promote differentiation; and couple-focused work to promote intimacy and mutuality (Foley & Gambescia, 2015; Weeks, Gambescia, & Hertlein, 2016). Perelman (2009) wrote that most clinicians still rely on masturbation exercises to treat the disorder. By completing these exercises, men can learn to increase their arousal utilizing a combination of physical stimulation and fantasy. In his "Sexual Tipping Point" (STP) model, Perelman (2016) advocates for an integrative approach to treating the disorder (and other sexual disorders), which considers both mental and physical factors. We now offer an example of the MCT approach in treating Delayed Ejaculation.

Joseph and Kerry: Conformity vs. Rebellion

Joseph and Kerry, both 38 years of age (see Figure 7.3), were referred by their fertility doctor because Joseph's delayed ejaculation prevented them from moving forward with fertility treatment. Joseph experienced delayed ejaculation approximately 25% of the time prior to fertility treatment, compared to 100% of the time during the treatment. There were no recent medical or medication changes for Joseph. The therapist referred Joseph to a urologist for an evaluation, which was unremarkable. Upon assessment, the couple was determined to have a *conformity vs. rebellion* master conflict.

Kerry and Joseph dressed extremely professionally and seemed to adhere to the rules at work and in treatment. By their appearance, the word "rebel" would never come to mind. However, each had another side: they did things their way. Joseph was employed as an actuary. He came from a middle-class Irish family. His parents were devout Catholics who proudly sent their three sons to Catholic schools. Joseph's father worked as an engineer; his mother was a housewife. Joseph described his childhood as rigid and overly scheduled with activities. He said his brothers were much taller and stronger than he was; he referred to them as "stereotypical jocks." Both brothers excelled at athletics, earning collegiate scholarships to Division 1 schools. In contrast, Joseph described himself as "cherub-looking." He was short, a bit overweight, and uncoordinated. He believed that his father favored his brothers.

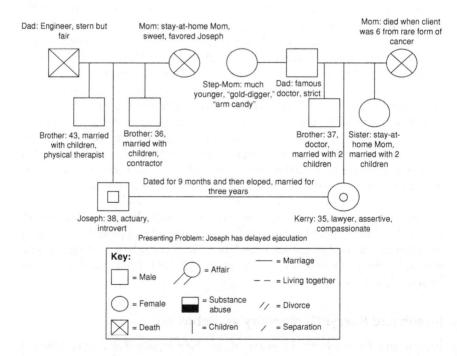

Figure 7.3 Joseph and Kerry.

What Joseph lacked in athletic ability, however, he made up for in intellect. His mother favored him for his brains and often told him he was superior to others, including his brothers. While this was a positive message, it did somewhat hinder Joseph's ability to relate to his peers, and as a result, he had few, if any, friends. Joseph said that he was often bored with his peers and refused to play sports or engage in anything active. He also rebelled against participating in school events. If it was expected of him, Joseph turned away, even to his own detriment. For example, he refused to go to his prom because he said, "that's what everyone else did." Joseph continued to replicate this pattern in college: he excelled in academics but resisted participating in his school's social life. While he did manage to have a couple positive relationships with women, they soon would fall prey to his general resistance and intermittent delayed ejaculation.

Joseph attended graduate school but left after one semester. True to form, he quit one semester shy of graduating because he felt that everyone expected him to complete his degree. Nonetheless, Joseph failed to mention this detail on his resume; he also kept it a secret from his mother, who often bragged to her friends about his academic accomplishments. And there is more rebellion: at his actuarial firm, Joseph upset his boss by refusing to take the required exams. He claimed that he did not need them to do his job effectively. Despite being very capable at his work, Joseph was often on the verge of getting fired because of his rebellious behavior. He had previously lost one job for failing to follow procedure, which he described as "stupid."

Joseph suffered from a medical disorder that required him to follow a specific diet. He would tell his doctor that he was adhering to her recommendations but continued to eat foods that were on the "strictly banned" list. When his wife would catch him breaking his dietary restrictions, she would become irate. If she asked him to do a household chore in a specific way, he insisted on doing it his own way even if it was less efficient.

Like Joseph, upon appearance, Kerry would hardly pass as a rebel. She was extremely poised, always well-dressed, and very conscious of manners. Kerry's mother died from a rare form of cancer when Kerry was 6 years old. She reported having few memories of her mother but was told she was "kind, sweet, and giving." Kerry's father, a prominent physician, remarried a woman 10 years his junior when Kerry was 10 years old. Kerry did not agree with her father's choice of mate; she "despised" this woman, whom she referred to as a "gold digger." Kerry explained that after marrying her father, her stepmother stopped working as a nurse and chose to play tennis and lounge around the house. Kerry's stepmother demonstrated little interest in motherhood, often leaving that job to hired help.

Kerry attended elite private schools and excelled academically. However, her social life suffered because she felt as if she did not fit in. Like

Joseph, Kerry refused to attend her prom, believing at the time that she "didn't need the experience." Later, she admitted that there was no point in going because she could not share the experience with her mother.

Kerry rejected many boys during her high school years. She gave the excuse that she was not interested in the "drama" of a relationship. She eventually excelled in college, but before attending, she took a took a year off to volunteer in a third world country; she said this gap in study "horrified" her father. Following college, Kerry took a "low-paying, non-profit job," refusing her father's financial help. She also rejected her father's financial assistance towards her law degree and opted for a lower tier school that offered her a scholarship. Unlike her adult siblings who continued to accept money from their father, Kerry wanted to make it on her own. But she admitted that there was also a little bit of an "f-ck you" to her dad. Kerry was labeled the "black sheep" and "rebel" of her proper family. Both Joseph and Kerry's families were disappointed in their union. Joseph's family preferred him to be with a "nice Catholic girl," and Kerry's family did not believe Joseph was of a high enough socioeconomic class. In addition, both families disapproved of the couple's elopement after nine months of dating. Most likely another act of rebellion.

Initially Kerry and Joseph had agreed not to have children, but the couple admitted in treatment that this decision was in part a rebellion against family pressure. Kerry, however, developed a change of heart. After a year of trying unsuccessfully to conceive, the couple sought out fertility treatment and discovered that Kerry would need hormones to become pregnant. To complicate matters, while Joseph conformed to having a child, he simultaneously rebelled by avoiding sex; he also noticed an increase in his delayed ejaculation. It was during this struggle to conceive that the couple finally began to see the true power and pervasiveness of their *conformity vs. rebellion* master conflict.

With treatment, Joseph and Kerry came to accept how their respective families of origin helped to create their *conformity vs. rebellion* master conflict and the impact it has had on their lives, especially their sexual problem. In addition, Joseph owned feeling conflicted about having a child. Part of him believed that he would enjoy being a father, but the other part was unsure of whether he desired the parental lifestyle. As Joseph struggled with this issue, Kerry applied for a master's degree program without consulting him. When Joseph discovered that she had signed up for her first class, he was hurt. To her credit, Kerry eventually admitted that her behavior was a rebellious act against Joseph but was most likely linked to her anger at her father and stepmother.

Rather than continue to sabotage the fertility treatment, Joseph concluded that he did not want a child. While Kerry was not surprised to hear this, she was devastated. She needed months to grieve Joseph's choice before proposing a compromise. Joseph was to support her through graduate school and a career change. The couple were also to purchase a home abroad (in a third world country). Joseph agreed and kept his word. The couple soon began to have sex on a regular basis, and Joseph achieved orgasm and ejaculated inside his wife. Consider this brief vignette challenging Joseph's defenses:

Kerry: I am really upset, because I feel like Joseph just isn't trying.
Joseph: I am! I wish I could ejaculate on command, but I just can't.
Kerry: It was never such a big problem before! But now that I've been asking for it, you can't do it at all.
Joseph: I don't understand why we can't go back to just trying the natural approach.
Therapist: Kerry, tell me what you meant by: "now that I've asked you for it, you can't."
Kerry: If someone tells Joseph to do something, he purposefully won't.
Joseph: It's just that the doctors don't know everything. Sometimes couples become pregnant after they have been told that they can't get pregnant.
Kerry: Joseph, I have a small window of time to get pregnant. But if you won't ejaculate inside of me during this time or at least come near me in a condom or something so that the sperm can be inserted, we will not get pregnant.
Therapist: Joseph, is that your understanding of the process? Do you realize that Kerry cannot get pregnant otherwise?
Joseph: That is what the doctor said. I just do not think I can reach orgasm this way.
Therapist: What way?
Joseph: All that pressure; it feels like a command.
Kerry: Okay, but there is no other way for me to get pregnant.
Therapist: Is it all about pressure?
Joseph: What do you mean?
Therapist: Well, didn't you recently get passed over for a promotion because you failed to adhere to the guidelines of your current position? Did you refuse to follow protocol because you felt pressure to do so?
Joseph: I think so.
Therapist: Well, I understand you were upset with all the "rules" of living when you were a kid, some of which you were good at, like academics, and others not so much, like sports and socializing. I'm just wondering if there is a part of you that wants to follow the rules and please others. For example, if you go to school and excel academically, you are conforming and validating your mother's positive perception of you. But there is another side—perhaps an angry side—that says, "fuck them all and the horses

	they rode in on." People like your father, brothers, some teachers, bosses, and others.
Joseph:	I'm not so sure I agree with that theory.
Therapist:	Of course you don't; that would be consistent. You conform by coming to therapy but usually disagree with the therapist.
Joseph:	Even if you're right, what does that have to do with getting pregnant?
Therapist:	Well, there does seem to be a pattern of resistance when you feel you are expected to do something. In fact, from the time you were a child, it seems that you conformed, but only to a certain extent. You did the same in college: you conformed by attending classes and doing well academically, but little else. And even with that, you quit graduate school so close to finishing. You agreed to participate in fertility treatment, but your heart isn't in it.
Joseph:	That might be true.

Summary

The purpose of this chapter was to describe in some detail how we conceive of master conflicts and their association with some of the major male sexual disorders. Time and space would not allow for the coverage of all such disorders, but some of the most common of these were addressed: Premature (Early) Ejaculation (PE), Erectile Disorder (ED), and Delayed Ejaculation. Although we utilized the *DSM-5* as a framework for defining male sexual symptoms, we have acknowledged our disappointment that this coveted reference has all but removed relationships as a primary causal factor in their attempts to define and classify such disorders. Nevertheless, we hold fast to our belief that underlying conflicts, particularly those in the context of a relationship, can be the primary cause of sexual disorders.

References

Abdel-Hamid, I.A., Abdel-Razek, M.M., & Anis, T. (2013). Risk factors in premature ejaculation: The neurological risk factor and the local hypersensitivity. In E. Jannini, C. McMahon, & M. Waldinger (Eds.), *Premature ejaculation: From etiology to diagnosis and treatment* (pp. 167–185). Italy: Spring-Verlag.

American Psychiatric Association (2013). *Diagnostic and statistical manual of mental disorders* (5th ed.). Arlington, VA; Author.

Apfelbaum, B. (2000). Retarded ejaculation: A much misunderstood syndrome. In S. Leiblum & R. Rosen (Eds.), *Principles and practice of sex therapy* (3rd ed., pp. 205–241). New York, NY: Guilford.

Apfelbaum, B. (2001). What the sex therapies tell us about sex. I.P. Kleinplatz (Ed.), *New directions in sex therapy: Innovations and alternatives*. (pp. 5–28). New York, NY: Brunner-Routledge.

Althof, S. (2013). Risk factors in premature ejaculation: The relational risk factor. In E. Jannini, McMahon, & M. Waldinger (Eds.), *Premature ejaculation: From etiology to diagnosis and treatment* (pp. 133–139). Italy: Springer-Verlag.

Althof, S. (2014). Treatment of premature ejaculation: Psychotherapy, pharmacotherapy and combined therapy. In Y. Binik & K. Hall (Eds.), *Principles and practice of sex therapy* (5th ed., pp. 112–137). New York, NY: Guilford.

Althof, S., & Rosen, R. (2010). Combining medical and psychological interventions for the treatment of erectile dysfunctions. In S. Levine, C. Risen, & S, Althof (Eds.), *Handbook of clinical sexuality for mental health professionals* (2nd ed., pp. 251–266). New York, NY: Routledge.

Arackal, B.S., & Benegal, V. (2007). Prevalence of sexual dysfunction in male subjects with alcohol dependence. *Indian Journal of Psychiatry*, 49, 109–112. doi:10.4103/0019-5545.33257

Awad, A., Alsaid, B., Bessede, T., Droupy, S., & Benoit, G. (2011). Evolution in the concept of erection anatomy. *Surgical & Radiologic Anatomy*, 33, 301–312. doi:10. 1007/s00276-010-0707-4

Belew, D., Klaassen, Z., & Lewis, R. (2015). Intracavernosal injection for the diagnosis, evaluation, and treatment of erectile dysfunction: A review. *Sexual Medicine Review*, 3(1), 11–23. doi:10.1002/smrj.35

Betchen, S. (2001). Premature ejaculation as symptomatic of age difference in a husband and wife with underlying power and control conflicts. *Journal of Sex Education and Therapy*, 26, 34–44.

Betchen, S. (2005). *Intrusive partners – elusive mates: The pursuer-distancer dynamic in couples therapy*. New York, NY: Routledge.

Betchen, S. (2009). Premature ejaculation: An integrative, intersystem approach for couples. In K. Hertlein, G.R. Weeks, & N. Gambescia (Eds.), *Systemic sex therapy* (pp. 131–152). New York, NY: Routledge.

Betchen, S. (2015). Premature ejaculation: An integrative, intersystems approach for couples. In K. Hertlein, G.R. Weeks, & N. Gambescia (Eds.), *Systemic sex therapy* (2nd ed., pp. 90–106). New York, NY: Routledge.

Chekuri, V., Gerber, D., Brodie, A., & Krishnadas, R. (2012). Premature ejaculation and other sexual dysfunctions in opiate dependent men receiving methadone substitution. *Addictive Behaviors*, 37, 124–126. doi:10.1016/j.addbeh.2011.08. Epub2011Aug.25

Corona, G., Jannini, E., Lotti, F., Boddi, V., De Vita, G., Forti, G., Lenzi, A., Mannucci, E., & Maggi, M. (2011). Premature and delayed ejaculation: Two ends of a single continuum influenced by hormonal milieu. *International Journal of Andrology*, 34, 41–48.

Foley, S., & Gambescia, N. (2015). The complex etiology of delayed ejaculation: Assessment and treatment implications. In K. Hertlein, G. R. Weeks, & N. Gambescia (Eds.), *Systemic sex therapy* (2nd ed., pp. 107–124). New York, NY: Routledge.

Gambescia, N., & Weeks, G. (2015). Systemic treatment of erectile disorder. In K. Hertlein, G. R. Weeks, & N. Gambescia (Eds.), *Systemic sex therapy* (2nd ed., pp. 72–89). New York, NY: Routledge.

Hall, K. (2015). Male hypoactive sexual desire disorder. In K. Hertlein, G.R. Weeks, & N. Gambescia (Eds.), *Systemic sex therapy* (2nd ed., pp. 55–71). New York, NY: Routledge.

Hidalgo-Tamola, J. & Chitaley, K., (2009). Type 2 diabetes mellitus and erectile dysfunction. *Journal of Sexual Medicine*, 6, 916–926. doi:10.1111/j,1743. 6109.2008.01116.x

Kaplan, H.S. (1989). *PE: How to overcome premature ejaculation*. New York, NY: Brunner/Mazel.

Laumann, E., Paik, A., & Rosen, R. (1999). Sexual dysfunctions in the United States: Prevalence and predictors. *Journal of the American Medical Association*, 281(6), 537–544.

Lew, M. (2004). *Victims no longer: The classic guide for men recovering from sexual child abuse*. New York, NY: Quill.

Lewis, R.W., Fugl-Meyer, K.S., Corona, G., Hayes, R.D., Laumann, E.O., Moreira. Jr., E.D., Rellini, A.H., & Segraves, T. (2010). Definitions/epidemiology/risk factors for sexual dysfunction. *Journal of Sexual Medicine*, 7(4pt2), 1598–1607.

Liang, C.Z., Hao, Z.Y., Li, H.J., Wang, Z.P., Xing, J.P., Hu, W.L., Zhang, X.S., Zhou, J., Li, Y., Zhou, Z.X., Tang, Z.G., & Tai, S. (2010). Prevalence of premature ejaculation and its correlation with chronic prostatitis in Chinese men. *Urology*, 76, 962–966. doi:10.1016/j.urology.2010.01.061

McMahon, C. (2013). Taxonomy of ejaculatory disorders and definitions of premature ejaculation. In E. Jannini, C. McMahon, & M. Waldinger (Eds.), *Premature ejaculation: From etiology to diagnosis and treatment* (pp. 53–69). Italy: Springer-Verlag.

Metz M., & McCarthy, B. (2004). *Coping with erectile dysfunction: How to regain confidence and enjoy great sex*. Oakland, CA: New Harbinger Press.

Metz, M., & McCarthy, B. (2007). Ejaculatory problems. In L. Vandecreek, F.L. Peterson, & J.W. Bley (Eds.), *Innovations in clinical practice: Focus on sexual health* (pp. 135–155). Sarasota, FL: Professional Resource Press.

Namavar, M.R., & Robati, R. (2011). Removal of foreskin in remnants in circumcised adults for treatment of premature ejaculation. *Urology Annals*, 3, 87–92. doi:10.4103/0974-7796.82175

Palmer, N., & Stuckey, B.G.A. (2008). Premature ejaculation: A clinical update. *Medical Journal of Australia*, 188(11), 662–666.

Perelman, M. (2009, February). Understanding and treating retarded ejaculation: A sex therapist's perspective. *International Society for Sexual Medicine* (ISSM). Retrieved from www.http:issm.info/news/review-reports-understanding-and-treating-retarded-ejaculation

Perelman, M. (2014). Delayed ejaculation. In Y. Binik, & K. Hall (Eds.), *Principles and practice of sex therapy* (pp. 138–155). New York, NY: Guilford Press.

Perelman, M. (2016). Why the sexual tipping point model? *Current Sexual Health Reports*, 7, 1–8. doi:10.1007/s11930-016-0066-1

Perelman, M., & Rowland, D. (2006). Retarded ejaculation. *World Journal of Urology*, 24(6), 645–652.

Plaut, M., Graziottin, A., & Heaton, J. (2004). *Fast facts: Sexual dysfunction*. Oxford, England: HealthPress.

Rosen, R.C., Miner, M.M., & Wincze, J.P. (2014). Erectile dysfunction: Integration of medical and psychological approaches. In Y. Binik & K. Hall (Eds.), *Principles and practice of sex therapy* (5th ed., pp. 61–85). New York, NY: The Guilford Press.

Rowland, D., Keeney, C., & Slob, A. (2004). Sexual response in men with inhibited or retarded ejaculation. *International Journal of Impotence Research*, 16(3), 270–274.
Segraves, R.T., & Balon, R. (2003). *Sexual pharmacology: Fast facts*. New York, NY: Norton.
Semans, J. (1956). Premature ejaculation: A new approach. *Southern Medical Journal*, 49, 353–358.
Shamloul, R., & Ghanem, H. (2013). Erectile dysfunction. *The Lancet*, 381(9861), 153–165.
Simopoulos, E.F., & Trinidad, A.C. (2013). Male erectile dysfunction: Integrating psychopharmacology and psychotherapy, *General Hospital Psychiatry*, 35(1), 33–38. doi:10.1016/j.genhopspsych.2012.08.008
Waldinger, M.D., Zwinderman, A.H., Schweitzer. D.H., & Olivier, B. (2004). Relevance of methodological design for the interpretation of efficacy of drug treatment of premature ejaculation: A systemic review and meta-analysis. *International Journal of Impotence Research*, 16, 369–381. doi:10.1038/sj.ijir.3901172
Weeks, G. R., Gambescia, N., & Hertlein, K. (2016). *A clinician's guide to systemic sex therapy* (2nd ed.). New York, NY: Routledge.
Wincze, J.P., & Carey, M.P. (2001). *Sexual dysfunction: A guide for assessment and treatment* (2nd ed.). New York, NY: Guilford.
Yuan, J., Hoang, A.N., Romero, C.A., Lin, H., Dai, Y., & Wang, R. (2010). Vacuum therapy in erectile dysfunction—science and clinical evidence. *International Journal of Impotence*, 22, 211–219. doi:10.1038/ijir.2010.4

Chapter 8

Selected Sexual Issues

Open Marriage (Swingers)

An alternative to traditional monogamy is "open marriage" (O'Neill & O'Neill, 1973). In this relationship lifestyle, couples agree that each partner may engage in a relationship outside the marriage—sexual or otherwise—without being considered unfaithful. Incidence rates for open marriage in the United States have been found to range from 1.7% to 9% (Blumstein & Schwartz, 1983; Haag, 2012; Spanier & Cole, 1975; Veaux & Rickert, 2014). But these figures do not accurately reflect the nuances of the open relationship. For example, polyamory and swinging are two styles of open relationships, but there are significant differences between the two. Swingers are very community-oriented and look to increase their sexual and social contacts while avoiding emotional attachment. Taormino (2008) wrote about swingers: "Swinging is about the context in which they practice their nonmonogamy, the way they socialize, and their community. It's about, as many refer to it, the *lifestyle*" (p. 61). In contrast, the polyamorous look to develop deep mutual friendships. While sex is usually included in polyamory, it is not the primary motivator for seeking another relationship (Zell, 1990).

Herbenek (2010) of the Kinsey Institute contended that swinging is a relatively uncommon practice in the United States. And because there are so few studies, it is hard to determine with any accuracy how many swingers exist. That and because few people want to admit to doing it. Some research, however, estimates that as of 2011, there were approximately 15 million American swingers practicing on a regular basis (Kerner, 2011). We certainly can attest to the fact that we are seeing more swinging couples in our practices in recent years.

Fernandes (2012) has studied swingers for many years and found that they averaged between the ages of 36 and 55, were married for at least 11–20 years, were equally distributed across all political parties, and were represented in all socioeconomic classes. The author also found that approximately 20% of swingers were bisexual, and although partner swapping and group sex were common activities, the most reported activity was man-woman-man threesomes.

Taormino (2008) conducted in-depth interviews with over a hundred male and female swingers. The author found that most male swingers identified as heterosexuals and most women as heterosexual, bi-curious, or bisexual. And while women were sanctioned to have sex with other women, male-male sex was usually not encouraged. Taormino also discovered that very few gay, lesbian, queer, or transgendered individuals identified as swingers.

Bergstrand and Blevins Williams (2000) conducted a study of 1,100 swingers in 1999 and 2000. The authors found that 89.4% of swingers were married or in a committed relationship. The majority were highly educated, predominantly white, and more likely to maintain religious affiliations than the general population. Of those interviewed, 78.5% were found to be happier in their marriages compared to 64% of married couples in the general population.

There are many potential venues for swingers to practice their lifestyle: private homes, hotels, private clubs, or via vacation destinations, such as cruises to exotic locations (Herbenick, 2010). Open relationships merit clear and strong boundaries (Easton & Hardy, 2009) and their own rules of etiquette (Taormino, 2008). Some swingers limit the number of sexual encounters to avoid emotional bonds from forming (Betchen, 2013); other swinging couples will only swing together; and still others split off and have sex on their own (Herbenick, 2010). Taormino (2008) reported that most swingers tend to practice "partnered nonmonogamy" (p. 61) with the objective to keep the "physical, emotional and psychological investment in other people low" (p. 56).

Bergstrand and Blevins Sinski (2009) contended that nonmonogamy may be a healthier and more practical approach to modern relationships. Nevertheless, when a swinging couple presents for treatment, it is usually for any one or more of the following reasons: (1) to improve relationship issues that have little to do with the couple's swinging; (2) to address more common relationship issues that have adversely impacted the couple's swinging; (3) to renegotiate the sexual boundaries; or (4) when one partner is struggling with the "lifestyle" (Betchen, 2013).

Madison and Carl: Conformity vs. Rebellion

Madison, 34, and Carl, 37 (see Figure 8.1), were a married couple with two children. Carl was a sculptor and Madison a school teacher. The couple presented for therapy because Madison had become emotionally involved with a man that she was swinging with and was threatening to end her marriage. Carl reported that the couple had been swinging for several years and never had any problems before. While most of their swinging was with couples

174 Case Studies

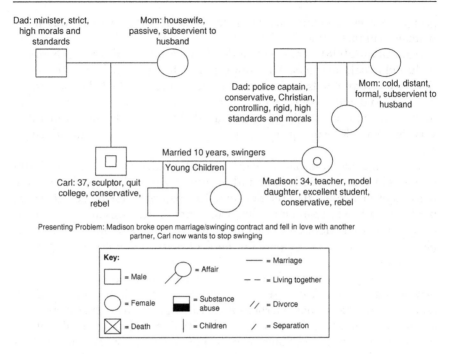

Figure 8.1 Carl and Madison.

that they had befriended over the years, they sometimes split up and chose partners on their own. This was one of those times.

Carl said that he felt betrayed by Madison. He also said that he wanted to save his marriage, but he did not think he could continue with it unless Madison reconciled her emotions for her lover, promised never to see him again, and agreed to stop swinging. Carl said he was still in love with Madison and did not want to take any more risks with his marriage. Several times he broke into a moral argument about saving his family. He specifically lectured Madison about the ills of developing emotions for her lover and putting their marriage and children at risk.

Madison resented what she called Carl's sermons. She said that he reminded her of her father. She also said that she was sick of Carl's need to control every aspect of their lives. She added that every decision she made had to be run by Carl, and that he insisted on veto power. While Madison said that Carl was most controlling in nonsexual areas (e.g., finances), he also insisted on sanctioning the individuals and couples they were to swing with. While Madison claimed that she stopped seeing her lover for the sake of the therapy, she would end her marriage if Carl did not allow her more freedom, especially in the nonsexual areas of their lives. Carl denied that he was as controlling as Madison contended.

Madison's family of origin assessment revealed that she grew up in a very conservative home. Her father was a police captain with high expectations and strict rules of conduct. Her mother was described as cold, distant, and formal. She apparently allowed her husband complete control but agreed with his values. Madison was an excellent student and engaged in several activities in high school. She said her parents saw her as a model daughter. But all was not as it appeared to be. Madison admitted to having sex, drinking, and taking drugs whenever she went out with her friends. She proudly claimed that she lost her virginity at 16 years old. Madison continued onto college and once again excelled academically. But she also continued her partying behavior to excess. Graduating with dual degrees in education and mathematics, Madison quickly obtained a job as a math teacher in a local elementary school.

Carl's father was a minister and his mother a "passive" housewife. Carl reported that his dad was "strict," and that although he agreed with his politics, he could not wait to escape his father's rule. Rather than please his parents and compete college, Carl left school his sophomore year and joined an art colony.

The couple were introduced by Carl's cousins. Carl and his cousins encouraged Madison to try swinging, and Madison liked it. Carl and Madison soon agreed to specific rules of conduct: (1) They would be completely open and honest about who they were sleeping with when they were not swinging together; (2) No sex with close friends; (3) No sex with anyone the other disapproved of; (4) No sex with anyone with a known sexually transmitted disease (STD); (5) No sex without protection; (6) No sex with someone more than a maximum of four times; and (7) No emotional involvement. When the couple started out, they were not polyamorous—they claimed to only be interested in experiencing a greater variety of sex.

The first thing the therapist noticed were the incongruences between each partner's physical presentation and their attitudes and behaviors. This was one of those "head scratching" moments that can help lead a clinician to a couple's master conflict. For example, Madison presented as conservative and referred to herself as a "soccer mom." She drove a minivan and wore large, goggle-like glasses and an oversized pink sweat suit. She did not appear flirtatious or sexually provocative. But when the therapist looked hard behind the glasses, there seemed to be lurking a beauty and sensuality that Madison was trying to hide. Carl was no less a mystery than his wife. He presented with long silver hair, a brown beard, and a few well-placed piercings and tattoos. But it was not long before he began complaining to the therapist about liberals, the lack of discipline in the United States, and the laziness of children in society. He was perhaps one of the most conservative individuals the therapist had ever met.

There was no doubt that Madison was an emotionally strong woman. She made it clear that if Carl tried to control her any more, she was going to leave him. Carl's first attempt to regain control of Madison was to threaten her financially. When this failed, he warned her that she was going to destroy their lives and the lives of their children. Soon he resorted to attacking her lover. Because nothing seemed to shake Madison from her stance, Carl finally gave in and told her that he would allow her to do anything she wanted if she would stop swinging and never see her lover again. Madison warned Carl that it might be too late for a change. She admitted that although she might be in love with this other man, she would nevertheless give the therapy a chance.

Over the course of two months, Madison agreed that Carl was less controlling. But she also admitted that she missed her lover. The therapist determined that each partner showed signs of a *conformity vs. rebellion* conflict dating back to their youth. Madison was the perfect student but acted out when she could. She now portrayed herself as a conservative housewife but in fact was a long-time swinger. Carl clearly had conservative values and presented as a hippie. The couple found this interesting, but by itself it did little to change their situation. The therapist then proceeded to link the conflict to their current symptom by showing the couple that their conflict was bound to become unbalanced because of a strong need to eventually rebel in some way. Carl did in fact enforce the rules more strictly than Madison preferred, and she did her best to rebel behind Carl's back, just as she did with her parents. Carl was unbalancing the couple's conflict with his need for control and Madison was as well by breaking the couple's agreed upon rules of swinging and pushing the couple to a crisis. Once the couple's shared conflict was explained to them, they began to broaden their process and search for other areas in which they conformed and rebelled. For example, Carl said that he had seminary training. As therapy endured, the couple admitted to numerous contrary acts in almost every phase of their lives as individuals and as a couple.

Despite the knowledge the couple gained about their master conflict, Madison rebelled against the therapy and decided that she was going back to her lover and ending the marriage. It did occur to the therapist that she may have never stopped the affair but used it to rebel against the treatment behind the therapist's back. Perceiving that he had little chance to save his marriage, Carl became angry and said that he was moving on. But not before he preached about the ills of Madison's ways and how terrible it was to destroy a family. The therapist gently pointed out that these were interesting words coming from a man who sanctioned his wife to have sex with others.

The following is an example of the therapist challenging the couple on their paradoxical behavior and linking it to their respective families of origin and, in turn, their sexual symptom. Notice that although a correlation was drawn between the couple's swinging and rebelling behaviors, the therapist refrained from judging the couple on either. In MCT, most often when two partners agree upon how to conduct themselves in their relationship, the therapist's job may well be over. There is no room in the MCT approach for moralizing or inflicting the therapist's personal values on the couple. The pros and cons of the couple's decision can and should be discussed, but without prejudice.

Therapist: It is most interesting to me just how similar you two are. Do you know what I mean?
Carl: You mean because we both swing.
Therapist: Well, that too. But I was thinking how you both present somewhat contrary to the way you are.
Madison: I get that. I look like a soccer mom in the day but am a bit wild at other times.
Therapist: Yes. And Carl looks like a bohemian but with very conservative values.
Carl: Yeah. I look like me and sound like my father.
Therapist: Yes. It's as if each of you are two people, just as you were in your families of origin: Madison, you were a star student on the outside, but you were a bit of a rebel, unbeknownst to your parents. Carl, you were more open with your rebelling by quitting school, but a conservative rule follower in other ways.
Carl: I quit college well before I told my parents. They thought I was still going for at least a year before I confessed.
Therapist: You make my point even stronger. I suspect you each demonstrated the same conflict: a *conformity vs. rebellion* conflict. That is, each of you has a need to conform to rules and a need to rebel against them. Having come from two strict backgrounds, it makes perfect sense that each of you would want to please your parents and yet resist their control.
Carl: I can see that. My dad was very strict.
Therapist: That was your experience. I am not passing judgment, but although you both look and sound quite conservative, you practice a form of relationship that is not that common in our society. Perhaps that too is a form of rebellion.
Carl: I can accept that.
Therapist: As long as the two of you agreed upon the rules of the game, you were fine. But Madison rebelled against your control and the rules of swinging. As a result, your shared conflict became unbalanced. I am not blaming you, Madison. It is what it is. The conflict that drew you together is now driving you apart.
Madison: I just do not think Carl can continue to give up control.
Therapist: I understand. But with this intractable stance, you might be rebelling now ... against the treatment?
Madison: Maybe, but I'll use what I learned in my next relationship. It does make some sense.

Carl: I get it, and I am not going to beg her to stay. Fine, rebel, Madison, but get a good lawyer to help you.
Therapist: I have a sinking feeling that the two of you are going to spend a lot of money on your new revolution.

Online Infidelity

According to the *AAMFT* (American Association for Marriage and Family Therapy, 2017), over half of the households in the United States have Internet service, and approximately 20–30% of Internet users go online for sexual purposes. Most of these users are male, 35 years of age, well-educated, and married. As many as 17% become addicted to these activities. Even if the user does not become addicted to online sexual activities, relationship problems may ensue if the usage is likened to an affair or offline infidelity (Whitty, 2005). Studies have suggested that online infidelity can evoke similar emotions to those of offline infidelity, such as anger, guilt, insecurity, pain, shame, and rejection (Hertlein & Blumer, 2014; Smith, 2011).

All experts do not agree on the definition of online infidelity (Nelson, 2000). Cooper and Griffin-Shelly (2002) defined it as an activity that "involves sexuality for purposes of recreation, entertainment, exploration, support, education, commerce, efforts to attain or secure sexual or romantic partners, and so on" (p. 3). Mao and Raguram (2009) recognized it as a "process whereby individuals already involved in a committed relationship seek to be involved in computer synchronous, interactive contacts with members of the opposite sex. A cyber affair can either be a continuous relationship specific to one online user or a series of random erotic chat room encounters with multiple online users" (p. 302). Hertlein and Webster (2008) regarded online infidelity as a perceived boundary violation or breach of relationship contract that merits a common definition agreed upon by both partners.

The use of technology "can enhance existing relationships or facilitate the development of new relationships, including illicit ones" (Cravens & Whiting, 2014, p. 4). In their book, *The Couple and Family Technology Framework: Intimate Relationships in a Digital Age*, Hertlein and Blumer (2014) addressed just how diffuse sexual boundaries have become with the addition of greater technology/social media. The upside for relationships is that partners can connect easily and often. More than ever, people can stay in constant contact via texting and email, among other means. The downside is that it is also easier to connect with those outside the primary relationship, such as ex-lovers, ex-spouses, and others from all over the world. In this sense, technology can provide "both a closeness function to the outsider and a distancing or separating function from the partner" (Hertlein & Blumer, 2014, p. 108). It is not unusual for a spouse who once had a crush on a high school classmate, for example, to finally get the chance to make an old fantasy come true. Rubin, 63, mentioned that he was leaving his wife of

30 years because the woman that his parents made him break up with when they were both 19 years old was now available. How did Rubin know this? The woman contacted him through Facebook. Rubin said that he was not necessarily unhappy with his wife. He simply could not pass up a chance to fulfill his fantasy. While there were other factors involved in this case, the point is that social media made it easier for Rubin to seriously engage his fantasy.

According to Cravens and Whiting (2014), despite the increase in Facebook relationship problems, most of the studies conducted in the field have focused on the Internet. The authors did their part, however, by comparing Internet activities and Facebook-specific behaviors. The results suggested that there were several similarities, such as: difficulty in defining infidelity; viewing online behaviors as infidelity; similar impact on the offline relationship; and disagreement about rules regarding specific behaviors. Perhaps most interestingly, Facebook was found to be more threatening to a relationship than the Internet in general, given the increased probability of an affair occurring online and offline.

Muise, Christofides, and Desmarais (2009) conducted a study on partner jealousy and gender difference in Facebook users. The results found 74% of the participants in their study were likely to add previous romantic or sexual partners as friends; 78% reported that their partner had friended previous romantic or sexual partners; and 92% of the study's participants reported that their partner was somewhat likely to add friends who they did not know. Last, women were found to score higher than men on Facebook jealousy.

The following case is not one of sexual addiction but rather one that we feel is reflective of the kind of case that we see most often. That is, one partner uses technology (e.g., the Internet or Facebook) to initiate and maintain sexual contact. The relationship might remain exclusively online. In this case, sexting and the exchanging of provocative emails may serve as vehicles to maintain the connection. The online relationship, however, may escalate to a more threatening physical or offline relationship.

Jared and Samantha: Security vs. Risk

Jared and Samantha (see Figure 8.2) are a couple in their middle 40s. Jared was an actuary and Samantha a paralegal. The couple had twin boys and had been married for 15 years. Jared presented as distraught. Proficient in computers, he had discovered that Samantha had been talking to various men in chatrooms and the material was sexual in nature. After being confronted, Samantha admitted that she was on the Internet because she was bored with the marriage. She complained that while Jared was a nice guy and a good provider, he was too cautious and lacked a sense of adventure. She said that he never initiated sex and would always veto any of her suggestions

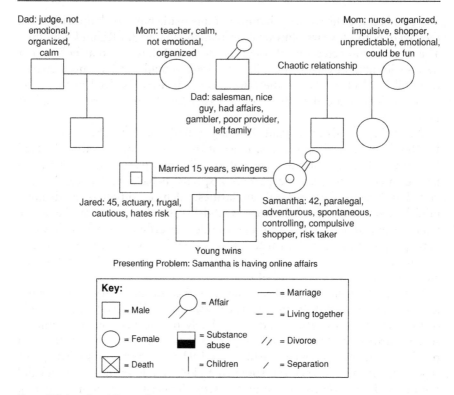

Figure 8.2 Jared and Samantha.

to have fun. Perhaps most damning was her accusation that Jared was cheap and put most of their earnings in retirement plans. Samantha said that she had always wanted to visit the seven continents before she died, but because of Jared, she would only see North America—the one she was living in. She added that she could not spend the rest of her life with Jared if he continued to force her to live his way. Samantha claimed that she was attracted to Jared's practical nature—that it gave her a sense of safety and security. But she never envisioned that he would be so controlling.

Despite feeling betrayed, Jared wanted to save his marriage. It was his idea to attend therapy over what he considered to be infidelity on Samantha's part. Jared admitted that he was frugal, but added that whatever financial precautions he took, he did so to insure the couple's economic future. He claimed that Samantha was a spendthrift and that they would have no retirement if he had let her chase her desires. He said that she does contribute to the couple's finances but she always spent more money than she had. He said that he had to bail her out of several thousand dollars in debt before they married. Jared made it clear that he loved Samantha's energy, but that she terrified him. He also reported that he was very attracted to Samantha, but she was a flirt—another characteristic that made him nervous.

Jared was the youngest of two brothers. His father was a judge and his mother a kindergarten teacher. The word he used to describe both of his parents and his household growing up was "calm." He said that he never heard his parents fight and that everyone got along with one another. He said his parents were always very careful with money and that his mother made sure the house was organized. On the other hand, Jared admitted that his family rarely went on vacations and that there was little affection or emotion displayed between family members. Education and discipline were role modeled.

Samantha was the oldest of three siblings. Her father was in sales, and her mother was a nurse. Samantha described her household as chaotic. Her father was a gambler and poor financial provider, and her mother was impulsive, disorganized, and highly emotional. Samantha was adventurous and admittedly out of control in her youth. She claimed that she dated a series of "bad boys," but with Jared she had finally found a "good guy."

After Jared had discovered her online behavior, Samantha said that she immediately stopped contacting men. While she was threatening Jared to loosen up his grip on her and the marriage, it was evident that she was not in a hurry to divorce. Applying MCT, each partner came to recognize and understand what was believed to be an unbalanced *security vs. risk* conflict. While Jared was cognizant that he was attracted to Samantha's sense of adventure, he had to connect it to his repressed feelings regarding his deprived, unemotional childhood. Only then could he understand that he was asking his wife to accept the same kind of life. He also needed to understand that his true financial situation did not merit the level of control he was employing in his marriage. Samantha was cognizant of her chaotic upbringing and her need for security. But she did not understand the kind of anxiety that she had internalized from such a lifestyle and that she was attempting to replicate this life by insisting that Jared enable some of her ill-thought-out adventures. In MCT terms, Samantha required a certain amount of adventure and the risk that often accompanied it, but she also wanted security. Jared missed adventure, but needed control and stability. Prior to treatment, the partners could not negotiate because neither would give up something to get something. But with their newfound insight, they eventually accepted compromise and demonstrated respect for what each brought to the marriage. The following is an example of how the therapist helped each partner connect their respective families of origin to the shared master conflict to build mutual empathy and trust:

Therapist: Jared, it sounds as if your upbringing was somewhat antiseptic.
Jared: What do you mean?
Therapist: No messiness for you; well under control.

Samantha: Yeah, boring.
Jared: I guess so, but we never had to worry about where the next dollar was coming from.
Therapist: True, but did you really think that your parents needed to be as careful as they were? I may be wrong, but it sounds to me as if they probably had enough money to be able to take a vacation or two every now and then.
Jared: If you're asking me if they were a bit extreme, then I would have to answer yes. My brother used to make fun of them all the time. I think it bothered him more than it bothered me.
Therapist: Didn't it ever get to you?
Jared: Well, when it was time for me to go to college I had to go to a state school to save money. Because my grades were good, I did resent that a bit.
Therapist: Did you tell your parents how you felt about the situation?
Jared: I tried, but they calmly told me that was the way it had to be.
Therapist: Doesn't sound like there was much emotion attached to the conversation.
Jared: My brother used to call them robots.
Therapist: So along came this exciting, adventurous woman, and you fell for her.
Jared: Yeah, she was the life of the party.
Therapist: But now she scares you.
Jared: Yes, I think she can be out of control. She almost destroyed our family with her behavior on the Internet.
Therapist: Do you really think that if you spend a little more money on having fun that you will go bankrupt?
Jared: Not really. But if I let Samantha do whatever she wants, we could end up that way.
Therapist: So, there *is* room for compromise? Particularly since a part of you seems to need some of what Samantha brings to the marriage. Because if you reject that side of her, you will then be demanding that you two live as your parents did. And this might encourage her to look elsewhere for excitement. I'm not condoning her behavior, but that is what happened, isn't it?
Jared: I can compromise.
Therapist: It sounds to me, Samantha, that you bought the side of Jared that would provide you with a sense of security. A far cry from the chaotic life you experienced as a child and young adult. But you also react as if this very side chokes the life out of living.
Samantha: It does make me wonder if I am wasting my life.
Therapist: Do you buy what Jared is saying about your spending habits?
Samantha: Yes and no. I can spend a lot of money. And I am very spontaneous. Jared needs time to get used to the idea of doing something.

	He has a need to plan it out. Make sure the price is right and that there are bathrooms readily available. I don't think that way. It's a drag to me. But I can overdo it at times. Truthfully, he is right when he says I don't know what will make me happy.
Therapist:	Perhaps something in-between. If you can accept that the price you will pay for your security is a few missing adventures, maybe the two of you can reach a compromise. Unless you insist on living the way you were raised.
Samantha:	Oh, no. I see your point.

Sexual Abuse

Child sexual abuse remains a common experience in the United States. Surveys have found that 26.6% of girls and 5.1% of boys reported sexual abuse and sexual assault by age 17 (Finkelhor, Shattuck, Turner, & Hamby, 2014). Other research suggested the rates for girls experiencing sexual violence may be even higher. The National Women's Law Center found that 31% of girls reported experiencing sexual assault and other forms of violence (Chaudhry & Tucker, 2017). Most of the professional literature tends to focus on father-daughter incest or stepfather incest (McCarthy & Breetz, 2010). Boys and girls may be abused in or outside the home, but more commonly by people they knew and trusted (Laurel House, 2017). Boys have been found to be abused more often outside the home by teachers, coaches, and family friends, among others (Stoltenborgh, van Ijzendoorn, Euser, & Bakermans-Kranenburg, 2011).

Compared to non-victims of child sexual abuse, victims are four times more likely to develop post-traumatic stress disorder (PTSD) as adults; three times more likely to experience major depression as adults; and four times more likely to abuse drugs (Zinzow et al., 2012). Other common problems include anxiety, increased feelings of guilt and shame, risk of suicidality, problems with body image, eating disorders, dissociative disorders, somatic symptoms (Hall & Hall, 2011), and a wide range of medical conditions, including chronic illnesses (Maltz, 2001). Some specific symptoms that abused males may experience are: (1) shame – born from the myth that this only happens to females; (2) fear of being gay – this does not happen to real men; (3) fear of being blamed – because males are always interested in sex, it must be the male's fault; and (4) fear of becoming an offender – males are offenders and females are victims (Laurel House, 2017). According to Lew (2004), if the male was abused by a female, he may have experienced a double bind: If it felt good, then it can't be abuse; if it was a shameful experience, he may wonder if he is gay.

Experiencing childhood sexual abuse can contribute to a myriad of relationship issues such as: problems with attachment and trust, sexual difficulties, greater relationship instability, and difficulties with boundaries.

184 Case Studies

Survivors of child sexual abuse are also more at risk for becoming involved in abusive relationships (Hall & Hall, 2011; Isley, Isley, Freiburger, & McMackin, 2008; Roberts, O'Connor, Dunn, Golding, & ALSPAC Study Team, 2004). Polonsky (2010) wrote: "Sexual abuse is always a breach of trust and boundaries, with consequences for attachments, trust, and sexuality" (p. 242). Successful treatment of adult survivors of child sexual abuse usually includes treating both traumatic stress related symptoms as well as relationship and related sexual issues. We believe MCT can be useful, as evidenced by treatment with the following couple:

Tom and Zoey: Specialness vs. Ordinariness

Tom and Zoey (see Figure 8.3) were a married couple in their 30s who sought treatment after four months of dating. This was Tom's second marriage. Tom had traveled the world as a professional drummer, but after a significant wrist injury and the dissolution of his band, he found himself unemployed. Zoey was employed as a marketing director. At the start of treatment, Zoey was pregnant with the couple's first child. The couple had

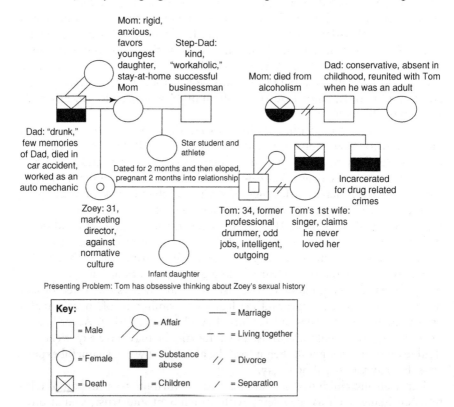

Figure 8.3 Tom and Zoey.

met at a video gaming conference and claimed to have experienced "love at first sight." They moved in together after just two weeks of dating and eloped after dating for two months. The couple said that they moved ahead quickly because they saw their relationship as special.

Tom and Zoey sought couples therapy because of Tom's obsessive thoughts regarding Zoey's past sexual experiences. These thoughts would sometimes leave Tom angry, irritable, and at times unresponsive. In some instances, he would verbally lash out at Zoey, cursing and calling her names. Zoey was upset by Tom's reactions but claimed to know how to "get him out of" his destructive state. Zoey valued her ability to rescue her husband and saw herself as special. Despite Tom's obsession with Zoey's sexual history, it was relatively uneventful. She had had no more than a handful of lovers. Nevertheless, Tom was bothered by her past. Triggers included any mention of past boyfriends and even old clothing that an ex-boyfriend may have touched.

Tom and Zoey expressed their commitment to improving the relationship. They each said that they had "never loved anybody else," even though both had been previously married. They also claimed that neither of them had ever achieved orgasm with another partner. They described themselves as "soul mates." Watching the couple interact reminded the therapist of a teen romance replete with giggling. The couple reported having sex daily, even throughout their pregnancy. Sexual contact, in fact, served to solidify their specialness; without it, they reported feeling anxious and insecure.

Zoey was the only child from her mother's first marriage. She had no memories of her father, who died in a car accident when she was 2 years old. Zoey's mother told Zoey that her father was a physically abusive "drunk" who had many affairs. Zoey had a distant relationship with her mother, who she saw as anxious and critical. Zoey was proclaimed the "matchmaker" of her mother's second marriage. Apparently, she picked her future stepfather out at a neighbor's party around age 3.

Zoey had a close relationship with her stepfather, whom she described as a stable man and a good provider. She remained an only child and was showered with attention by both her mother and stepfather until the age of 8, when her sister was born. From that point forward, Zoey felt that her parents favored her younger sister, who happened to be a phenomenal scholar and talented athlete. Zoey had gone from special to ordinary with the birth of her sister.

Tom grew up in a poor urban area in the South. His father left his mother when Tom was 5 years old. Tom's mother passed away shortly after due to an alcohol-related illness, leaving him in the care of his mother's sister, who was also an alcoholic. Because Tom's aunt was a mentally unstable alcoholic, Tom was charged with raising himself and his two younger brothers. Tom's aunt was often drunk in front of him and his brothers and often brought random men to the family home, exposing him and his brothers to her various sexual encounters. She also sexually molested Tom and his brothers on numerous occasions. When she was in a good mood, she would praise Tom for his caretaking skills. But when she was in a bad mood, she would taunt him about the smallness of his penis.

At 16, Tom ran away to Los Angeles with a girlfriend. Despite having no formal musical training, he found himself a professional drummer, and by 20 he and his band were signed by a major record label. Tom was a talented musician, and his rise to fame solidified his specialness; it also distinguished him from his brothers, who succumbed to drug addiction and crime. At age 28, Tom married a backup singer who he met on tour. Unfortunately, the ill-fated marriage failed, primarily because of Tom's infidelity.

Tom remained estranged from his aunt until her death from an alcohol-related illness. Soon thereafter, Tom and his father repaired their relationship. Tom's middle brother died from a heroin overdose shortly after his aunt's passing, and his youngest brother was incarcerated for drug-related offenses. Since the dissolution of his band, Tom struggled to find employment. He resisted taking a "boring 9 to 5 desk-job," which he perceived as ordinary. Rather, he worked odd jobs and gave drum lessons.

While Tom did not meet the full diagnostic criteria for PTSD, he did show signs of it, such as lashing out. Even though the couple claimed that they wanted Tom's emotional outbursts to end, the therapist suspected the couple might sabotage these efforts because of the specialness each received from these outbursts. For example, Tom sought added time with an independent therapist, which helped him to heal from his traumatic past. As a result, he felt more secure in the relationship, causing him to decrease the need to be rescued. In this sense, his health took away Zoey's main source of specialness. And while Tom's anxiety improved, Zoey's worsened.

Tom seemed to adjust to the idea of finding healthier ways to experience specialness easier than Zoey did, which he suspected was partially because he was able to return to his drumming. Tom also saw his new role as a father to a little girl as a very special one. Zoey experienced the new role of being a mother as a threat to her specialness. For instance, initially her family was very excited about the pregnancy, but once the baby arrived, they offered little help, choosing to spend more time at her sister's collegiate sports tournaments. And although she loved that Tom showered their infant daughter with affection, she couldn't help but feel jealous.

As a compromise to what the therapist perceived as a shared *specialness vs. ordinariness* master conflict, the couple chose to move closer to Tom's father and stepmother, who wanted to be involved in raising their grandchild. Tom and Zoey implemented scheduled date nights, which helped Zoey to feel special, as did the added attention of her in-laws. Zoey's return to work also helped her to build confidence and solidify her specialness. She returned to her status in the company as one of their best employees.

While these behavioral suggestions and experiences were helpful, they would have had less of an impact without the insight gained by the couple regarding their master conflict and how it was linked to each partner's family of origin. The following brief vignette demonstrates how the therapist intervened to increase this insight:

Therapist: We've talked before about your *specialness vs. ordinariness* conflict. Zoey, I do wonder if treating Tom's trauma symptoms supports this type of conflict.

Zoey: What do you mean?

Therapist: Even though a part of you dislikes Tom's jealous outbursts, perhaps another part of you needs to play the role of savior.

Zoey: I certainly don't like it when he verbally lashes out at me.

Therapist: Of course not. But you did admit that after you bring him back, you feel closer to him. Because you have the key to rescue him, you are indeed special to him.

Tom: It's true. No one else has ever been able to help me through these periods. Just like no one has ever made me feel so loved the way Zoey does.

Therapist: So, it might stand to reason that if Tom improves, your special powers will no longer be needed, and you will be just an "ordinary whore" [a phrase Tom would literally use when he lashed out].

Zoey: If you're right, I'm not doing it on purpose. When we first started dating [turns to Tom], you promised me we would never spend a single night apart. And just a week ago, you brought up the idea of you going away for two weeks to record in Los Angeles. What changed?

Therapist: Perhaps you worry that you are no longer special in Tom's eyes. If you are ordinary, he might lose interest in you. Just like your parents lost interest in you after your "special" younger sister was born.

Zoey: [Becoming visibly upset]. That makes some sense.

Tom: I know I made that promise to you, but maybe it was not realistic.

Zoey: So, what other promises have you made to me that you now view as unrealistic?

Tom: As I feel better, I notice that I want to do some things independent of you; which is normal for a healthy relationship. It doesn't mean I don't love you.

Zoey: [Crying] It feels that way.

Therapist: Maybe we need to find other ways for both of you to feel special to each other that does not involve playing out Tom's past trauma.

Tom: Zoey, I do not want to keep pushing my crap from my mother onto you.
Therapist: What do you mean, Tom?
Tom: I think I obsess about Zoey's sexual history because I fear replicating a relationship with my aunt. I know that sounds gross, but I think on some level it's true [turns to Zoey]. My aunt was an abusive slut. When I think about you being with other people, even if we weren't together at the time, I see you as a whore like my aunt, and I lash out.
Therapist: I would offer a slightly different slant. The sexual abuse was no doubt a horrific experience. But you weren't the only one abused, and as such, you were ordinary. You were abused just like the other kids in the home. But you countered this ordinariness by taking on the role of the competent parent and attending to your siblings. You also became an accomplished musician. In real time, by obsessing about Zoey's sexual history and likening her to your mother, you hang onto the abuse that makes you ordinary. Zoey's tolerance of the abuse enables her ordinariness. But to regain the specialness she had before her younger sister was born, she takes on the role of the "good mother" and comes to your rescue, which makes you feel special as well. The cycle then repeats itself as you both continue to collude to maintain your shared *specialness vs. ordinariness* master conflict.
Tom: That's heavy.
Zoey: I never thought of that one. But it makes sense.

Summary

The primary reason for including this chapter in a book on MCT is to show just how applicable this model can be with couples who suffer from an assortment of sexual symptoms. We did not address all the sexual issues in couples that we believe could be alleviated with MCT. Rather, we chose to select a series of those that appear to be prominent in today's work with couples and those that might be of most interest to our readers: Open Marriage (Swingers), Online Infidelity, and Sexual Abuse. The dialogue that we have included in each of these cases should give the readers some insight into the mechanics of the MCT approach.

References

American Association for Marriage and Family Therapy (2017). Online infidelity. Retrieved from www.aamft.org/imis15/AAMFT/Content/Consumer_Updtaes/Online_Infidelity.aspx

Bergstrand, C., & Blevins Williams, J. (2000). Today's alternative marriage styles. *Electronic Journal of Human Sexuality*, *3*. Retrieved from http://questia.com/library/journal1G1-154817866/today-s-alternattive-marriage-styles-the-case-of-swingers

Bergstrand, C., & Blevins Sinski, J. (2009). *Swinging in America: Love, sex and marriage in the 21st century*. Santa Barbara, CA: Praeger/ABC-CLIO.

Betchen, S. (2013, July 4). The slippery slope of open marriage: A dynamic more complex than you think. Retrieved from http://psychologytoday.com/blog/magnetic-partners/201307/the-slippery-slope-open-marriage

Blumstein, P., & Schwartz, P. (1983). *American couples: Money, work, sex*. New York, NY: William Morrow.

Chaudhry, N., & Tucker, J. (2017). Let Her Learn: Stopping School Pushout. Retrieved May, 2017, from https://nwlc.org/wp content/uploads/2017/04/final_nwlc_Gates_OverviewKeyFindings.pdf

Cooper, A., & Griffin-Shelly, E. (2002). Introduction: The Internet: The next sexual revolution. *Sexual Addiction & Compulsivity*, *7*(1–2), 5–29. doi:10.1080/10720160008400205

Cravins, J., & Whiting, J. (2014). Clinical implications of Internet infidelity: Where Facebook fits in. *American Journal of Family Therapy*, *00*, 1–15. doi:10.1080/01926187.2013.874211

Easton, D., & Hardy, J. (2009). *The ethical slut: A practical guide to polyamory, open relationships & other adventures*. (2nd ed.). Berkeley, CA: Celestial Arts.

Fernandes, E. (2012). The swinging paradigm: Are swingers freaks, deviant sex predators? Retrieved from http://elisabethsheff.com/2012/09/27/guest-blog-froms wingign-expert-dr-edward-fernandes

Finkelhor, D., Shattuck, A., Turner, H.A. & Hamby, S.L. (2014). The lifetime prevalence of child sexual abuse and sexual assault assessed in late adolescence. *Journal of Adolescent Health*, *55*, 329–333.

Haag, P. (2012). *Marriage confidential: Love in the post-romantic age*. New York, NY: Harper-Perennial.

Hall, M., & Hall, J. (2011). The long-term effects of childhood sexual abuse: Counseling Implications. Retrieved from http://counselingoutfitters.com/vistas/vistas11/Article_19.pdf

Herbenick, D. (2010, January). Q & A: How common is the "swing" lifestyle? *Kinsey Confidential*. Retrieved from http://kinseyconfidential.org/common-swing-lifestyle/

Hertlein, K., & Blumer, M.L.C. (2014). *The couple and family technology framework: Intimate relationships in a digital age*. New York, NY: Routledge.

Hertlein, K., & Webster, M. (2008). Technology, relationships, and problems: a research synthesis. *Journal of Marital & Family Therapy*, *34*, 445–460. doi:10.1111/j.1752-606.2008.00087.x

Isley, P.J., Isley, P., Freiburger, J., & McMackin, R. (2008). In their own voices: A qualitative study of men abused as children by Catholic clergy. *Journal of Child Sexual Abuse*, *17*(3–4), 201–215.

Kerner, I. (2011, September 15). Would you ever swing? CNN Health. Retrieved from http:// thechart.blogs.cnn.com/2011/09/15/would-you-ever-swing

Laurel House (2017). *Male adult survivors of child sexual abuse*. Retrieved from www. laurelhouse.org.au/?page_id=20

Lew, M. (2004). *Victims no longer: The classic guide for men recovering from sexual child abuse*. New York, NY: Quill.

Maltz, W. (2001). *The Sexual Healing Journey*. (Rev. ed.). New York, NY: Harper Collins.

Mao, A., & Raguram, A. (2009). Online infidelity: The new challenge to marriages. *Indian Journal of Psychiatry, 51*, 302–304. doi:10.4103/0019-5545.58299

McCarthy, B., & Breetz, A. (2010). Confronting male hypoactive sexual desire disorder. In S. Leiblum (Ed.), *Treating sexual desires disorders: A clinical casebook* (pp. 75–91). New York, NY: Guilford.

Muise, A., Christofides, E., & Desmarais, S. (2009). More information than you ever wanted: Does Facebook bring out the green-eyed monster of jealousy? *Cyberpsychology & Behavior, 12*, 441–444. doi:10.1089/cpb.2008.0263

Nelson, T. (2000). *Internet infidelity: A modified Delphi study* (Unpublished doctoral dissertation). Purdue University.

O'Neill, N., & O'Neill, G. (1973). *Open marriage: A new lifestyle for couples*. New York, NY: Avon.

Polonsky, D. (2010). The bisexual challenges and dilemmas of young single men. In S. Levine, C. Risen, & S. Althof (Eds.), *Handbook of clinical sexuality for mental health professionals* (pp. 231–249). New York, NY: Routledge.

Roberts, R., O'Connor, T., Dunn, J., Golding, J., & ALSPAC Study Team. (2004). The effects of child sexual abuse in later family life; mental health, parenting and adjustment of offspring. *Child Abuse & Neglect, 28*(5), 525–545.

Smith, B. (2011). Are Internet affairs different? *American Psychological Association, 42*, 48–51.

Spanier, G., & Cole, C. (1975). Mate swapping: Perceptions, value orientations, and participation in a midwestern community. *Archives of Sexual Behavior, 4*, 143–159. doi:10.1007/BF01541079

Stoltenberg, M., van Ijzendoorn, M.H., Euser, F.M., & Bakermans-Kranenberg, M.J. (2011). A global perspective on child sexual abuse: Meta-analysis of prevalence around the world. *Child Maltreatment, 16*, 79–101. doi:10.1177/1077559511403920

Taormino, T. (2008). *Opening up: A guide to creating and sustaining open relationships*. San Francisco, CA: Cleis Press.

Veaux, F., & Rickert, E. (2014). *More than two: A practical guide to ethical polyamory*. Portland, Oregon: Thorntree Press.

Whitty, M. (2005). The realness of cybercheating: men's and women's representations of unfaithful Internet relationships. *Social Science Computer Review, 23*(1), 57–67. doi:10.1177/0894439304271536

Zell, M.G. (1990). A bouquet of lovers: Strategies for responsible open relationships. Retrieved from http://caw.org/content/?q=bouquet

Zinzow, H.M., Resnick, H.S., McCauley, J.L., Amstadter, A.B., Ruggiero, K.J., & Kilpatrick, D.G. (2012). Prevalence and risk of psychiatric disorders as a function of variant rape histories: results from a national survey of women. *Social Psychiatry and Psychiatric Epidemiology, 47*(6), 893–902.

Epilogue

We have always been of the mindset that we borrow from others before us, either consciously or unconsciously. Even the works of the greatest of minds have been influenced by predecessors, contemporaries, or by experiences that have resonated with them; and these influences are not necessarily restricted to their fields of expertise. We think that was made clear in the opening chapter. For example, in *Chapter 1. Introduction*, we wrote that Nietzsche was impressed with the pre-Socratic Heraclitus (Kaufman, 1974). But he also admired the playwright Goethe and was enamored with the work of the philosopher Schopenhauer. Both Nietzsche and Schopenhauer were interested in the function that the "will" played in the lives of people and existence in general. Schopenhauer believed that the essence of humanity is expressed in will and his concept of the *will to live*. But it is will that drives human beings in the relentless pursuit of desires that can never be completely satisfied—a pointless existence that can only lead to suffering (Schopenhauer, 1818/1966). From this position, we mark the Buddhist warning to avoid an attachment to craving (Abelson, 1993). Nietzsche eventually rejected his hero's perspective on this matter and took a more optimistic view. He saw will as the "driving force" in life. Working to better oneself, to achieve, and to reach great heights was life-affirming for Nietzsche. He referred to this concept as the *will to power* (Nietzsche, 1883–1885/1966).

Nietzsche was also influenced by the great composer Wagner (Köhler, 1998). Nietzsche believed Wagner to be a creative genius, and he loved the revolutionary spirit of his work. He considered the composer one of "the most important men in German arts and letters since Goethe's death" (Kaufman, 1974, p. 30). Although Nietzsche eventually rejected Wagner (Nietzsche, 1888/1967), he remained impressed with the composer's opera, *Tristan and Isolde*. Nietzsche claimed that the musical drama had a profound impact on his book, *The Birth of Tragedy*. To Nietzsche, the opera illustrated the Dionysian/Apollonian struggle and the re-emergence of tragedy and redemption that gave meaning to existence (Nietzsche, 1872/2000); it also depicted Schopenhauer's concept of insatiable will. Wagner, too, was a great admirer of Schopenhauer.

Beethoven was mentored by the Austrian composer Joseph Haydn, but he openly acknowledged the influence of Goethe on his music. Rolland and Pfister (1931) wrote of Beethoven: "From his earliest days he had steeped his mind in Goethe's work" (p. 4). In *Egmont*, Beethoven constructed a set of musical pieces based on Goethe's play of the same name (Goethe, 1788/2017). James Joyce was said to be enamored with the great playwright Henrik Ibsen (Joyce, 1999). Joyce admired Ibsen's courage and sense of realism. To Joyce, Ibsen was the model of the artist who rebelled against conventional creative approaches. In his drama *A Doll's House*, the playwright countered the mores of the times by allowing his protagonist, Nora, to leave her husband (Ibsen, 1879/2016). Kenner (1951) wrote:

> Ibsen represented for Joyce, first and foremost, a remarkable prototype of the successful provincial artist—one who might offer not only a paradigm of personal integrity but a set of strategies for dealing with a starved milieu and a half-baked culture.
>
> (p. 77)

Pulling from a variety of the arts to inspire one's creative process is not unusual. But this process is not limited to those in the humanities. Albert Einstein was said to be influenced by Max Planck, the father of quantum theory, but he was also inspired by the music of Mozart. A violinist, Einstein claimed that Mozart's music was his creative outlet. He shared with Mozart a somewhat eccentric personality and could relate to the composer's ability to create under stress. Einstein once said that, like physics, Mozart's music "was so pure, that it seemed to have been ever-present in the universe, waiting to be discovered by the master" (Miller, 2006, para. 3). He considered great scientists to be artists (Calaprice, 2011).

If many of the greatest works of civilization were influenced by the work of others, surely the same can be said for the creations of us lesser mortals. In MCT, we have borrowed certain aspects from psychoanalytic theory and technique (Freud, 1910/1957), Bowen theory (Bowen, 1978), and principles and practice of sex therapy (Kaplan, 1974, 1983). After many years of treating couples with sexual problems, combining certain aspects of each model has yielded the most significant positive results, offering the breadth and depth needed to tackle the most complex relationship dynamics. Whether these couples chose the arduous task of balancing their conflicts and alleviating their symptoms, or to end their relationships, the counterintuitive style of MCT provoked movement, even if in a shocking way. For example, informing a couple that they may long to achieve success but simultaneously strive to fail is a difficult concept to comprehend. They may accept the need to achieve but outright reject the unconscious wish to sabotage their success. Accepting both sides of a conflict offers a couple too much responsibility for their symptoms—a burden they tend to reject with a vengeance. In a similar vein, Freud (1919/1955) wrote: "In actual fact, indeed, the neurotic patient presents with a torn mind, divided by resistances" (p. 161). The therapist who wishes to think better of a couple's motivations will most likely reject this approach.

We have been told time and again by colleagues, students, and supervisees that MCT, more than any other approach, makes better sense of a couple's nonsensical behavior and challenges their resistances more effectively. We are not surprised by this assertion, given that our model is based in part on the absurd and the tendency to normalize it. Although we developed our model specifically to treat couples with sexual problems, we have found that it is easily applicable to treating individuals with sexual problems. Kaplan (personal communication, October 7, 1987) warned to promise no more than limited gains under such conditions. And we acknowledge this, especially if there is a treatment-resistant partner at home supposedly waiting for a cure. But even under these conditions, we have achieved success. Consider a man who reported for individual therapy because of delayed ejaculation. Although he was attracted to his girlfriend, he could not ejaculate inside of her. Once he accepted his *commitment vs. freedom* conflict and located the origin of it, his symptom dissipated, and he married. Another example is that of a single man with PE who entered individual treatment. By uncovering an *adequacy vs. inadequacy* conflict, in combination with the aid of stop-start exercises, condom use, and the SSRI paroxetine (Paxil), he learned to control his ejaculatory process in the dating world.

MCT is also quite useful in treating individuals with non-sexual symptoms in individual or conjoint treatment. People of all walks of life who feel stuck have found its application life enhancing, such as: a man who could not free himself enough to marry the woman he loved because she did not share his cultural or religious background; the small businessman who could not meet his expenses; the executive who was having difficulty succeeding in the corporate world; the athlete who could not achieve peak performance or excel when the pressure was at its highest; and the politician who sabotaged his or her future. Problems such as these and more may be treated successfully with master conflict therapy. One prominent example comes to mind. A professional golfer could not lower his golf score to his satisfaction. His history revealed a *success vs. sabotage (big vs. small)* master conflict that, once controlled, enabled him to finally achieve his goal. While his conflict put up a fierce battle, the man fought it with equal tenacity and won. But his true reward came not in the form of a lower golf score; this man's ultimate triumph was in fighting the good fight and regaining control over his master conflict; this is what gave him the ability to decide his own fate on the golf course.

We have been informed that MCT is quite adaptable to other major models of treatment and *vice versa*. Most notably, Emotionally Focused Therapy (EFT) (Johnson, 2004), and Internal Family Systems (IFS) (Schwartz, 1997).

Although we have limited knowledge of these approaches, a practitioner of EFT claimed that he has successfully melded it with MCT by considering the couples he treats as having internalized conflicts with intimacy and attachment. A colleague who favored IFS said that the concept of integrating parts of oneself fit nicely with the MCT approach. To those with a territorial bent, such overlap may prove unsettling. But we accept the concept as flattery given our belief that most, if not all, therapeutic models share much in common. A close colleague who claimed to routinely combine EFT and MCT in his clinical work proposed a follow-up book that would illustrate the ways in which MCT could be used with other models. Perhaps this is a concept worth considering.

In conclusion, we will use a sports metaphor: in writing this book, we have left everything we had to give on the field of play. And while we have thoroughly exhausted ourselves, there is always more. We are aware that the concept of conflict predates the pre-Socratics, but such an exploration is beyond the scope of this book. Our objective was to trace some of the major theories that may have directly influenced psychoanalytic conflict theory and in turn MCT. After attending one of our workshops, a colleague commented that our model reminded him of a concept in Chinese philosophy born in the 3rd century BCE, referred to as the Yin and Yang. According to the *I Ching*, two opposites, Yin and the Yang, exist as inseparable. They are contradictory concepts that attract and complement each other. Yang is considered a positive attribute. It is bright and symbolizes "the masculine, the firm, the strong, the odd numbers, as well as all active things." Yin is shaded and symbolizes "the feminine, the yielding, the weak, the even numbers, as well as all passive things" (Huang, trans. 1998, p. 4). Neither Yin nor Yang is better than the other. As one "reaches its peak, it starts to decline as the other rises"; a rotation "fundamental to the Chinese conception of human life" (Redmond, trans. 2017, p. 340). It is believed that a balance between the two poles must be achieved to experience peace and harmony. Sound familiar?

References

Abelson, P. (1993). Schopenhauer and Buddhism. *Philosophy East and West*, 43(2), 255–278.
Bowen, M. (1978). *Family therapy in clinical practice*. New York, NY: Aronson.
Calaprice, A. (Ed.). (2011). *The ultimate quotable Einstein*. Princeton, NJ: Princeton University Press and The Hebrew University of Jerusalem.
Freud, S. (1910/1957). Five lectures on psycho-analysis, Leonardo da Vinci and other works. In J. Strachey (Ed. and Trans.), *The standard edition of the complete psychological works of Sigmund Freud* (Vol. 11, pp. 9–238). London, England: Hogarth Press and the Institute for Psychoanalysis.
Freud, S. (1919/1955). An infantile neurosis and other works. In J. Strachey (Ed. and Trans.), *The standard edition of the complete psychological works of Sigmund

Freud (Vol. 17, pp. 159–168). London, England: Hogarth Press and the Institute for Psychoanalysis.
Goethe, J.W. (1788/2017). *Egmont: A tragedy in five acts.* A. Swanwick (Trans.), Middletown, DE: CreateSpace Independent Publishers.
Huang, A. (Trans.). (1998). *The complete I Ching* (10th ed.). Rochester, NY: Inner Traditions.
Ibsen, H. (1879/2016). *A doll's house and other plays.* New York, NY: Penguin Classics.
Johnson, S. (2004). *The practice of emotionally focused couple therapy* (2nd ed.). New York, NY: Routledge.
Joyce, J. (1999). *On Ibsen.* Los Angeles, CA: Green Integer.
Kaplan, H.S. (1974). *The new sex therapy: Active treatment of sexual dysfunctions.* New York, NY: Times Books.
Kaplan, H.S. (1983). *The evaluation of sexual disorders: Psychological and medical aspects.* New York, NY: Brunner/Mazel.
Kaufman, W. (1974). *Nietzsche: Philosopher, psychologist, antichrist.* Princeton, NJ: Princeton University Press.
Kenner, H. (1951). Joyce and Ibsen's naturalism. *The Sewanee Review*, 59(1), 76–96.
Köhler, J. (1998). *Nietzsche & Wagner: A lesson in subjugation.* New Haven, CT: Yale University Press.
Miller, A. (2006, January 31). A genius finds inspiration in the music of another. *The New York Times.* Retrieved from www.nytimes.com/2006/01/31/science/a-genuis-finds-inspiration-in-the-music-of-another.html
Nietzsche, F. (1872/2000). *The birth of tragedy.* In D. Smith (Trans.), Oxford World Classics. Oxford, UK: Oxford University Press.
Nietzsche, F. (1883–1885/1966). *Thus spoke Zarathustra.* (Trans. W. Kaufmann). New York, NY: Viking.
Nietzsche (1888/1967). *The birth of tragedy and the case of Wagner.* W. Kauffmann (Trans.). New York, NY: Vintage.
Redmond, G. (Trans.). (2017). *The I Ching: Book of Changes.* London, England. Bloomsbury Academic.
Rolland, R., & Pfister, G.A. (1931). *Goethe and Beethoven.* New York, NY: Harper & Brothers.
Schopenhauer (1818/1966). *The world as will and representation* (Vol. 1). E.F.J. Payne (Trans.). New York, NY: Dover Publications.
Schwartz, R. (1997). *Internal family systems therapy.* New York, NY: Guilford.

Index

abuse 61–2, 77–8, 183–8
acceptance vs. rejection 22, 31–2, 79
addiction 27, 36, 77, 161
Addyi (flibanserin) 3
adequacy vs. inadequacy 21, 32–3, 46–7, 72–3, 78, 79–80, 81–3, 84, 86, 92–3, 120–1, 122–3, 159–62, 193
ADHD 39
affairs (sexual) 34, 38, 39, 40–1, 42, 44, 45–6, 53, 89–90, 92–4, 96–7, 143–5, 172–8, 178–83; online infidelity 178–83
anxiety 6–7
Aristotle 9, 12–13
assessment 99; absenteeism 52–3; commitment 64–5; content 74–6, 124–6; contradictions 78–80; couple dynamics 53–4; culture 85–90; genogram 53–73; incongruent feelings and behaviours 76–85; infidelity 66–8; initial interview 55–7; medication 71; parental influences 60–2, 66–70; problem longevity 59–60; process 74–6, 124–6; race 91–4; reactions 81–5; sexual history 56–64; sexual orientation 94–9; siblings 72–3; structure 51–2; therapy history 71–2

balance 27–9
Berlin, Isiah 6
big vs. small *see* success vs. sabotage
Bowen Theory (psychodynamic systems) 4, 16–17, 54–5, 192

caretaking *see* getting one's needs met vs. caretaking

chaos *see* control vs. chaos (out-of-control)
characteristics of 22–4
childhood 23, 42–3, 44, 97–8, 164–6; sexual abuse 183–8; siblings 72–3, 148–9, 158
children 70–1
choice 6–7; consequences 8; life partner 7–8, 24
closeness vs. distance 22, 33–4, 72–3, 79, 90, 96–7, 136–40
commitment 26–7, 64–5
commitment vs. freedom 34–5, 193
communication 3, 26
conflict 4–6, 14–17, 22–4, 31, 46–7, 192–4; acceptance vs. rejection 22, 31–2, 79; adequacy vs. inadequacy 21, 32–3, 46–7, 72–3, 78, 79–80, 81–3, 84, 86, 92–3, 120–1, 122–3, 159–62, 193; closeness vs. distance 22, 33–4, 72–3, 79, 90, 96–7, 136–40; commitment vs. freedom 34–5, 193; conformity vs. rebellion 21–2, 35, 80, 87–8, 163–8, 172–8; control vs. chaos (out-of-control) 21, 35–6, 61; getting one's needs met vs. caretaking 21, 28, 36–7, 72–3; giving vs. withholding 7, 22, 28–9, 37, 61, 62, 73, 75–6, 113–17, 141–5; Greek philosophy 8–13; justice vs. injustice 26, 38, 46–7, 72–3, 74–5, 79, 83, 92, 129; legitimacy vs. illegitimacy 38–9, 62; management *see* treatment; opposites 8–13, 16; others (conflict adjustment) 46; person vs. object 39–40, 81, 88–9; players 5; power of 25–7, 29–30; power vs. passivity 5, 7–8, 40–1, 72–3, 79–80, 81;

resolution vs. misery 41, 77; satisfaction vs. disappointment 41–2, 79–80; security vs. risk 42–3, 89–90, 179–83; self vs. loyalty (others) 43, 63, 72–3, 77–8, 87–8, 95–6, 97–8, 127, 146–50; specialness vs. ordinariness (less than ordinary) 43–4, 72–3, 108–12, 184–8; success vs. sabotage (big vs. small) 6–7, 21–2, 28, 44–5, 46–7, 61, 77, 79–80, 84, 92, 130, 155–8, 193; trust vs. distrust 5, 45–6, 74, 92, 93–4; witnesses 5–6
conformity vs. rebellion 21–2, 35, 80, 87–8, 163–8, 172–8
content 74–6, 124–6
contradictions 78–80
control vs. chaos (out-of-control) 21, 35–6, 61
culture 85–90, 160–1

delayed ejaculation 125–6, 162–8
depression 6–7, 33, 36–7, 97–8
disappointment *see* satisfaction vs. disappointment
discrimination 25–6, 32–3, 38, 92–3, 94–5
distance *see* closeness vs. distance
distrust *see* trust vs. distrust
drive 27

Einstein, Albert 192
emotionally focused therapy (EFT) 193–4
Empedocles 10, 17
erectile disorder (ED) 3, 32, 37, 56–7, 71, 77, 78, 91, 108, 158–62
exercises 112–17, 136, 141, 144, 149, 154, 159, 163

factors, influencing 23, 25–6, 85, 149; culture 85–90
fantasy 63
female orgasmic disorder 135–40
female sexual interest/arousal disorder 3, 56–7, 145–50
fetish 40–1, 45, 64
flibanserin (Addyi) 3
freedom *see* commitment vs. freedom
Freud, Sigmund 4–6, 8, 16–17, 76, 192–3; Greek philosophy 8–13; Friedrich Nietzsche 13–14; Oedipus complex 5, 8, 15; psychoanalytic conflict theory 4

genito-pelvic pain/penetration disorder (GPPPD) 37, 56–7, 113–17, 140–5; exercises 112–13, 141
genogram 53–73
getting one's needs met vs. caretaking 21, 28, 36–7, 72–3
giving vs. withholding 7, 22, 28–9, 37, 61, 62, 73, 75–6, 113–17, 141–5
Goethe 191–2
Greek philosophy 8–13

Hippocrates 9–10

Ibsen, Henrik 192
illegitimacy *see* legitimacy vs. illegitimacy
imposter syndrome 38–9
inadequacy *see* adequacy vs. inadequacy
infertility 41
infidelity 34, 38, 39, 40–1, 42, 44, 45–6, 53, 89–90, 92–4, 96–7, 143–5, 172–8, 178–83; online infidelity 178–83
influencing factors 23, 25–6, 85, 149; culture 85–90
injustice *see* justice vs. injustice
internal family systems (IFS) 193–4
internalization 23
inverse reactions 84–5

jealousy 36, 38
Joyce, James 192
justice vs. injustice 26, 38, 46–7, 72–3, 74–5, 79, 83, 92, 129

legitimacy vs. illegitimacy 38–9, 62
life partner 7–8, 21–2; attraction 62; choice 7–8, 24; sexual relationship 34, 36, 36–7, 40, 65–6, 74–5, 79–80
loyalty *see* self vs. loyalty (others)

management *see* treatment
masturbation 62–3, 64
mental illness 27, 37
misery *see* resolution vs. misery
mixed-agenda couples 52–3

neutrality 117–18
Nietzsche, Friedrich 13–14, 22–3, 191

objectification *see* person vs. object
objectivity 119–24
Oedipus complex 5, 8, 15

online infidelity 178–83
open marriage 172–8
opposites 8–13, 16
ordinariness *see* specialness vs.
  ordinariness (less than ordinary)
origins of 14–17
overreactions 83

pain, tolerance of 25
parental influences 5–6, 32, 34, 38, 43, 45, 68–9, 77, 84, 95–6, 114–17, 136–40, 142–5, 146–50, 175; marriage 69–70, 109–12; sex 60–2
partner 21–2; attraction 62; choice 7–8, 24; sexual relationship 34, 36–7, 40, 65–6, 74–5, 79–80
passivity *see* power vs. passivity
person vs. object 39–40, 81, 88–9
Plato 9, 11–12, 13
pornography 35, 64, 74
power of a conflict 25–7, 29–30
power vs. passivity 5, 7–8, 40–1, 72–3, 79–80, 81
premature ejaculation (PE) 39, 52–3, 56–7, 58–9, 154–8
problem-solving capability 26
process 74–6, 124–6
psychoanalytic conflict theory 4
psychodynamic systems 4, 16–17, 54–5, 192
Pythagoras 9

race 39, 43, 91–4; discrimination 32–3, 38, 92–3
reactions 81–5
rebellion *see* conformity vs. rebellion
rejection *see* acceptance vs. rejection
relapse strategies 130
relationship conflicts 23–4; commitment 26–7; symptom development 27–9
resolution vs. misery 41, 77
responsibility 26
risk *see* security vs. risk

sabotage *see* success vs. sabotage (big vs. small)
satisfaction vs. disappointment 41–2, 79–80
Schopenhauer 191
security vs. risk 42–3, 89–90, 179–83
self vs. loyalty (others) 43, 63, 72–3, 77–8, 87–8, 95–6, 97–8, 127, 146–50

sensate focus exercises 112–13, 136, 149
sexual abuse 183–8; affairs 34, 38, 39, 40–1, 42, 44, 45–6, 53, 89–90, 92–4, 96–7, 143–5, 172–7, 178–83; exercises 112–17, 136, 141, 144, 149, 154, 159, 163; fantasy 63; fetish 40–1, 45, 64; history 56–64; open marriage 172–8; orientation 32, 43, 62, 94–9; relationship 34, 36–7, 40, 65–6, 74–5, 79–80
sexual disorders 56–7, 168; delayed ejaculation 125–6, 162–8; erectile disorder (ED) 3, 32, 37, 56–7, 71, 77, 78, 91, 108, 158–62; female orgasmic disorder 135–40; female sexual interest/arousal disorder 3, 56–7, 145–50; genito-pelvic pain/penetration disorder (GPPPD) 37, 112–17, 140–5; premature ejaculation (PE) 39, 52–3, 56–7, 58–9, 154–8
siblings 72–3
sildenafil citrate (Viagra) 3, 71, 159
social class 77–8
Socrates 9, 11–12
specialness vs. ordinariness (less than ordinary) 43–4, 72–3, 108–12, 184–8
success vs. sabotage (big vs. small) 6–7, 21–2, 28, 44–5, 46–7, 61, 77, 79–80, 84, 92, 130, 155–8, 193
swingers 172–8

trauma 26, 28, 82–3
treatment 24, 29, 107–8, 130–1, 150–1; adequacy vs. inadequacy 120–1, 122–3, 159–62; balance 118–24; boundaries 119; broadening the process 124–6; closeness vs. distance 136–40; conformity vs. rebellion 163–8, 172–8; exercises 112–17, 136, 141, 144, 149, 154, 159, 163; giving vs. withholding 113–17, 141–5; neutrality 117–18; relapse strategies 130; security vs. risk 179–83; self vs. loyalty (others) 127, 146–50; specialness vs. ordinariness (less than ordinary) 108–12, 184–8; stage 1: exposing contradictions and conflict 108, 113–14; stage 2: origin of the conflict 109–10, 114–15; stage 3: options on a behavioural level

110, 115–16; stage 4: options on a psychodynamic level 110–11, 116–17; stage 5: resolution of underlying conflict and increased differentiation 111–12, 117; success and failure 126–8; success vs. sabotage (big vs. small) 155–8; termination 128–30; therapist's objectivity 119–24
trust vs. distrust 5, 45–6, 74, 92, 93–4

unconscious 23
underreactions 81–3

vaginismus *see* genito-pelvic pain/penetration disorder (GPPPD)
Viagra (sildenafil citrate) 3, 71, 159

Waelder 8
withholding *see* giving vs. withholding

Yin and Yang 194